THE HESITANT HAND

THE HESITANT HAND

TAMING SELF-INTEREST IN
THE HISTORY OF ECONOMIC IDEAS

Steven G. Medema

PRINCETON UNIVERSITY PRESS   PRINCETON AND OXFORD

Copyright © 2009 by Princeton University Press
Published by Princeton University Press, 41 William Street,
Princeton, New Jersey 08540
In the United Kingdom: Princeton University Press, 6 Oxford Street,
Woodstock, Oxfordshire OX20 1TW
press.princeton.edu
All Rights Reserved

Second printing, and first paperback printing, 2011
Paperback ISBN 978-0-691-15000-0

The Library of Congress has cataloged the cloth edition of this book as follows
Medema, Steven G.
The hesitant hand : taming self-interest in the history of economic ideas /
Steven G. Medema.
p.   cm.
Includes bibliographical references and index.
ISBN 978-0-691-12296-0 (cloth : alk. paper)
1. Free enterprise—History. 2. Economic policy—History. 3. Economics—History.
4. Economic history. I. Title.
HB95.M43 2009
330.1—dc22   2009004860

British Library Cataloging-in-Publication Data is available

This book has been composed in Galliard
Printed on acid-free paper. ∞

Printed in the United States of America

3 5 7 9 10 8 6 4 2

For Carolyn

[B]y directing [his] industry in such a manner as
its produce may be of the greatest value, he
intends only his own gain, and he is in this,
as in many other cases, led by an invisible
hand to promote an end which was no part
of his intention. Nor is it always the worse for the
society that it was no part of it. By pursuing
his own interest he frequently promotes that
of the society more effectually than when he
really intends to promote it.

—Adam Smith, *An Inquiry into the Nature
and Causes of the Wealth of Nations*

[T]he working of self-interest is generally beneficent, not because of some natural coincidence
between the self-interest of each and the good
of all, but because human institutions are arranged so as to compel self-interest to work in
directions in which it will be beneficent.

—Edwin Cannan,
Economic Review, July 1913

The invisible hand which guides men to
promote ends which were no part of their intention, is not the hand of some god or some
natural agency independent of human effort;
it is the hand of the lawgiver, the hand which
withdraws from the sphere of the pursuit of
self-interest those possibilities which do not
harmonize with the public good.

—Lionel Robbins,
*The Theory of Economic Policy in
English Classical Political Economy*

Contents

Acknowledgments

THIS BOOK draws on work previously published by the author, at times in combination with others. Chapter 1: "The Economic Role of Government in the History of Economic Thought," in Jeff Biddle, John B. Davis, and Warren J. Samuels, eds., *The Blackwell Companion to the History of Economic Thought* (Oxford: Blackwell, 2003), 428–44. Chapter 2: "The Hesitant Hand: Mill, Sidgwick, and the Evolution of the Theory of Market Failure," *History of Political Economy* 39 (Fall 2007): 331–58. Chapter 3: "Marshallian Welfare Economics and the Welfare Economics of Marshall," in Tiziano Raffaelli, Giacomo Becattini, and Marco Dardi, eds., *The Elgar Companion to Alfred Marshall* (Cheltenham: Edward Elgar, 2006), 634–47. Chapter 4: "Marginalizing Government: From *La Scienza delle Finanze* to Wicksell," *History of Political Economy* 37 (Spring 2005): 1–25. Chapter 5: "Of Pangloss, Pigouvians, and Pragmatism: Ronald Coase on Social Cost Analysis," *Journal of the History of Economic Thought* 18 (Spring 1996): 96–114; and, with Nahid Aslanbeigui, "Beyond the Dark Clouds: Pigou and Coase on Social Cost," *History of Political Economy* 30 (Winter 1998): 601–25. Chapter 6: " 'Related Disciplines': The Professionalization of Public Choice Analysis," *The History of Applied Economics: History of Political Economy Annual Supplement* 32 (2000): 289–323. Chapter 7: "Wandering the Road From Pluralism to Posner: The Transformation of Law and Economics, 1920s–1970s," in Mary Morgan and Malcolm Rutherford, eds., *The Transformation of American Economics: From Interwar Pluralism to Postwar Neoclassicism: History of Political Economy Annual Supplement* 30 (1998): 202–24; and "Legal Fiction: The Place of the Coase Theorem in Law and Economics," *Economics and Philosophy* 15 (October 1999): 209–33. I would like to thank these publishers and my coauthor for their permission to use portions of these works here.

As always, I get by with a little help from my friends. The list of those from whom I have received invaluable advice, comments, and information about various facets of this project over the past decade or so is extensive. Thanks go to Douglas Allen, Nahid Aslanbeigui, Roger Backhouse, Bradley Bateman, Ana Maria Bianchi, Jeff Biddle, Piero Bini, Peter Boettke, Tony Brewer, James Buchanan, Loïc Charles, Ronald Coase, the late Bob Coats, Robert Cooter, Marco Dardi, John Davis, Robert Ellickson, Walter Eltis, Ross Emmett, Jerry Evensky, Philippe Fontaine, Nicola Giocoli, Craufurd Goodwin, Peter Groenewegen, Marco Guidi, Claire Hammond, Dan Hammond, Elizabeth Hoffman, David Levy, Alain Marciano, Deirdre McCloskey, Nicholas Mercuro, Leon Montes, Laurence Moss, Denis O'Brien, Sir Alan Peacock, Sandra Peart, Richard Posner, Tiziano Raffaelli, Ingrid

Rima, Malcolm Rutherford, Warren Samuels, Bo Sandelin, Ian Steedman, Gianfranco Tusset, Thomas Ulen, Karen Vaughn, Richard Wagner, John Whitaker, Donald Winch, and Amos Witztum. Numerous anonymous referees have provided comments and suggestions on previous drafts of this material and have helped me to clarify my thinking on certain points raised herein. Roger Backhouse is due particular thanks for his extensive commentary on the manuscript and for forcing me to clarify my arguments in many places, including several where we see things somewhat differently. Warren Samuels got me interested in the analysis of the economic role of government in the history of economic thought during my graduate student days and has been a source of much advice and inspiration along the way. Of course, all of these individuals are completely absolved from any responsibility for whatever is flawed in this discussion.

I have had the good fortune to present this work in many places around the globe. I am grateful for all of the stimulating comments and discussion that attended these various presentations, which include the Workshop in the History of Economic Thought and Methodology at Michigan State University; the J. M. Kaplan Workshop in Political Economy, the Workshop in Politics, Philosophy, and Economics, and the Public Choice Workshop at George Mason University; the Austrian Economics Workshop at New York University; the Workshop on the Cambridge School of Economics in Tokyo, Japan; the Summer Institute for the Preservation of the Study of the History of Economic Thought at George Mason University; seminars at the University of Nice/LATAPSES, the University of Aix-Marseilles III, the École normale supérieure de Cachan, and the University of Reims; and the 2006 AISPE conference in Padova, Italy, as well as various conferences conducted by the *History of Political Economy* journal, the History of Economics Society, the U.K. History of Economic Thought group, and the European Society for the History of Economic Thought. Particular thanks go to Piero Bini, Gianfranco Tusset, and Katia Caldari, who invited me to give a keynote address on this subject to the 2006 AISPE conference in Padova, and to Richard Arena (Nice), Alain Marciano (Reims), and Philippe Fontaine (Cachan), who have hosted me during several extended visits to French universities.

Special thanks go to James Buchanan, Betty Tillman, and Jo Ann Burgess for their assistance and hospitality during the author's visit to Buchanan House. Permission to quote from the archival materials is gratefully acknowledged. Excellent research assistance on the various projects that evolved into this book was provided by Tammy Baker, Mary Therese Cogeos, Jason Huston, and Matt Powers.

I am very grateful for the continued financial support that the Earhart Foundation has provided for my research, including much of that which is contained in this book. Thanks also go to the National Endowment for the

Humanities, which awarded me a 2005 Summer Stipend to help support the writing of this book.

I have said before that my editor at Princeton University Press, Peter Dougherty, is a man sui generis. His colleagues have recently recognized this by anointing him Director of the Press, but he has been kind enough to keep his hand in things on the editorial side and has helped to see this project through to completion. This is our fourth book together, and I am immensely grateful for all of the assistance, advice, and, most of all, friendship that he has provided along the way.

A special debt is owed to Brad, Gary, Roger, Werner, Bob, and Sharon, for reasons known only to them.

Finally, Carolyn, Alex, and Christopher have been patient attendants through much of this process and are the source of much joy, support, and inspiration. Along with Ashley and Jim, they constantly show me that while writing is one of life's greatest pleasures, it pales in comparison to the joys of family life. At the center of all of this is my wife, Carolyn, and it is to her that this book is dedicated—with much love and affection.

THE HESITANT HAND

WHEN ADAM SMITH wrote about an "invisible hand" translating the pursuit of self-interest to the larger interests of society as a whole, he launched a debate over the impact of self-interested behavior that continues to this day in academic, political, and popular realms—most recently in the context of the current economic crisis, which is widely seen as the consequence of self-interest (and, in the limit, greed) run amok. Smith was not the first to assert that the pursuit of self-interest could have beneficial effects or that government policies closer to the laissez-faire end of the spectrum would be in the best interests of the nation. Vincent de Gournay, Pierre de Bois-guilbert, and Bernard Mandeville had been making statements at least as strong as this for decades before Smith wrote his *Inquiry into the Nature and Causes of the Wealth of Nations* (1776). Smith was the first, however, to construct an analytical system that purported to demonstrate the beneficial effects of the working of self-interest, and his system provided the background against which subsequent debates took place.

The idea that people behave in self-interested fashion within the economic realm goes back at least to the ancient Greeks, and while the form and content of the self-interest assumption has varied over time, it remains central to economic analysis to this day. There is a tendency on the part of the uninitiated to believe that "self-interested" means "selfish." But such is not the case. Economists have never assumed that people care only about themselves or that they are greedy. What they *have* consistently assumed is that people will do the things that they believe will make them the happiest, given the various circumstances of their lives, and that businessmen will pursue profits. Yes, there are variations on this assumption—from the notion that people behave "as if" they were pursuing their self-interest, to the idea that people "tend to" pursue their self-interest, to the very strong assumption that people are rational maximizers of their satisfactions who function as lightning calculators of benefits and costs. The common denominator, though, is that self-interest is a motivating force in individual behavior, and this perspective has been part of the analysis of economic activity since ancient times.

Throughout the history of economic thought, the analysis of the impact of self-interested behavior has been hand-in-glove with discussions of the appropriate role for government within the economic system. The two are linked by a concern that self-interested behavior, channeled through markets, sometimes does not generate outcomes that are in the best interests of society as a whole, and by an attendant belief that government action may be able to remedy these problems. The debate surrounding the current economic crisis reflects exactly this, with economists and policymakers concerned that the regulatory environment did not provide a system of checks sufficient to rein in potential base effects of self-interested behavior within the financial system and that government regulations need to be put into place to prevent the recurrence of these problems in the future.

Modern economics is very much bound up in the analysis of the economic role of government as a response to the operation of the forces of self-interest: specifically, whether self-interest leads to "optimal" (read: efficient) results, or whether there is "market failure"—to use the term that is commonplace in the literature. Nevertheless, the relationship between self-interested behavior, the market, and the theory of the economic role of government has a centuries-long historical lineage. This book attempts to bring out some key facets of this history and, in particular, the relatively underexplored history of this topic from the mid-nineteenth century onward.

Nearly all of the economic literature prior to the late eighteenth century expressed significant qualms about the effects of self-interested behavior on social welfare and held out state intervention as the only means to mitigate these problems. Smith's *Wealth of Nations* played a pivotal role in the elaboration of a political economy more inclined to see self-interest working toward the greater good. Smith argued that the pursuit of self-interest will often redound to the larger interests of society via the "invisible hand," and that governmental interference with this tends to work contrary to the interests of the nation. The classical economists of the nineteenth century elaborated and refined Smith's prescription, but the basic message—that markets tend effectively to reconcile self-interest and social interest—remained central to the analysis.

The tide began to turn back in the mid-1800s, as political economists became increasingly concerned about the ability of the invisible hand to channel self-interested behavior to society's benefit, though there was still great pessimism about the degree to which the state could improve on market performance. Over the course of the next century, however, concerns about the efficiency of markets increased, while the qualms about the capabilities of government progressively receded—to the point where, by the middle of the twentieth century, orthodox economic analysis had not only a very expansive conception of market failure, but also a clear picture of how the very visible hand of government could bring about efficiency where the invisible hand failed to do so.

The second half of the twentieth century brought a challenge to this conception of the relative efficacy of market and state, spearheaded by economists at the universities of Chicago and Virginia. The first piece of this challenge was the argument that self-interest operates in the governmental realm as well as the market one, and that self-interested behavior by voters, legislators, and bureaucrats generates government failures that parallel those on the market side. The second critique of the orthodox approach was that the market is more capable than commonly recognized. It was argued that outcomes identified as market failures were not necessarily so, and that ostensible limitations of markets could be overcome by setting them within an appropriate legal framework. In sum, the new view proposed that orthodox claims regarding both the failure of the market and the abilities of government to improve things were overblown.

The Chicago and Virginia attacks on the theory of market failure were bound up in an expansion of the boundaries of economics that was gaining momentum in the 1960s and 1970s. This movement reflected an increasingly strongly held belief—among economists, to be sure, but among others as well—that economics, with its assumption of self-interested behavior across the social realm, could inform our understanding of activities once considered to be no part of the purview of the economist. Central here was the application of economic analysis to legal and political behavior, which allowed economists to weigh in on a broader set of government policy topics than ever before. Legal and political rules and outcomes could be evaluated against the same dictates of optimality as were standard market phenomena, and the results of the analysis often called into question the received view of government and the market.

The focus of this book is the interplay of self-interest, market, and state in economic analysis from the mid-nineteenth century up through the latter stages of the twentieth. We will begin by sketching the larger historical context of this debate, from the ancient Greeks through the writing of Adam Smith. The relatively slight attention given to Smith and the classical economists of the first half of the nineteenth-century—such as Thomas Robert Malthus and David Ricardo—is justified by the quality work that has already been done on this period by scholars such as D. P. O'Brien, Lionel Robbins, Warren Samuels, and Donald Winch, rather than a commentary on the import of this literature. The subsequent discussion focuses on key moments in the modern history of our subject: the work of John Stuart Mill and Henry Sidgwick in elaborating an increasingly broad theory of market failure; the growing optimism about the ability of government to remedy market failure in the work of the Cambridge school of Sidgwick, Alfred Marshall, and A. C. Pigou, and the subsequent elaboration of the neoclassical theory of market failure; the attempts by a group of scholars working in Italy to develop an economic policy analysis that included a theory of the political process; Ronald Coase's challenge to Pigou and the neoclassical theory of market failure; the development of public choice analysis—the economics of politics; and the evolution of law and economics. Both of the latter endeavors are significant for bringing self-interest into the policy-making arena—the former showing the potential for government failure and the latter how the legal system can help facilitate market success in situations where market failure was thought to be inevitable.

While the focus of this book is almost exclusively on "microeconomic" analyses of market failure and governmental responses to it, these movements have their parallels on the macro side: Say's Law being of a piece with the affirmative view of the system of natural liberty during the classical era, the correspondence between Keynesian macro theory and Pigovian welfare economics regarding the broad scope for government intervention, and the rise of rational expectations theory and its policy invariance results at the same time that the work of the Chicago and Virginia schools was gaining converts to non-interventionism on the micro side. Then again, these parallels seem fairly natural, given that the policy issues of macroeconomics—stabilization policy and income distribution policy—are themselves responses to market failures of the stability and distribution types.

In examining the history of the to-and-fro relationship between self-interest, market, and state in economic theorizing, we thus make no pretense of comprehensiveness. There is certainly far more to the theory of the economic role of government than the role and effects of self-interest, and much is left out by so confining our focus. Nonetheless, the fact is that those writing economics have been wrestling with the impact of self-interested behavior on social and economic outcomes for more than two millennia, and Nobel prizes continue to be awarded for work that furthers our understanding of how to channel self-interest in socially beneficial directions.[1] In the pages that follow, we attempt to tell the story of how this dance among self-interest, market, and state has unfolded.

[1] The 2007 Nobel Prize award is an excellent example of this. The work of Leonid Hurwicz, Eric Maskin, and Roger Myerson on mechanism design examines the properties of optimal allocation mechanisms, particularly when individuals have private information.

CHAPTER ONE

Adam Smith and His Ancestors

WHEN ADAM SMITH suggested that "an invisible hand" would tend to harmonize individual and social interests, and that attempts by the state to interfere with this would run counter to the national interest, he was living in the midst of a society dominated by a morass of regulations on trade. There were taxes and protective tariffs, of course, but there were also countless regulations and monopolies, many of which would seem incredible today: apprenticeship laws, regulations on the quality of goods, primogeniture mandates, laws of settlement, corporation laws, and sundry guild controls. These measures established a web of monopoly privileges that often generated substantial riches for their beneficiaries. Though governments were influenced by ideas about trade, what they created was an irrational patchwork of regulations: monopolies that had been created so that governments could raise money by selling them, regulations that existed to make it easier for taxes to be levied, regulations imposed because powerful merchants had argued for them. Competition was hampered on all sides.

How did men think about these problems of economic policy—about their origins and about the means of dealing with them? Economic analysis did not begin with Adam Smith. Indeed, it is not possible to understand Smith without a working knowledge of what came before him—as far back, at least, as the ancient Greeks. It was a commonplace from the Greeks onward to see individuals as tending to pursue their self-interest, but this self-interested behavior was thought to engender results contrary to the national interest unless restrained by the long arm of the state. The base effects ascribed to self-interest, as well as the content given to the national or social interest, varied across authors and over time, but the necessity of employing government to harness self-interest was a recurring theme.

One of the defining features of economic thought and analysis prior to the nineteenth century was its naturalistic or natural law orientation.[1] Individual and class roles within the socioeconomic system, the legitimacy of actions, and the goals to be pursued were among the factors considered to be given by a higher authority and thus beyond human control. Harmonization of individual and social life with the dictates of nature

---

[1] See, for example, Schabas (2006).

was paramount for proper social ordering, and good governance entailed putting into place a system of earthly laws that facilitated this. The role of government was thus something given rather than something to be worked out in pragmatic fashion. We find in this early "economic" literature no theory of governmental behavior to speak of, no serious analysis of the ability of government to carry out the tasks ascribed to it by the authors. What we see instead—in many cases, at least—is an assumed natural order of things and consequent statements of how government should act so as to facilitate the operation of a social-economic system that comports with the dictates of natural law.

ADAM'S ANCESTORS

The Greeks and the Scholastics: Pursuit of a Higher Good

The profound influence of Greek thinking on Western intellectual life is most prominently evidenced in areas such as philosophy, rhetoric, and political theory, but it also extends into economics.[2] One would search in vain for a Greek treatise on economics: the Greeks would have thought absurd the idea that one could make a study of the economic system as an autonomous subject. For the Greeks—as for most economic commentators prior to the nineteenth century—the economy was but one piece of a larger social system, and this led them to examine economic issues as one facet of a broad-based social theory.

The two centuries prior to the time of Plato and Aristotle had been a period of economic liberalization, and with this came an enormous surge in commercial activity—including international trade. Moreover, tremendous economic upheaval and social instability accompanied the rapid commercial expansion, and this greatly influenced Plato and Aristotle's economic thinking. They believed that the instability resulted from the pursuit of financial gain, which, as the fable of Midas made clear, both knew no limits and brought with it dire consequences. Just as Midas had destroyed himself in the pursuit of gold, so too had the pursuit of wealth imperiled Greek society. It was partly in response to this threat that Plato and Aristotle undertook to contemplate what life would look like in the ideal state, and their analysis was built around the question of what, in such a state, would constitute "the good life"? It was clear to them that economic growth had undesirable effects, and they stressed the need for an economic system that generated a relatively stationary level of economic activity. Their ideal

---

[2] Excellent discussions of Greek economic thought can be found in Todd Lowry's *The Archaeology of Economic Ideas* (1987) and Barry Gordon's *Economic Analysis before Adam Smith* (1975).

system was one in which the citizens of the state had a reasonable standard of economic well-being, and in which economic relationships satisfied the dictates of justice. The task for government here was to structure a system of laws that would facilitate this.

Both Plato and Aristotle were deeply suspicious of the ability of the forces of material self-interest to generate a just and harmonious social order. Self-interest and the pursuit of financial gain, they thought, tended to go hand-in-hand, and the negative consequences of this were observable all around them. Not surprisingly, then, they frowned upon commercial activity in general, seeing it as, at best, a necessary evil that allowed people to acquire the possessions sufficient to meet their needs. The potential for earning vast sums of money through trade, however, made commerce an irresistibly attractive line of work for many Greek citizens and thus something destined to continue to expand in scope and influence unless somehow checked. Relatively strict limits on commercial activity were thought by the philosophers to be the most straightforward means of attaining their objectives for the ideal state, and this is where the state was to play a central role within the Greek system. Aristotle, seeing no other means for the achievement of satisfactory economic coordination, advocated fairly wide-ranging governmental control over economic activity. He saw the market as "a creature of the state" (Lowry 1987: 237) and suggested that regulation was something that could and should be readily applied to deal with any problems that cropped up (*Politics* 1327a). So important was this aspect of the government's operations for Aristotle that among the "indispensable offices" of the state, he listed first "the office charged with the care of the marketplace" (*Politics* 1321b18; Lowry 1987: 237).

To rein in self-interest and avoid the potential problems that its unrestrained exercise could cause, Plato and Aristotle advocated policies including a prohibition on lending at interest, the elimination of profits, and statutory fixing of prices—all of which they believed would help to keep commercial activity in check. Moreover, while both Plato and Aristotle recognized that the development of an economic system that could generate a satisfactory level of material well-being required harnessing the power of the division of labor, they objected to the internationalization of the division of labor—foreign trade—owing to the base influences they believed it would introduce (and had already introduced) into society. The philosophers recommended various government actions to mitigate incentives to seek private gain through foreign trade, including the creation of separate domestic and international trading currencies. Such a dual-currency system would make it easier for the state to control the extent of international trading activity and allow for the confiscation of illicit gains.

Given that politics and economics were part of the same body of analysis for Plato, it is not surprising that his distrust of self-interested individual action bled over into the political arena. The ideal state could not, for Plato, evolve via democratic action; he opposed participatory governance and did not believe that the citizens could understand how to achieve the efficient outcomes of the ideal state unless they submitted themselves to the guidance of a ruler possessing superior intelligence.[3] The idea that the state should be governed by such a ruler-expert was a reflection of Plato's conception of the division of labor, which, in turn, gave effect to his belief that each person has a single task for which he is best suited by nature. This ruler would have the flexibility to adapt the laws of the state to meet situational needs, something that was not so easily done in a system governed by laws rather than by an individual. Although not himself immune from the influence of self-interest, this ruler could be trusted to govern in the interests of society as a whole because to act unjustly would be damaging to his psychic harmony and thus contrary to his self-interest. Given that the ruler ruled justly, obedience on the part of the subjects would be in their self-interest. It was thus part of the ruler's task to get his subjects to understand that their interests were served by submission to his rule. The result, as Todd Lowry (1987: 93) has pointed out, would be a state that was "rationally organized ... an efficient, static, changeless society administered by experts."

The intellectual legacy left by the ancient world, and by Aristotle in particular, began to gain currency in the thirteenth century. This marked the beginning of the Scholastic period, which was characterized by a renewed emphasis on learning, the application of rationality or reason, and, with this, the rise of the university as a home for learning and scholarship. Scholastic scholarship, like that of the Greeks, ranged over a broad spectrum of topics and included the systematic analysis of matters economic. That there were certain significant parallels between the respective analyses of the Greeks and the Scholastics is not surprising, as Thomas Aquinas (1225–74), the foremost of the schoolmen, made the reconciliation of Holy Scriptures and the teachings of the Church with the rule of reason, particularly as manifested in the writings of Aristotle, the centerpiece of his work. One sees in Aquinas a tendency for those things that Aristotle considered "unnatural" to be found inconsistent with scripture, and conversely, in keeping with Aquinas's view that religion and reason should lead one to the same conclusions.

Scholastic economic commentary was motivated by and bound up with the discussion of Christian morality and ethics.[4] The Scholastics' contempla-

---

[3] Aristotle shared Plato's nondemocratic bent but did not go all the way with the philosopher-king brand of expert advocated by Plato. See Kraut (2002) and Keyt and Miller (1991).

[4] On Scholasticism generally, see Gordon's *Economic Analysis before Adam Smith* (1975) and Odd Langholm's *The Legacy of Scholasticism in Economic Thought* (1998).

tion of the relationship between man and his Creator necessarily involved a consideration of relations between individuals in a social context, the biblical mandate to "love they neighbor as thyself" being on essentially equal footing with the command to "Love the Lord thy God with all thy heart, and with all they soul, and with all thy mind, and with all thy strength."[5] The attempt to work out the practical content of this led the Scholastics to consider the operation of the commodity exchanges and the monetary system. The Scholastic inquiry into social-economic issues was motivated by the basic question, "What ought a Christian man to do?" Justice was central, of course, but its attainment on this earth was rendered problematic by man's sinful nature. One of the effects of sin was that individuals were more concerned with self than with others,[6] and the results were seen to be both contrary to the will of God and (perhaps as a consequence) harmful to the social order.

The influence of man's sinful nature came through in a variety of ways in both the commodity and money markets. Though the Scholastics tended to be more favorably disposed toward commercial activity than the Greeks, it was not because the Scholastics approved of the unbridled pursuit of wealth. Rather, they were generally of the mind that market outcomes would satisfy the dictates of justice in the absence of monopoly or fraud. The problem, of course, was that monopoly and fraud were seen to be regular consequences of unrestrained behavior, as sellers would attempt to exploit consumers by charging the maximum price that they could get away with, whether for goods or, in the case of usury, for the use of money. In the former instance, regulations were considered appropriate means of preventing unjust pricing practices. In the case of usury, Aquinas followed Plato and Aristotle in supporting prohibitions on lending at interest—grounding this in the Old Testament biblical dictum that "thou shalt not charge interest to any of my children that is poor by thee"—although this view eroded slowly over time as later Scholastic writers came to understand the opportunity cost associated with lending.[7]

While the Scholastics devoted a great deal of effort to the question of usury between the thirteenth and sixteenth centuries, monetary issues in general were a significant economic problem during this period, and they attracted plenty of commentary from the Scholastic writers. Monarchs in need of funds to finance military expansion and regal lifestyles regularly succumbed to the temptation to debase the national currency, calling in old

---

[5] Mark 12:30–31 (King James version).

[6] Indeed, the command to "love thy neighbor as thyself" may be seen as a response to exactly this problem.

[7] See Aquinas ([1274] 1948). The reader may find Aquinas's interpretation of this passage a bit broad, as it could be said to apply only to the poor or, say, fellow Jews ("thy neighbor"). See the discussion in Gordon (1975) for further commentary on this.

coins and reminting at the same face value but with reduced precious metals content—meaning that more coins were available after the reminting and so leaving a "surplus" to be pocketed by the monarch. The citizens were no less in need of funds, and they responded similarly—by clipping coins and selling the clipped bits of gold and silver. Commoner and Crown alike were thus subject to the temptations of self-interest. The effects of this pursuit of gain were clear: currency destabilization that resulted in significant macroeconomic fluctuations. One Scholastic response to these problems was to support measures that would eliminate such practices. The authority of the monarch, however, rendered debasement prevention laws problematic, and the technology of coining at that time made it virtually impossible to prevent clipping. One artifact of this dilemma was widespread Scholastic support for some degree of price control—in this case, the regulation of prices within certain upper and lower limits. If controlling the quality of the currency was problematic, price controls could at least serve to mitigate the extent of the fluctuation in the value (or purchasing power) of money over time.

The self-interested behavior arising from man's sinful nature was also at the heart of the Scholastics' support for private property. Plato was a staunch supporter of common property, but Aristotle was equally adamant that private property was necessary in that people would not take sufficient care of things owned in common because the benefit of such care did not redound to them. Not surprisingly, the Scholastics followed Aristotle, but gave the position religious underpinnings. Most of the Scholastic writers had taken vows of poverty, and many were mendicants, which made it logical that they would consider common property as the ideal. Nonetheless, they were very much of the mind that private property was optimal for society as a whole. The problem with common property, they said, was the negative incentive effects that it provided for sinful, worldly people—these being sufficiently severe to render common property unworkable. The one exception to this position, it seems, was the communal monastic institutions—the monks' discipline of mind presumably placing them above the self-interested actions that were thought to be so problematic for laymen.

For both the Greeks and the Scholastics, then, relatively extensive regulation of economic activity—whether by governmental, religious, or other authorities—was thought to be a necessary tool for bringing about a harmonious social-economic order. There was not so much an overarching theory of the state here as there was a set of supposedly naturally ordained ends that authorities could (and, indeed, necessarily should) assist society in attaining. In particular, the operation of the forces of self-interest was said to promote outcomes inconsistent with those prescribed by nature or by God, and regulatory action was necessary to prevent, or at least minimize, the more base impacts of self-interested behavior.

Mercantilism's Golden Rule

Self-interest began to take an entirely different form in the economic writings of the sixteenth and seventeenth centuries. The literature of this period was produced not by theologians writing manuals on doctrine or the Christian life, but by businessmen and merchants who wrote pamphlets in an attempt to influence government policy and popular sentiment in ways that promoted their particular interests. Significantly, the dissemination of this pamphlet literature was greatly aided by the advent of the printing press. While self-interested advocacy was often the motivation for this work, many of these writers appealed (for obvious reasons) to the larger national interest to justify their proposals. In spite of its polemical nature, however, this work evidenced systematic methods of analysis that were absent from many earlier economic writings, as a result of which certain insights were gained into the workings of the economic system.

The mercantile period, as this era came to be known,[8] saw a shift in the focus of the analysis away from moral concerns to those of a more worldly nature. Mercantilist doctrines were aimed at promoting economic growth and consolidating the power of the nation-state, including the provision of revenues sufficient to meet its needs. The means for achieving these ends was the accumulation of gold and silver bullion, on the grounds that a nation's wealth and political-economic power were directly tied to its stocks of precious metals.[9] One avenue for increasing the nation's bullion stock was via the colonization of the metals-rich New World. Trade, however, offered a second avenue: Selling one's goods to other nations brought bullion into the country, while importing the goods produced by other nations sent it out. Precious metals accumulation, then, was directly tied to the magnitude of a nation's trade surplus. The link between bullion accumulation and the self-interest of those promoting it was simple: The maximization of the trade surplus meant protecting domestic industry from foreign competition and promoting the sale of domestically produced goods on world markets—all of which worked to the advantage of certain domestic business interests. Those who stood to gain from these policies sought to gain popular support for them by appealing to a larger national interest—national wealth, political power, increased employment—that would ostensibly be served if the policies were enacted. That political and economic objectives here were mutually reinforcing—and

---

[8] The term "mercantilism" was coined in the 1760s—and so relatively late in the mercantile era—by the Marquis de Mirabeau, but it achieved canonical status when Smith used the term to describe the trade policies that he was attacking in *The Wealth of Nations*.

[9] Eli Hecksher's *Mercantilism* offers the most expansive treatment of the subject. Lars Magnusson's *Mercantilism: The Shaping of an Economic Language* (1994) is a useful recent treatment.

worked to the benefit of the mercantile interests—can be seen when one notes that bullion accumulation went hand-in-hand with the development of military strength, including naval power, which at once protected both nation and trade shipments; with the acquisition of colonies, which brought empire, sources of raw materials for manufacturing, and markets for exports; and with the slave trade, which offered up low-cost labor.

While the justice-related questions that so concerned the ancient Greeks and the Scholastics were largely absent from the mercantilist literature, there was a degree of continuity with Greek and Scholastic thought in the view that individual self-interest, if given free rein, would run counter to the national interest, and that broad-based government intervention in economic activity was necessary to minimize these tendencies.[10] Self-interested behavior, in the mercantilist view, would lead to diminishing bullion stocks, and thus reduced national wealth—and for two reasons. First, traders would see the opportunity for gain from the importation of foreign goods, and the payment for those goods would be made in bullion. Second, self-interest on the part of consumers was bound to lead to what the mercantilist writers considered "excessive" consumption of both domestic and foreign goods, and especially luxuries. The former would diminish the quantity and raise the price of domestically produced exports, thereby reducing their competitiveness on world markets, while the latter increased the quantity of imports. The effect of all of this would be to harm the nation's trade balance and thus its stock of precious metals.

Given that people's natural inclinations would lead them to pursue courses of action that worked against the national interest, bullion accumulation, and thus the maintenance of a favorable balance of trade, required the implementation of a wide-ranging scheme of economic policy that would check this self-interested behavior. Import restriction and export promotion were only the most obvious policies proposed by the mercantilist writers. Even here, however, there were trade-offs to be dealt with. A number of writers recognized, for example, that outright prohibitions on imports and excessively high tariffs would serve only to encourage smuggling and even destroy markets for one's exports. Moreover, exceptions were allowed for consumer necessities and raw materials that could not be produced at home in the necessary quantities. Beneficial export policies were thought to include the removal of customs duties and other export impediments, subsidies for the export of manufactured products, and restrictions on the export of raw materials—the last of these because

---

[10] It should be noted here that the continuity was hardly intentional. The mercantilist literature is noticeably devoid of references to previous economic thinking.

these raw materials could be used by other nations to produce manufactured goods that would compete with domestically produced products. These policies, then, would result in the export of products with the highest value added, thus bringing in the largest possible quantity of bullion in payment. The policies advocated by the mercantilist writers, however, went well beyond these basic import and export controls to include the regulation of precious metals exchanges—including prohibitions on bullion exports, exchange rate controls, and protecting the quality of coinage—and related regulations restricting the hoarding of bullion and its conversion into plate, jewelry, and so forth, to ensure sufficient currency in circulation to fuel the nation's economic activity. Strategic policies that would favor certain important national industries and protect infant industries were also much in vogue, as were labor-related policies—including loose immigration and tight emigration rules, and subsidies to encourage workers to relocate to manufacturing centers—that would serve to keep labor supply up and wages low, thus facilitating the price-competitiveness of exports. In general, the rod against which policy proposals should be measured was, for the mercantilists, the effect they would have on the nation's stock of precious metals.

While its rhetoric centered on the pragmatic idea of nation-state building, the mercantilist mode of reasoning was not without its own natural law aspect. As Jacob Viner (1937: 100–101) has pointed out, the mercantilists

> managed ingeniously to adapt the doctrine of [divine] providence to their own particular views ... [using] the doctrine either to justify the restriction of certain products to Englishmen, on the ground that Providence had assigned them to this country, or appealed to the doctrine in support of that branch or type of trade which they wished to have fostered, while completely forgetting the doctrine when attaching other branches or types of trade.

In fact, these appeals to providence, often couched in nationalistic garb, regularly served as a mask to shield what was really self-interested advocacy on the part of the author: the attempt to use governmental policy to support private interests. Yet there was more to the natural law aspect than just this effort to mask self-interest. Mercantilism departed from previous thinking by viewing the economic system as "an independent territory with its own distinctive laws." Here, economic welfare depended greatly on "the statesman's ability to rule according to the laws dictated by an independent economic realm," this being necessary owing to the inability of self-interested private action, as translated through the market mechanism, to promote most effectively the interests of the nation, whether this be measured by political power or precious metals stocks (Magnusson 1993: 6–8).

Physiocracy

The French mercantile apparatus had its origins in the policies laid out by Jean Baptiste Colbert (1619–83), who was finance minister during the reign of Louis XIV. In an effort to provide sufficient revenues to finance the Crown, and so solidify its power, Colbert introduced a wide-ranging set of policies that benefited the manufacturing sector, in the mercantile way, while retarding the development of the agricultural sector. Legal barriers to the movement of foodstuffs within the country caused some regions to experience severe shortages of food while other regions had surpluses. The monarchs did not help matters. Profligate court spending and the need to finance military activities meant that substantial tax revenues were necessary. The nobles were exempt from taxes, which meant that the tax burden fell on the common people. There was little money available for investment in agriculture, which caused a progressive deterioration of agricultural output and thus returns on investment. These problems were further exacerbated by the movement of the population from the countryside to the cities. As a result, food was in extremely short supply, and life for the common people of France during this period was very difficult.

Given the extent of these hardships, it is not surprising that the backlash against mercantilist thinking was first evidenced in a significant way in France in the eighteenth century. Vincent de Gournay—who is widely credited with popularizing the expression, "laissez-faire, laissez-passer"[11]—and Pierre de Boisguilbert attempted to make the case for economic liberalism against the restrictions on resource movement imposed by Colbert.[12] The most prominent strain of anti-Colbertism to emerge in France, however, was the product of that group of intellectuals known then as "les économistes" but who later became known as the Physiocrats. Led by François Quesnay (1694–1774), and Victor Riqueti, Marquis de Mirabeau (1715–89), the Physiocrats were the first organized group—or "school"—of economic thinkers, and their doctrine was very much a reaction against Colbert's mercantilist policies that promoted French manufacturing at the expense of agriculture. As Quesnay and Mirabeau pointed out in their classic work, *La Philosophie Rurale*, first published in 1763,[13] these policies, combined with wars and high tax burdens, served to impoverish the agricultural peasant proprietors and thus retarded productivity advances in the agricultural sector, where the continued use of cattle rather than horses to plow land

[11] See, for example, Higgs (1897: 67).

[12] For an excellent treatment of Boisgilbert, see Faccarello (1999).

[13] *Philosophie Rurale* went through several subsequent revisions. See Meek (1962) and the introduction to the works of Quesnay (2005) for an analysis of the evolution of this work and its arguments.

yielded output levels per acre significantly lower than those of nations such as England.

The Physiocrats were very much a product of the enlightenment mentality of eighteenth-century France. The world as they saw it consisted of a set of self-evident truths arising from natural law—the term "physiocracy" means "rule of nature"—and they believed that these truths could be discovered through human reason. Quesnay, who was the personal physician to Madame de Pompadour, the mistress of King Louis XV, exemplified this link between the natural and social realms. His medical science perspective infused his political economy, which posited an essential commonality between the body human and the body social, with each governed by its own particular set of laws set down by nature.[14] These natural laws extended to the economic system and, according to the Physiocrats, the state that governed best would govern in accordance with them.

For the Physiocrats, agricultural production was the cornerstone of economic activity. The reasoning behind this position was straightforward: agriculture alone, they said, generated a *produit net*—a net product, a surplus of output over input. Manufacturing was said to be sterile. In the Physiocratic system, the net product was the sole source of funds for investments in increased agricultural productivity, as well as the source of the tax base.[15] Quesnay and the Physiocrats saw the growth of this surplus as the only possible source for the financial capital needed to advance the technology of French agricultural production to match that of other nations. The mechanics of this were elegantly demonstrated in Quesnay's *Tableau Économique*—the economic table—which was devised and employed to show exactly this relationship between investments in agriculture and the growth of the net product, and rendered with a degree of scientific sophistication heretofore unseen in economic argumentation.[16]

Given the importance of the net product for economic development, it is not surprising that the Physiocrats made its increase the goal for society. It was against this rod—rather than the stock of precious metals—that the efficacy of all policy proposals was to be judged. As Mirabeau put it in a letter to Rousseau (quoted in Meek 1962: 20),

> The whole moral and physical advantage of societies is ... summed up in one point, *an increase in the net product*; all damage done to society is determined by this fact, *a reduction in the net product*. It is on the two scales

---

[14] On the relationship between Quesnay's political economy and his medical background, see Groenewegen (2001).

[15] Given that the manufacturing sector generated no surplus over costs, the Physiocrats argued that any tax ultimately came out of the net product, whether directly or indirectly.

[16] Quesnay's works (2005) show many of the tableaux that Quesnay and Mirabeau employed, and a number of these are reproduced, with commentary, in Meek (1962).

of this balance that you can place and weigh laws, manners, customs, vices, and virtues.

From a Physiocratic perspective, then, the mercantilists had things exactly backward in promoting manufacturing. Self-interested behavior, however, was also a big part of the problem, according to the Physiocrats.[17] First, it generated an enormous demand for manufactured goods, and luxuries in particular. Secondly, the significant returns available in the manufacturing sector, especially in light of the mercantilist policies in place, attracted resources from profit-seeking entrepreneurs that could otherwise have been invested in agriculture. Given that any expenditures on the production and consumption of manufactured goods inevitably reduced the net product, self-interest and social interest were once again seen to be in conflict.

The importance of the net product, and thus of agricultural production, set the Physiocrats steadfastly against policies that restricted agricultural production for the benefit of the manufacturing sector—such as the prohibitions on agricultural exports that served to keep food prices, and thus manufacturing wages, low. In rejecting the mercantilist policy scheme, Quesnay argued that the sole function of the state is the provision of security: national defense and the appropriate system of laws—those that harmonized with natural law. The Physiocratic position on government interference with commerce and its consonance with the laissez-faire views set out by Gournay and Boisgilbert is nicely illustrated in Quesnay's essay on "Corn," where he argues that "all trade ought to be free.... It is enough for the government to watch over the expansion of the revenue of the kingdom's property; not to put any obstacles in the way of industry; and to give the people the opportunity to spend as they choose." ([1757] 1993: 79). Elsewhere, in his "General Maxims for the Economic Government of an Agricultural Kingdom," Quesnay says that "complete freedom of trade should be maintained; for THE POLICY FOR INTERNAL AND EXTERNAL TRADE WHICH IS THE MOST SECURE, THE MOST CORRECT, AND THE MOST PROFITABLE FOR THE NATION AND THE STATE, CONSISTS IN FULL FREEDOM OF COMPETITION" ([1767] 1993: 237).[18] This freedom of trade or competition entailed freedom in the production and circulation of goods, the reduction or elimination of transport tolls, improvement of transportation infrastructure, and the substitution of a single tax on the net product for the arbitrary tax system that so oppressed the agricultural sector.

It would seem from all of this that the Physiocrats were attempting to establish a case for the market, and hence the beneficial working of self-interest. It would be incorrect, though, to label their system one of laissez-

---

[17] On the importance of self-interest for Quesnay, see his "Essai Physique sur L'Économie Animale" (reprinted in Quesnay 2005), as well as the discussion in Steiner (1994, 1998) and Faccarello and Steiner (2006).

[18] The French version of the "Maxims" is reprinted in Quesnay (2005).

faire, in spite of their claims regarding noninterference and a minimalist state. In fact, the "appropriate system of law" to which Quesnay referred added up to a rather activist state. In addition to their support for the loosening of restrictions on agricultural production, the Physiocrats also pushed for the implementation of policies that would favor the agricultural sector, including agricultural price supports, legal ceilings on interests rates to hold down the cost of borrowing for agricultural proprietors, limitations on the importation of foodstuffs, and restrictions on the export of manufactured products—this last on the grounds that export promotion led to political pressures to hold down food prices in order to keep manufacturing wages, and thus costs, low. Quesnay even suggested that the government needed to educate citizens in the basic principles of natural law, lest they make improper decisions ([1767] 1993: 213). That is, far from proposing a minimalist and inactive state, the Physiocrats looked to achieve their aims through the state's agency, replacing mercantilist policies with those that favored the agricultural sector and the interests it represented.[19] That the Physiocrats were not truly disposed to noninterference—or willing to trust self-interested behavior to properly allocate resources—can be seen in Quesnay's statement that "the government's economic policy should be concerned only with encouraging productive expenditures and trade in raw produce ... " ([1767] 1993: 233) and in his harnessing of the rhetorical power of the *Tableau* to "demonstrate" both the error of Colbert's policies and the beneficial effects of the policies favored by the Physiocratic writers.[20]

Self-interest, then, could not be relied upon to promote the growth of the net product any more than it could be trusted to promote stability, Christian justice, or bullion accumulation. Left to their own devices, people would spend and invest in ways inimical to the national welfare, and the power of the state was the only means by which the social interest could be effectively promoted. And, as was the case for Plato, Quesnay and the Physiocrats placed great emphasis on the role of the expert—in this case, the monarch—who alone was sufficiently in tune with natural law to govern according to its dictates.

THE HAND OF ADAM

The Physiocratic revolt against mercantilist policies was picked up and extended by Adam Smith in his *Inquiry into the Nature and Causes of the Wealth of Nations* (1776). Smith was born in 1723 in the Scottish coastal

---

[19] See Samuels (1962: 149) and Groenewegen (2002: 216).

[20] Even Gournay and Boisgilbert were not immune from this somewhat selective invocation of laissez-faire. See, for example, Pitvay-Simoni (1997).

village of Kirkcaldy, and his education under Francis Hutcheson at the University of Glasgow imbued him with the Scottish Enlightenment perspective.[21] This enlightenment mentality had many facets, including a broad-based view of human motivation—as against, for example, the strong self-interest view that Bernard Mandeville extolled in his *Fable of the Bees* (1714)—and a concern with the origins, development, and structure of civil society. These characteristics are reflected in the emphases on moral philosophy and political economy in the Scottish Enlightenment tradition, and Smith, who spent more than a decade as a professor of moral philosophy at the University of Glasgow (where he inherited Hutcheson's chair), evidences both of these emphases in his writings.

While of common purpose with the Physiocrats in their attack on mercantilism, Smith, who had spent several months in their company in 1766, also considered Physiocratic doctrine erroneous.[22] For Smith, the wealth of a nation consisted in the value of its produce rather than in the national stock of precious metals or, as with the Physiocrats, the net product of agriculture. The role for government within the economic system, then, was to facilitate the growth of national wealth, so defined. In this sense, Smith demonstrated an important commonality with the mercantilist and Physiocratic writers, but, as he himself recognized, accomplishing the goal of maximizing the value of output required a very different role for government than that posited by earlier writers.

This Scotsman understood full well the complexity of the human psyche and wrote about it eloquently and at great length in his *Theory of Moral Sentiments* (1759), the book that gave Smith his wide reputation and was, in fact, more influential during his own lifetime than was *The Wealth of Nations*. Even so, Smith shared with his ancestors the view that individuals are motivated primarily by self-interest in economic affairs. Smith's position, in a nutshell, was that individuals tend to be motivated most strongly by benevolence in dealings with those closest to themselves (such as immediate family), but that the force of benevolence weakens—and that of self-interest strengthens—as one moves progressively farther away from the self. Given that relations between individuals tend to be relatively anonymous in the realm of economic affairs, Smith considered self-interest to be the

---

[21] On the Scottish Enlightenment generally, see Broadie (2003). Ian Simpson Ross's *The Life of Adam Smith* (1995) provides a detailed analysis of Smith's life and work. The secondary literature on Smith is voluminous. For a selection of perspectives on Smith, see Hollander (1973), Skinner (1996b), Rothschild (2001), Winch (1996), and Haakonssen (2006).

[22] Smith spent 1764–66 in France as a tutor to the young Duke of Buccleuch, giving up his university professorship to do so. He developed good relations with several of the Physiocrats, including Quesnay, and, in spite of his criticism of the Physiocratic system, insisted that it was "perhaps, the nearest approximation to the truth that has yet been published upon the subject of political œconomy" (from *Wealth of Nations*; see [1776] 1981: IV.ix.38).

dominant motive in that arena. As he says early on in *The Wealth of Nations*, "In civilized society [man] stands at all times in need of the cooperation and assistance of great multitudes, while his whole life is scarce sufficient to gain the friendship of a few persons." As a result, this help must come primarily from relative strangers, and Smith contends that "it is in vain for him to expect it from their benevolence only." He is more likely to secure their assistance if he is able to "interest their self-love in his favour, and show them that it is for their own advantage to do for him what he re-quires of them." Smith then goes straight to the point: "It is not from the benevolence of the butcher, the brewer, or the baker, that we expect our dinner," he says, "but from their regard to their own interest. We address ourselves, not to their humanity but to their self-love, and never talk to them of our own necessities but of their advantages" ([1776] 1981: I.ii.2). The other-regarding aspect of our nature, then, cannot be expected to play a governing role in the marketplace.

What distinguished Smith from his ancestors on this score was not that he saw self-interest as a dominant feature of commercial life; after all, we have already seen that self-interested behavior was a centerpiece of the earlier literature, and Smith, like his predecessors (but unlike, say, Mande-ville), disapproved of many of the manifestations of self-interested behavior. Rather, the distinguishing feature of Smith's analysis was his attitude toward its effects ([1776] 1981: IV.ii.4):

> Every individual is constantly exerting himself to find out the most advanta-geous employment for whatever capital he can command. It is his own ad-vantage, indeed, and not that of society, which he has in view. But the study of his own advantage naturally, or rather necessarily, leads him to prefer that employment which is most advantageous to the society.

Smith was arguing here that the individual pursuit of self-interest serves the best interests of society as a whole, that self-interest and the social inter-est are partners rather than enemies. So understood, the operation of self-interest is something to be facilitated rather than restrained. It hardly needs noting that this marked a significant break with past economic thinking.

Such a dramatic departure cries out for an explanation: How does this coincidence of private and social interests occur? Here, Smith is at once vividly descriptive and maddeningly vague in making what is assuredly his most famous pronouncement. Smith contends that a person will attempt to employ his capital where he expects that it will yield for him the high-est return, and, in doing so, "He generally ... neither intends to promote the public interest, nor knows how much he is promoting it." Yet, Smith argues, even though intending his own gain, "he is in this, as in many other cases, led by an invisible hand to promote an end which was no part of his intention"—that end being the interest of society as a whole ([1776]

1981: IV.ii.9). An invisible hand—this is as specific as Smith gets. What Smith meant by this is anyone's guess, and plenty of guesses have been offered, ranging from God to government.[23] But whatever it is, Smith was convinced of its propensity to channel self-interest in socially useful directions.

This perception of an essential congruence—some would say, more strongly, a harmony—between private and social interests explains the strong parallels in Smith's critiques of mercantilism and Physiocracy. Smith saw that self-interest, if channeled in the proper directions, could work in the national interest. If not so channeled, however, it would lead to all manner of conspiracies to restrain trade. The mercantilists and Physiocrats, in contrast, believed that its operation tended to work directly counter to the national interest and needed to be forcibly checked by the state. Smith saw the respective favoritisms of the mercantilists and the Physiocrats, as well as the policy schemes that attended them, promoting flows of labor and capital resources into these favored sectors at rates in excess of what would arise naturally via the operation of self-interest. The problem, of course, was that if the resource-flows generated by the motive of self-interest promoted the greatest increases in national wealth, then measures that worked to deflect resources from these courses would necessarily restrict economic growth by comparison. In Smith's words ([1776] 1981: IV.ix.50),

> [E]very system which endeavors, either, by extraordinary encouragements, to draw towards a particular species of industry a greater share of the capital of the society than what would naturally go to it; or, by extraordinary restraints, to force from a particular species of industry some share of the capital which would otherwise be employed in it; is in reality subversive of the great purpose which it means to promote. It retards, instead of accelerating, the progress of society towards real wealth and greatness; and diminishes, instead of increasing, the real value of the annual produce of its land and labour.

This idea was at the heart of Smith's argument for (relatively) free trade. To take just one example cited by Smith, to produce at home that which could be produced more cheaply abroad—as mercantilist policies advocated—serves only to reduce the value of the nation's output, enriching the individual businessman who is the beneficiary of the protection while harming the interests of society as a whole.

What is often lost in the discussions of Smith's critiques of mercantilism and Physiocracy is that Smith never questions the internal logic of either system. The mercantile literature does a very good job of laying out a pro-

[23] See Samuels (2009a,b).

gram for promoting precious metals accumulation and the Physiocrats for promoting the growth of agricultural output. The problem, for Smith, was that both the mercantilists and the Physiocrats had misapprehended the nature of wealth, and as a result believed that the growth must be facilitated by governmental support for a particular segment of the economy. There was thus a perceived disconnect between self-interested behavior and the growth of national wealth, and this could, in their view, be resolved only via state action. Against this, Smith argued that the growth of national wealth, properly understood, was facilitated by self-interested action and that attempts to interfere with it in the national interest managed to work exactly contrary to that interest.

None of this is meant to suggest that Smith saw self-interested behavior as an unmitigated good nor that he believed people *ought to* behave in self-interested fashion. For example, Smith understood, with the Scholastics, that businessmen were constantly looking to exploit any possible advantage in ways detrimental to both consumers and their fellow producers. In one of many cutting remarks that he made about the business class, Smith said, "People of the same trade seldom meet together, even for merriment and discussion, but the conversation ends in a conspiracy against the publick, or in some contrivance to raise prices" ([1776] 1981: I.x.c.27). Smith believed, however, that competition, if allowed to flourish and supported by appropriate legal structures, would be the rule rather than the exception, and that such an environment would greatly curtail the extent to which the base effects of self-interest could manifest themselves.

While showing a healthy degree of confidence in the effects of self-interested behavior when channeled through the market, Smith's position is grounded in more than a basic optimism about private activity. He also had a very negative view of the abilities of statesmen and civil servants—one that was quite justified by the state of politics in Britain during the period, which is often described as being "shot through with corruption and venality" (Prest 1991: 68).[24] Indeed, *The Wealth of Nations* is replete with pejorative characterizations of government agents, such as Smith's reference to "that insidious and crafty animal, vulgarly called a statesman or politician" ([1776] 1981: IV.ii.39)—a personal favorite of Frank Knight, one of the founders of the Chicago school. Not surprisingly, this dim view of government officials translated into a belief on Smith's part that the state tends not to be capable of improving upon the results of private activity. Smith found it perfectly evident that "any individual" can judge the disposition of his resources "much better than any statesman or lawgiver can do for him" ([1776] 1981: IV.ii.10). In fact, he says,

[24] See also Hill (2006) and the references cited by Hill and by Prest (1991).

The statesman, who should attempt to direct private people in what manner they ought to employ their capitals, would not only load himself with a
most unnecessary attention, but assume an authority which could safely be
trusted, not only to no single person, but to no council or senate whatever,
and which would nowhere be so dangerous as in the hands of a man who
had folly and presumption enough to fancy himself fit to exercise it. ([1776]
1981: IV.ii.10)

Where the state had for centuries been characterized as the savior from
the negative influences of self-interest, Smith was arguing the reverse. The
expert had been transformed into the delusional bumbler, susceptible to
capture by a business class always looking to further its own interests at the
expense of the public. It is not just that self-interest does the job, then—it
does it *better* than can the state. In fact, Smith suggests that the force of
self-interest is sufficiently powerful and positive that it can even overcome
some degree of mismanagement by politicians ([1776] 1981: IV.ix.28).[25]

All of this having been said, Smith did not see the situation as hopeless
where government was concerned. In fact, he subscribed to what might
be called an "improvability thesis" regarding state action. He was of the
mind that much of what he considered bad policy resulted from ignorance
and prejudice on the part of government agents, and he held out hope
that the extent of this could be reduced—and legislative performance thus
improved—if government officials were properly instructed.[26] *The Wealth
of Nations*, of course, was a recipe for exactly that.

Smith's take on things, in short, is that markets are quite successful at
facilitating the growth of national wealth and that government interference
with this process will tend to be more harmful than helpful. All of this was
nicely summed up by Smith ([1776] 1981: IV.ix.51) when he was rounding
out his critique of mercantilism and Physiocracy and giving his summary
prescription for enhancing the wealth of the nation:

All systems either of preference or restraint, therefore, being thus completely
taken away, the obvious and simple system of natural liberty establishes itself
of its own accord. Every man, as long as he does not violate the laws of justice, is left perfectly free to pursue his own interest his own way, and to bring
both his industry and his capital into competition with those of any other

[25] What makes Smith's position here all the more interesting is that he spent that last part
of his career in the civil service, as Commissioner of Customs for Scotland. That his time in
the civil service seemingly did not cause him to revise his views (Smith made multiple revisions to *The Wealth of Nations* during this period) suggests that his bureaucratic sojourn may
have only served to confirm his original position.

[26] On this aspect of Smith, see Stigler (1971). Stigler is critical of Smith for failing to realize
that politicians, too, are inevitably self-interested and as such beyond having their performance enhanced by instruction.

man, or order of men. The sovereign is completely discharged from a duty, in the attempting to perform which he must always be exposed to innumerable delusions, and for the proper performance of which no human wisdom or knowledge could ever be sufficient; the duty of superintending the industry of private people, and of directing it towards the employments most suitable to the interest of the society.

This is all well and good, of course, but it leaves one wondering what, for Smith, is the appropriate role for government within such a system. He suggests that there are only three duties that fall to the state ([1776] 1981: IV.ix.51):

> According to the system of natural liberty, the sovereign has only three duties to attend to; three duties of great importance, indeed, but plain and intelligible to common understandings: first, the duty of protecting the society from the violence and invasion of other independent societies; secondly, the duty of protecting, as far as possible, every member of the society from the injustice or oppression of every other member of it, or the duty of establishing an exact administration of justice; and, thirdly, the duty of erecting and maintaining certain publick works and certain publick institutions, which it can never be for the interest of any individual, or small number of individuals, to erect and maintain; because the profit could never repay the expence to any individual or small number of individuals, though it may frequently do much more than repay it to a great society.

Smith's "certain publick works and certain publick institutions" is actually a reasonably broad category and includes not only the standard roads, bridges, canals, and harbors—which serve to facilitate commerce—but also education, to counteract what he saw as the mind-numbing effects of the division of labor, temporary monopolies given to joint-stock companies to facilitate new trade avenues, and religious instruction for clergy.[27]

One would be severely mistaken, though, in thinking that Smith actually confined the operations of the state to this narrow band. Smith was certainly in favor of doing away with the trade restrictions of the mercantilists, apprenticeship and settlement laws (which inhibited the free flow of labor), legal monopoly, and the laws of succession that impeded free trade in land. Yet, in addition to the basic governmental functions noted in the previous paragraph, he also allowed for exceptions to his generally free-trade attitude to encourage and protect industries essential to national defense

---

[27] Smith's list of appropriate governmental functions is virtually identical to that offered by Sir William Petty in his *Treatise of Taxes and Contributions* (1662), the exception being the social safety net included by Petty. The absence of such in Smith may owe to his belief in the ability of labor markets to clear relatively quickly and thereby eliminate involuntary unemployment.

and to level the playing field for domestic products subject to tax at home, and he suggested that retaliatory tariffs would be beneficial if (although only if) they induced other countries to lower their trade barriers. Beyond this, Smith offered at least a degree of support for regulations dealing with public hygiene; legal ceilings on interest rates to prevent excessive flows of financial capital into high-risk ventures; light duties on imports of manufactured goods; the mandating of quality certifications on linen and plate; certain banking and currency regulations to promote a stable monetary system; various regulations that were in the interest of the laboring classes (to offset employers' bargaining power advantage); and the discouragement of the spread of drinking establishments through taxes on liquor, as well as various other regulations that would compensate for the imperfect knowledge and foresight—what is sometimes called diminished telescopic faculty—of individuals.[28] All of this has led Jacob Viner to conclude that while Smith's "one deliberate and comprehensive generalization" regarding the proper functions of the state would "narrowly restrain" its activities, the actual range of activities pointed to by Smith was so extensive that if Smith "had been brought face to face with a complete list of the modifications to the principle of laissez faire to which he at one place or another had granted his approval, I have no doubt that he would have been astounded at his own moderation" (1927: 102).

Smith, then, was not a doctrinaire advocate of laissez-faire. He had an inherent suspicion of the ability of government to manage economic affairs properly, but he also recognized that there were various policy actions that could improve the national welfare, and that the ability of government officials to govern wisely could be improved if they were properly instructed.[29] At least as important, though, was Smith's recognition that the market does not operate absent government; indeed, Smith calls political economy "a branch of the science of a statesman or legislator" ([1776] 1981: IV.i.1), making it, in part at least, a branch of jurisprudence. Smith found in the system of natural liberty a regulating mechanism that previous commentators had been unable to discern—a coordinating force that would keep self-interest from becoming totally destructive.[30] Yet, he also understood that governmental action supplies the legal-institutional process through and within which markets function. It was not government that Smith opposed. Both the *Wealth of Nations* and his *Lectures on Jurisprudence*

---

[28] See Skinner (1996a) for an excellent elaboration of Smith's rather broad-based conception of the appropriate functions for the state.

[29] See Viner (1927: 112).

[30] While Smith's writings have a natural law flavor to them—as evidenced, for example, in his use of the invisible hand and system of natural liberty concepts—his views on the appropriate role for government are not so much derived from a broad set of general principles as from the examination of specific circumstances and problems.

(1978) show that he fully understood the integral relationship between government and economy. What Smith was after was the appropriate set of policies that, working in tandem with the self-interest that he believed governed behavior in the economic realm, would facilitate the growth of national wealth.

So yes, Smith had turned the tables in arguing and elaborating an analytical system of political economy, which showed that self-interest, channeled through the market, could be trusted to move resources into the uses most conducive to the growth of national wealth.[31] But it is also important to be clear on what Smith had *not* done here. Smith was not, as some have imagined, a proto-modern.[32] Smith's view of man is not economic man with his rational, single-minded pursuit of his self-interest. Ronald Coase has argued quite correctly that "Adam Smith would not have thought it sensible to treat man as a rational utility-maximiser. He thinks of man as he actually is—dominated, it is true, by self-love but not without some concern for others, able to reason but not necessarily in such a way as to reach the right conclusion, seeing the outcomes of his actions but through a veil of self-delusion" (1976: 545–46). Furthermore, Smith did not argue that private action was optimal, in the modern efficiency sense, nor even that it was always superior to governmental alternatives. Smith considered the link between private and social interests partial and imperfect, but he was also of the mind that self-interest, properly channeled, tended to engender positive results, rather than negative ones, and that government interference with its operation in the economic sphere would generally lead to inferior results.

Self-interest, then, had finally found legitimacy.

[31] Bear in mind that the Physiocrats, for all of their laissez-faire rhetoric, did not trust self-interest to grow the net product, but instead urged policies that favored agriculture. Moreover, while Gournay and Boisgilbert may have been more laissez-faire oriented than the Physiocrats, they both advocated policies at odds with their rhetoric and had only minimal impact on subsequent literature, as compared to Smith.

[32] See, for example, Evensky (2005), Samuels and Medema (2005), and Medema (2009a).

CHAPTER TWO

Harnessing Self-Interest

MILL, SIDGWICK, AND THE EVOLUTION
OF THE THEORY OF MARKET FAILURE

ON MAY 31, 1876, the Political Economy Club of London held a dinner to mark the centenary of the publication of the *Wealth of Nations*. Those present included prominent politicians, academics, businessmen, civil servants, and aristocrats. Mr. Robert Lowe, an able exponent of Benthamite utilitarianism and the Chancellor of the Exchequer (1868–73) under Prime Minister William Gladstone, opened the discussion by singing the praises of Adam Smith and the *Wealth of Nations*, holding forth the opinion that "[t]he test of science is ... prediction, and Adam Smith appears to me in the main to satisfy that condition."[1] Lowe praised Smith for his demonstration that governmental attempts to divert capital from its natural flows between sectors were bound to be injurious, and that man most effectively promoted the interest of society when he pursued his own interest.

As we saw in chapter 1, the preclassical commentators had looked for a means to coordinate or restrain the base effects of self-interested behavior and saw no means other than government regulation and religious control—both of which were rather centralized, authoritarian, and pessimistic regarding the effects of self-interested behavior. The idea that self-interest could somehow be massaged or channeled to work to the advance the general welfare of society was essentially absent.[2] Lowe's comments reflected a sense that Adam Smith had found in the system of natural liberty a means for harmonizing, to a greater or lesser extent, self-interest and social interest, allowing the market to function with far less direct control by government than had been deemed necessary by most of his predecessors. In this chapter we will look briefly at how the classical economists of the first half of the nineteenth century built on this aspect of Smith's work before we turn our attention to how, over the last half of the nineteenth century, the pendulum began to swing back to a greater degree of suspicion about the effects of self-interested behavior. Specifically, as against the classical faith in the system of natural liberty and the attendant suspicion of state inter-

---

[1] Quoted in Hutchison (1953: 2); on Lowe, see Maloney (2005).

[2] Courts, monarchs, and legislative bodies did begin to lay the legal foundations for a market economy in the fourteenth through seventeenth centuries.

vention, we observe in the literature assertions of a rather extensive set of divergences that the market could not satisfactorily coordinate—market failures—and the argument that government could serve as an efficient coordinating force.

This transformation in perspective over the course of the nineteenth century was the product of multiple forces. Externally, economists of the late nineteenth and twentieth centuries saw the effects on society, both positive and negative, of widespread industrialization, and this caused some to begin a rethinking of certain aspects of the received view of the market. There were, however, also methodological factors at work. The onset of the marginal revolution in the 1870s also precipitated a change in the way that economists went about their *analysis* of the economic role of government. As William Baumol (1952b: 154) has pointed out,

> With the Jevonsian revolution, French, Italian and English speaking authors were led, under the influence of positivist philosophy, to shy away from ethically normative discussion. Discussion of the duties of the state had generally amounted to a specification of the authors' preconceptions as to what ought to be, and this sort of analysis was not in keeping with the new approach.[3]

Writings on public finance no longer began with an elaboration of the appropriate role of government;[4] rather, they were confined to a discussion of how the revenues necessary for the operation of government should be garnered. The analysis of the appropriate role for government became bound up in the newly emerging welfare economics. At least as important, though, was a second internalist force: The *tools* of marginal analysis made possible the derivation of market optimality conditions and thus the *demonstration* of the potential failings of the system of natural liberty. With this came the related demonstration of the possibilities offered by governmental policy actions for promoting, rather than diminishing, social welfare, and these were now grounded in definitions of social welfare that went beyond mere wealth.

The theory of market failure brought analytical refinement to a centuries-old concern with the impact of self-interested behavior on economic activity, and in this chapter we attempt to shed some light on the transition from the fairly non-interventionist approach of the classical tradition to the more interventionist orientation that came to characterize neoclassical welfare theory and public economics. The argument here is that this transition occurred via a two-stage process, in which John Stuart Mill and Henry Sidgwick were central players. The first step involved the elaboration

---

[3] The Italian perspective is taken up by James Buchanan (1960) and in chapter 4, infra.

[4] Sir William Petty's *Treatise of Taxes and Contributions* (1662) is an excellent early example of this method—one we see carried though in Smith's *Wealth of Nations* (1776) as well.

of a greatly expanded theory of the failure of the system of natural liberty—akin to what we today call "market failure"—as against the classical
success story.[5] Mill was instrumental in this expansion, and it continued
at the hands of Sidgwick. The second stage involved the move to a much
more markedly positive assessment of the possibilities of corrective policy
actions undertaken by the state than we find in the classical tradition, and
it was here that Sidgwick took center stage. All of this fed into Pigovian
welfare theory, the market failure aspect of which, at least, came to dominate professional discourse. At this stage, we will examine how the writings
of Mill and Sidgwick represent a departure from that which came before,
the forces that led them to their respective views, and the role that these
ideas played in the development of the more expansive role for government
evidenced in early stages of welfare economics. Before doing so, however,
we need to set some context in the rise of utilitarianism and the evolution
of nineteenth-century classical political economy.

UTILITARIANISM

The evolution of political economy in the century following Smith's writing was profoundly influenced by the rise of utilitarianism, which received
its major impetus from the work of Jeremy Bentham in the late eighteenth
and early nineteenth centuries, and, in particular, from his *Introduction to
the Principles of Morals and Legislation* (1823).[6] Bentham ([1823] 1970:
I.1) saw the principle of utility, grounded in a calculus of pleasures and
pains, as the basis of individual decision-making and the ethical standard
for judging action:

> Nature has placed mankind under the governance of two sovereign masters,
> *pain* and *pleasure*. It is for them alone to point out what we ought to do, as
> well as to determine what we shall do.

For Bentham, individual decision-making was grounded in "psychological
hedonism," the notion that people make decisions based on calculations of
pleasure and pain, seeking to maximize the former and minimize the latter.
This hedonic calculus was consistent with the principle that individuals are
motivated by self-interest, while also allowing for the possibility that the
individual may increase his own happiness through altruistic actions. It also

---

[5] This has several aspects: stability failure, distribution failure, and allocation failure. The
focus of this chapter is on the last of these. Backhouse (2006) contains an excellent treatment of the ethical underpinnings of the Cambridge tradition, including their relationship
to distributional issues.

[6] This work was originally published in 1789.

provided an analytical engine for thinking about self-interested behavior in a more formalistic way, which took on increasing import in the last third of the nineteenth century.

It was the ethical strand of utilitarianism—utilitarianism as a moral standard for judging action—that had the greatest impact on social thought. Ethical utilitarianism offered a consequentialist ethic that judged an action right or good if it promotes the happiness of all those who are affected by it—rather than simply promoting the happiness of the person(s) undertaking the action—and conversely. Bentham's ethical utilitarianism was grounded in three fundamental premises. First, the interests of society are the sum of the interests of all of the individuals who make up that society. Second, each individual is the best judge of his or her own happiness. Third, each individual has the same capacity for happiness as every other individual. Utility, for Bentham, was not a simple construct; the utility associated with an act was said to be a function of the intensity, duration, certainty, propinquity (nearness or remoteness), fecundity (more or less of the same will follow), purity (pleasure won't be followed by pain, or vice-versa), and extent (number of people affected) of the pleasure or pain sensations. Measurement problems made the actual adding up of utilities problematic, but it was felt that this general approach could nonetheless serve as a useful ethical guide. One of the more noteworthy aspects of Bentham's calculus is that the interests of all individuals in society counted equally, which gave it simultaneous individualistic and egalitarian aspects.

Utilitarianism thus offered a means by which to assess individual and social action. The best courses of action were those that produced the greatest happiness for the members of society, and it was against this measuring rod that moral and legal rules, social-political institutions, and governmental policies should be judged. That is, policy evaluation was to be grounded in a rational empirical appraisal of the effects of policies on human happiness. The role of the legislature here was in some sense to resolve the conflicts between the effects of individuals' hedonic calculations and the utilitarian ethical creed. Bentham's utilitarian analysis of law had a similar cast, calling attention to the social consequences of individual acts. Theft, for example, has negative impacts that go beyond the harm to the actual victim: It threatens the status of private property and the stability of society. Bentham used this insight—which we would today call an externality argument—as the basis for his contention that the penalty for theft should include punishment that goes beyond righting the wrong done to the individual victim, in order to deter people from engaging in theft.

Bentham's utilitarian approach to questions of social, legal, and economic policy was to have a profound effect on the evolution of political economy and, in particular, on the analysis of the relationship between self-interested action and the best interests of society.

NINETEENTH-CENTURY CLASSICAL ECONOMICS:
PRAGMATISM MEETS SELF-INTEREST

The misleading nature of the caricature of the nineteenth-century classical economists as die-hard proponents of laissez-faire who held a homogeneous view of the economic role of government has long been evident to serious students of the history of economic thought.[7] Lionel Robbins (1952) elegantly laid out the case for the reformist nature of the classical economists, who were critical of a number of the institutional arrangements of their time and highly optimistic that the insights of political economy could be used to point economic policy in a direction that would benefit society. This new science would be an indispensable part of the policy-making process and help to arrest the more negative effects of partisan advocacy within it.

The nineteenth-century classical economists, like Smith before them, had a strong belief in the market as a vehicle for successfully coordinating economic activity, but they also understood that the market could operate satisfactorily—harmonizing actions of self-interested agents with the interests of society as a whole—only within a framework of legal, political, and moral measures that facilitated certain forms of action while simultaneously restricting others. Yes, there is a hostility to government that is evidenced in varying degrees throughout classical economics, largely a legacy of Smith's harsh critique of mercantilism—a critique which continued pretty much unabated in the nineteenth century. On the whole, however, classical political economy evidences a relatively pragmatic view of the economic role of government, one borne of the utilitarianism that underlay the approach of many of the classical writers.[8]

The transmission of Bentham's ideas into political economy during this period was facilitated by the Philosophic Radicals, a group that included David Ricardo, James Mill, and John Stuart Mill among its most prominent members.[9] The Philosophic Radicals were ardent advocates for social and economic reform. On the social side, this included an expanded franchise and more frequent elections, which they hoped would facilitate policy-

---

[7] For more extensive treatments of the classical view, see O'Brien (1975, 2004), Robbins (1952), and Samuels (1966). A more broad-based overview of fiscal theory can be found in Musgrave (1985).

[8] My use of the term "pragmatism" here refers not to the philosophical pragmatism of William James, John Dewey, and Charles Sanders Peirce, but to more general notions such as "a method of understanding facts and events in terms of cause and effect, and of inferring practical lessons or conclusions from this process," or "attention to facts, as opposed to opinion, ideals, or emotion; realism" (*Oxford English Dictionary* [online version], *OED* hereafter).

[9] William Thomas (1979) and Joseph Hamburger (1965) present excellent analyses of the Philosophic Radicals and their activities.

making on a utilitarian basis. On the economic side, they were ardent free traders. Utilitarianism could be (and was) used to justify policy schemes ranging from extreme laissez-faire to wide-ranging intervention, depending on the situation and on who was doing the weighing of benefits and costs.[10] On the one hand, it provided the basis for the opposition to many forms of intervention, including impediments to trade, that one finds within nineteenth-century classical political economy. There was also, however, strong utilitarian-based support for many forms of social legislation—for example, regarding the Poor Laws, sanitation, and education for the children of the working classes—that the classical economists believed would promote increased social happiness.[11] And while the impact of policies on national wealth continued to be a significant feature of political economy, one of the significant aspects of the utilitarian standard was that it allowed for the evaluation of economic outcomes on grounds other than wealth, while not excluding it.

That unquestioned laissez-faire was not the order of the day is evident throughout the classical writings. Witness J. R. McCulloch's contention that "The principle of *laisser-faire* may be safely trusted to do in some things but in many more it is wholly inapplicable; and to appeal to it on all occasions savours more of the policy of a parrot than of a statesman or a philosopher."[12] In a letter to Macvey Napier, editor of the *Edinburgh Review*, on December 23, 1830, McCulloch, a disciple of Ricardo, noted in a similar vein that "[t]he question is not whether any regulation interferes with the freedom of industry, but whether its operation is on the whole advantageous or otherwise."[13] Likewise, Nassau Senior argued that "the only rational foundation of government, the only foundation of a right to govern and a correlative duty to obey, is expediency—the general benefit of the community. It is the duty of a government to do whatever is conducive to the welfare of the governed."[14] At the end of the classical period, we have J. E. Cairnes' assertion that "[t]he maxim of *laissez-faire* ... has no scientific basis whatever" but is instead a "mere handy rule of practice," though "a rule in the main sound" (1873: 244).[15]

---

[10] For example, Bentham's own ideal bureaucracy included a very wide range of bureaus and associated governmental functions. See Robbins (1952: 42).

[11] Edwin Chadwick, one of Bentham's most prominent disciples, played a significant role here, both through his writings and his work on the Poor Law Commission.

[12] J. R. McCulloch (1848: 156), quoted in Robbins (1952: 43). See Chadwick (1842).

[13] Quoted in O'Brien (1970: 286, n.2).

[14] Nassau Senior (1928: 2:302), quoted in Robbins (1952: 45).

[15] See also Dunbar (1886: 19–23) for a late-nineteenth-century commentary. It is worth pointing out that the utilitarian wing of classicism, which includes Bentham and James Mill in the early part of the nineteenth century, was somewhat more overtly and self-consciously interventionist than the rest of classicism during that period.

The point to be taken here is that, far from being anti-government apologists for the business class, the classical economists were concerned with what set of policies would promote society's best interests, and they were vociferously opposed to policies—like those of mercantilism, but also many others—that they believed served the interests of particular groups at the expense of the larger population. In this regard, their position was remarkably like that of Smith. Their consumption-oriented view led them to the belief that freedom of choice was desirable for consumers, and that freedom for producers was the most effective means of satisfying these consumer desires. It was thought that the impersonal forces of the market, working through the system of natural liberty, would then serve to harmonize these interests—or at least would do so to a greater and more beneficial extent than would other systems—and that the most basic function of government was the establishment and enforcement of a system of laws that would control, channel, and restrain certain aspects of individual action, and liberate and facilitate others, in such manner that the individual pursuit of self-interest would lead to the greatest happiness. So central was the state in this process that Lionel Robbins, looking back at this period a century later, was led to suggest that Smith's "invisible hand" is actually government itself. The hand "is not the hand of some god or some natural agency independent of human effort," said Robbins. Rather, "[I]t is the hand of the law-giver, the hand which withdraws from the sphere of the pursuit of self-interest those possibilities which do not harmonize with the public good" (1952: 56).

In other words, the classical period saw the continued transformation of self-interest from something base whose effects should be negated by a wide-ranging program of governmental restrictions to a view of self-interest as a driving force toward increased economic welfare for all when channeled through the competitive market process. Even a problem as seemingly severe as the population problem is kept in check, in Malthus' (1798) system, by the operation of the forces of self-interest.[16] This presumption in favor of private enterprise in English classical political economy, however, did not derive simply, or perhaps even primarily, from a positive view of the system of natural liberty, or, as Sidgwick put it, from the sort of "shallow optimism" that could be found in the attitudes of Frédéric Bastiat and his followers,[17] in the political agitation of the Anti-Corn Law League

---

[16] Malthus claimed that calculations based on self-interest would cause men to forgo marriage when population-driven increases in food prices made it too costly to provide properly for both self and family (the "preventive check"). The attendant reduction in fertility would then temporarily relieve the population pressure on the food supply. In the second edition of 1803, Malthus expanded this to include the more moderate *delay* of marriage, which he called the "prudential check."

[17] See, for example, Bastiat's *Economic Harmonies* (1850).

and the Manchester school, and in the journalism of John Wilson and the London *Economist*.[18] Rather, the classical predisposition against interference was rooted in pessimism borne of "a conviction that however bad things might be naturally, direct interference by Government could only make them worse" (Sidgwick [1885] 1904: 181–82). This perspective is amply evidenced in Smith's strident criticisms of government agents and of governmental attempts to channel resources in directions they would not naturally flow, and his attitude on this score was carried through a century of classical political economy.

How, then, did the tide begin to turn?

JOHN STUART MILL, INDIVIDUAL LIBERTY,
AND THE PROBLEM OF EXTERNAL EFFECTS

The starting point for this transition is John Stuart Mill, whose writings on political economy, utilitarianism, liberty, and governance brought a new level of sophistication and nuance to the analysis of economic policy issues.[19] An enigmatic genius, Mill was educated by his father to be a disciple of both Bentham and Ricardo.[20] The younger Mill drew significantly on the work of each in the process of creating an approach to economic theory and policy that was both familiar and creatively original. Indeed, Mill's perspective is emblematic of a continuity within the classical tradition reaching back to Smith but at the same time marks a transition toward an increasing recognition of market failures that, over the course of the next century, became a centerpiece of the Cambridge school's welfare theory and, later, orthodox welfare economics. The seriousness of the issue of the appropriate role for the state, both within the economic sphere and without, and the contentious nature of the debate on this topic is, for Mill ([1859] 1992:20–21), both reflected in and a result of the fact that

> [t]here is ... no recognized principle by which the propriety or impropriety of government interference is customarily tested. People decide according to their personal preferences. Some, whenever they see any good to be done, or evil to be remedied, would willingly instigate the government to undertake

[18] On the Manchester school, see Grampp (1960). On Wilson and the *Economist*, see Gordon (1955).

[19] In fact, John Stuart Mill's views on the economic role of government are on display throughout his voluminous writings See *The Collected Works of John Stuart Mill*, in thirty-three volumes, published by the University of Toronto Press, several volumes of which have recently been issued in paperback by Liberty Fund. See Hollander (1985) for a detailed treatment of Mill's contributions.

[20] Mill's *Autobiography* (1873) describes his rather unique upbringing.

the business; while others prefer to bear almost any amount of social evil, rather than add one to the departments of human interests amenable to governmental control.[21]

Mill went on to observe that the absence of a generally accepted rule or principle for assessing the usefulness of government action means that both sides are often wrong in their assessments—"the interference of government is, with about equal frequency, improperly invoked and improperly condemned" ([1859] 1992: 21).

Mill thought it absolutely necessary to have in place a framework for assessing the propriety of government interference.[22] The elaboration of such a framework was his goal in writing *On Liberty* (1859), and it is also the subject of Book V of his *Principles of Political Economy* (1871).[23] Bentham had been concerned with this same issue in his attempt to distinguish between the agenda and non-agenda of government. Not surprisingly, his criterion was utilitarian: "[T]he interposition of government may be desirable or not, according to the state of the account—according as the inconveniences attached to the measures in which the interposition of government consists, preponderate or fail of preponderating over the advantage attached to the effect which it is proposed should be produced" ([1793–95] 1839: 34). Though he too was a utilitarian, Mill went in a slightly different direction than Bentham.

Mill believed that there is "a limit to the legitimate interference of the collective opinion with individual independence"; moreover, "to find that limit, and maintain it against encroachment, is as indispensable to a good condition of human affairs as protection against political despotism" ([1859] 1992: 14).[24] For Mill, the appropriate rule or limit is not arbitrary—there *exists* a limit to what is legitimate, and it is something to be *discovered*, not something to be worked out via the utilitarian (or any other) calculus. Moreover, Mill was very explicit in setting out exactly what this limit is: There is "a circle around every individual human being which no government . . . ought to be permitted to overstep," and, as Mill saw it, this circle "ought to include all that part which concerns only the life, whether inward or outward, of the individual, and does not affect the interests of others, or affects them only through the moral influence of example"

---

[21] See also Mill ([1871] 1909: 795–95, 941–42).

[22] Mill used the terms "interference" and "intervention" interchangeably in his *Principles*.

[23] Mill's *Principles* was originally published in 1848, but his treatment of the present subject is remarkably consistent across editions. All references herein are to the "Ashley" version of the seventh (1871) edition, which was published in 1909.

[24] This concern about impingements on individual independence can also be found in Mill's writings on socialism—a system that he said would probably significantly exacerbate this "great growing evil" ([1879] 1967: 746)—and in his *Principles* ([1871] 1909: 942–43).

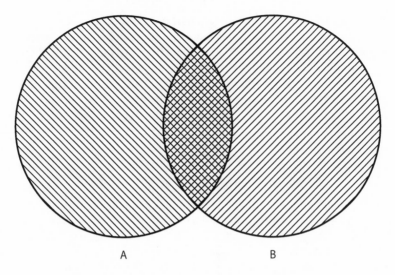

Figure 2.1. The intersection of individual interests.

([1871] 1909: 943).[25] For government to intervene for a person's own good, whether physical or moral, does not fall within these limits ([1859] 1992: 22). Mill was clearly arguing here for freedom of individual action where spillovers—or externalities—are absent. Where spillovers do exist, however, the situation is altered: "Whenever ... there is a definite damage, or a definite risk of damage, either to an individual or to the public, the case is taken out of the province of liberty, and placed in that of morality or law" ([1859] 1992: 147).[26] Looking at this principle from the perspective of the individual's obligation, Mill said that "[t]he liberty of the individual must be thus far limited; he must not make himself a nuisance to other people" ([1859] 1992: 101). In those instances where the individual does not exercise sufficient forbearance to accomplish this, a potential role for the state arises.[27]

Mill's view of the matter is illustrated in figure 2.1. Here, there are two parties, A and B, each with a respective set of interests. Mill's theory

[25] The same perspective can be found *On Liberty*, where Mill argues that "the sole end for which mankind are warranted, individually or collectively, in interfering with the liberty of action of any of their number, is self-protection. That the only purpose for which power can be rightfully exercised over any member of a civilized community, against his will, is to prevent harm to others" ([1859] 1992: 21–22). Mill said that "the object of " *On Liberty* is to assert this "one very simple principle" ([1859] 1992: 21).

[26] See also Mill ([1871]1909: 943).

[27] Mill ([1871]1909: 943). Mill is not asserting this as a hypothesis to be examined and tested; rather, he said, it is an "indispensable" principle ([1859] 1992: 134).

recognizes that A and B do not exist in isolation; in the intersection of these sets—the cross-hatched area—their interests are in conflict. For Mill, any portion of the hatched shaded area within A is inviolable: there are no spillovers onto B from actions within this area, and hence no legitimate grounds for state interference with A's liberty. In the cross-hatched area—where there are spillovers or collisions of interests between A and B—the situation changes. The protections afforded to individual liberty disappear and allow for the potential exercise of government interference with individual action.[28]

Mill was cognizant of the ubiquity of these external effects, in the sense that a gain for A sometimes (even often) implies a loss for B ([1859] 1992: 169):

> In many cases, an individual, in pursuing a legitimate object, necessarily, and therefore legitimately causes pain or loss to others, or intercepts a good which they had a reasonable hope of obtaining. Such oppositions of interest between individuals often arise from bad social institutions, but are unavoidable while those institutions last; and some would be unavoidable under any institutions.

The issue, then, is not one of eliminating spillovers, for that is impossible. The problem is to determine how society should deal with these spillover effects in their various manifestations.

There is an extremely important asymmetry in Mill's prescription here. While Mill offered severe strictures against violations of individual liberty in the *absence* of externalities, he does not turn around and argue *for* intervention in those situations where externalities *are* present: "[I]t must by no means be supposed," he said, "because damage, or probability of damage, to the interests of others, can alone justify the interference of society, that therefore it always does justify such interference" ([1859[1992: 169). In terms of figure 2.1, the mere existence of a conflict between A's and B's respective interests—the cross-hatched area where the two circles overlap— is not in itself sufficient to justify government intervention, even though the lack of such conflict is sufficient to rule it out.

It is in the analysis of spillover effects that we see Mill's utilitarian side come to the fore, with implications for those on *both* sides of the debate over the limits of state action. Mill criticized both "supporters of interference ... content with asserting a general right and duty on the part of government to intervene, whenever its intervention would be useful" and "the *laisser-faire* school," which would restrict the operation of government to "the protection of person and property against force and fraud."

---

[28] Note that Mill failed to appreciate the reciprocal nature of the spillover issue (that one cannot label A or B as *the* cause of the harm)—a point made forcefully by Ronald Coase (1960) a century later. See chapter 5, infra.

For Mill, such trite offerings are not at all helpful because the issue of the appropriate boundaries for government action "does not ... admit of any universal solution" ([1871] 1909: 941–42). Indeed, even where government intervention may be warranted, Mill suggested that the appropriate *form* of such action will vary, depending on the nature of the market failure. Mill distinguished between two forms of government action: the authoritative, in which certain types of conduct are prescribed or proscribed, and the nonauthoritative, where government provides, for example, advice, information, services, and institutions, which are thereby available to the citizenry but do not impinge upon freedom of choice and action. Because prescription and proscription *do* limit individual freedom, Mill argued that they have "a much more limited sphere of legitimate action" and require "a much stronger necessity"—specifically, harmful spillover effects—to justify them ([1871] 1909: 942).

Where, then, did Mill wish to draw the line between acceptable and unacceptable government interference in the presence of spillovers? The pragmatic nature of nineteenth-century classicism, most amply evidenced in its utilitarian strain, comes out here perhaps more strongly and explicitly in Mill than in any of his predecessors or contemporaries. The criterion for the boundaries of the appropriate functions of government, he contended, is not strict or a priori, but rather is a matter of "expediency" ([1871] 1909: 800):

> [T]he admitted functions of government embrace a much wider field than can easily be included within the ring-fence of any restrictive definition, and ... it is hardly possible to find any ground of justification common to them all, except the comprehensive one of general expediency; nor to limit the interference of government by any universal rule, save the simple and vague one, that it should never be admitted but when the case of expediency is strong.

A simple suggestion, an assertion, or a bit of evidence that government intervention can improve the situation, then, is not sufficient; in Mill's mind, the case must be a "strong" one.[29]

The "necessary" functions of government, in which the case for expediency is obvious, are, for Mill, much broader than simplistic discussions would indicate. Indeed, he said, those who suggest that the functions of government should be limited to "protection against force and fraud" are

---

[29] We shall return later to the rationale behind the "strong" qualifier.

One class of spillovers that Mill ruled out of bounds for government on expediency grounds is those that naturally and inevitably occur within the context of a competitive market system. Life, according to Mill, is often a zero-sum game, as in, for example, when A gets the job and B does not. But, he said, society correctly "admits no right, either legal or moral, in the disappointed competitors, to immunity from this kind of suffering; and feels called on to interfere, only when means of success have been employed which it is contrary to the general interest to permit—namely, fraud or treachery, and force" ([1859] 1992: 169–70).

espousing "a definition to which neither they nor any one else can deliberately adhere, since it excludes ... some of the most indispensable and unanimously recognized duties of government" ([1871] 1909: 941). In addition to duties such as national defense and the provision of protective justice, they range across laws governing the many facets of inheritance, property, and contracts; the protection of those unable to look after themselves; the coining of money; the establishment of a standard set of weights and measures; the paving, lighting, and cleaning of roadways; the provision and improvement of harbors and lighthouses;[30] the undertaking of surveys in order to have accurate maps and charts; and the construction of dykes and embankments.

Mill also took pains to show that the application of government to many of these generally accepted tasks is not necessarily as circumscribed as some allege. Even things supposedly as simple as the "enforcement" of property and contract are, in fact, quite extensive and open-ended in nature. In the case of property,

> It may be imagined, perhaps, that the law has only to declare and protect the right of every one to what he himself has produced, or acquired by the voluntary consent, fairly obtained, of those who produced it. But is there nothing recognized as property except what has been produced? Is there not the earth itself, its forests and waters, and all other riches, above and below the surface? These are the inheritance of the human race, and there must be regulations for the common enjoyment of it. What rights, and under what conditions, a person shall be allowed to exercise over any portion of this common inheritance cannot be left undecided. No function of government is less optional than the regulation of these things, or more completely involved in the idea of civilized society. ([1871] 1909: 797)

The situation with contracts is quite similar. Mill pointed out that, in actuality, government does not limit its concern to "a simple enforcement" of that which is the product of voluntary consent. Rather, governments "take upon themselves to determine what contracts are fit to be enforced" ([1871] 1909: 798). What Mill offered here was at least as much a philosophical discussion of the law-making function of government as it was a normative discussion of appropriate tasks for the state. For, once one admits of the need for government enforcement of property and contract, the range of activities that are necessarily opened up to government action is very extensive, as Mill made clear.

There is another set of problems with self-interested action, though, where the appropriate remedy is somewhat less obvious. These are cases in which individuals may well not be the best judges of their own interests, and which may have consequences for others, including for society as a

---

[30] On the lighthouse example, see note 52 in this chapter.

whole. Mill ([1871] 1909: 953–79) gave several examples. First, people are not always the best judges regarding education, whether for themselves or their children, and here Mill made both the individual and the positive externality arguments in support of some degree of public provision of education. Second, limited foresight sometimes causes people to enter into contractual arrangements that bind them for longer periods than they might otherwise agree to, and such contracts—especially perpetuities—should not be enforced in all cases. Third, monopoly power attends the provision of certain public utilities, and government regulation or management may thus be necessary in the public interest. Fourth, strategic considerations may prevent individuals or firms from taking actions that might work to the great benefit of society, unless government enforces that behavior upon all participants in the market. Mill cited as an illustration the problem of labor shortages for producing goods and services and for building infrastructure in the New World because of the rush to acquire landholdings. The issue, Mill said, is that

> [h]owever beneficial it might be to the colony in the aggregate, and to each individual composing it, that no one should occupy more land than he can properly cultivate, nor become a proprietor until there are other laborers ready to take his place in working for hire; it can never be in the interest of an individual to exercise this forbearance, unless he is assured that others will do so too. Surrounded by settlers who have each their thousand acres, how is he benefited by restricting himself to fifty? Or what does a labourer gain by deferring the acquisition altogether for a few years, if all other labourers rush to convert their first earnings into estates in the wilderness a few miles apart from one another? ([1871] 1909: 966)

Such forbearance, according to Mill, does nothing to remedy the shortage of laborers and will leave the individual in a position inferior to that of his fellows. Thus, said Mill, "It is in the interest of each to do what is good for all, but only if others will do likewise ([1871] 1909: 966).[31] This led Mill to endorse Edward Gibbon Wakefield's (1829) plan of "systematic colonization," wherein Wakefield proposed that a high price be set on all unoccupied lands, and recommended that the associated rents from the sale of these lands be used as a source of funds to transport immigrants to the New World to increase the labor pool. Fifth, public charity is likely to be insufficient if left to private means. Sixth, colonization offers various benefits to the nation, including lowering population pressures by spreading people to (relatively) unoccupied parts of the world, but it may not repay individual interests to undertake all of the necessary startup

---

[31] A suggested remedy was to limit land ownership until one had worked a number of years as a laborer. Mill also cites the example of reductions in work hours, which no individual firm has the incentive to undertake, knowing that others will not match their action.

costs. The same, he said, may be true of the development of certain infant industries.[32] Seventh, the resources devoted to the discovery of new
knowledge via geographic and scientific exploration and the maintenance
of a learned class are likely to be insufficient if these matters are left to
individual action.

Mill found these failings sufficiently significant that the "presumption
in favour of the competition of the market does not apply" to them. Nevertheless, he said, this does not mean that government intervention is the
answer, either. Mill was prepared only to say that, in these instances, "the
balance of the advantages *may* be in favour of some mode and degree of
intervention by the authorized representatives of the collective interest
of the state" ([1871] 1909: 953, emphasis added). In most of the aforementioned cases, Mill's preference—if there indeed is to be government
intervention—was for "nonauthoritative" actions.[33] Government, he insisted, should not monopolize activities such as education, public charity,
colonization, scientific exploration, and the maintenance of a learned class
simply because they will not be provided in sufficient amounts through
voluntary mechanisms.[34] The utility of state action does not mean that
society could not benefit from the presence of private alternatives to the
government-sponsored activities.

What remains to be explained is why a utilitarian like Mill would argue
that simple expediency is not sufficient to trigger state intervention. Why,
that is, must the case for expediency be strong? We have seen that Mill suggested an extensive list of divergences between private and social interests,
and this seems to contradict George Stigler's contention that Mill's position
is grounded in the beneficial effects of individual liberty.[35] We thus need to
explain why this wide range of market failures does not, for Mill, give rise
to an equally wide range of appropriate government interventions. The
answer lies in Mill's perceived limitations of the state, whose management
he characterized as "proverbially jobbing, careless, and ineffective" ([1871]
1909: 960).[36] In spite of his relatively extensive elaboration of legitimate
governmental functions, Mill thought that government is poorly organized

[32] Mill ([1871] 1909: 922).

[33] See p. 37, infra.

[34] The reader may notice a terminological tension here between the negative consequences
of self-interested action and the notions of "negative" and "positive" externalities. It bears
emphasizing that the limitations of natural liberty—market failures, if you will—pointed to
by Mill (and, as we shall see, by Sidgwick) fall into both negative externality and positive externality (including public goods) categories. In both cases, however, these problems derive
from *negative* aspects of self-interested behavior. Thus, for example, the free-rider problem is
a "negative" force giving rise to an underprovision of goods with "positive" external effects.

[35] See Stigler (1965: 6, n. 9).

[36] Jobbing is "[t]he act or practice of turning a public office or a position of trust to personal gain or political advantage; the use of something corruptly or unscrupulously for personal gain" (*OED*).

to carry out many of the tasks that people would wish it to undertake, and that, even if it were well organized, the related information issues and incentives are such as to make private efforts superior to governmental ones in carrying out many tasks ([1871] 1909: 945–47). Moreover, he suggested that the expansion of government—such as to deal with a wider range of market failings—would serve only to exacerbate these problems.

Some of the arguments underlying Mill's position are spelled out in works that more overtly tackle the role and operation of government, including *Considerations on Representative Government* (1861), *On Liberty* (1859), and his essay dealing with "Centralisation" (1862).[37] For example, Mill believed that government was afflicted by "general ignorance and incapacity, or, to speak more moderately, insufficient mental qualifications, in the controlling body" ([1861] 1977: 436). This belief, in turn, was at least in part a result of his view that government jobs do not "hold out sufficient prospects of emolument and importance to attract the highest talents" ([1859] 1992: 199)—a rather ironic stance for someone who was himself a civil servant. Even though he was a strong proponent of the extension of the franchise, Mill certainly did not see democracy as any sort of panacea: "The natural tendency of representative government, as of modern civilization," he said, "is towards collective mediocrity" ([1861] 1977: 457).[38] The result is "the government of mediocrity," which leads to nothing more than "mediocre government" ([1859] 1992: 118). Yet Mill was not keen on having the best and the brightest filling governmental positions either. Given their limited numbers, utilizing a large share of these individuals in government posts would virtually eliminate the important outside check on government that they could provide. Mill also felt that even the best and the brightest were not immune from the pressures of interests that diverge from those of the larger community, nor from bribery and other forms of corruption that can come with such pressures. In the end, he concluded, government by the brightest would not necessarily be superior to "government by the mediocre."[39]

Mill's assessment of the prospects for effective government intervention in nonobvious situations was quite pessimistic—at least as regards more-or-less democratic forms of government: "No government by democracy or a numerous aristocracy," he said, "either in its political acts or in the opinions, qualities, and tone of mind which it fosters, ever did or could rise above

---

[37] Mill's dim view of the operation of government is also reflected in his chapters on socialism ([1879] 1967: esp. 739–42).

[38] Likewise, in *On Liberty*, Mill said that "the general tendency of things throughout the world is to render mediocrity the ascendant power among mankind" ([1859] 1992: 118). Mill attributes part of this trend to the extension of the franchise (1861: 457).

[39] See, for example, Mill ([1859] 1992: 202; [1861] 1977: 436, 441, 444–45; [1862] 1977: 607–8).

mediocrity" ([1859] 1992: 119).[40] This statement suggests that Mill did not see cause for optimism on the horizon, either. It is because of this pessimism about the ability of government intervention to make matters better rather than worse—a perspective that one finds throughout his writings—and not from a faith in the system of natural liberty, that we find Mill arguing that a society should restrict "to the narrowest compass the intervention of a public authority in the business of the community" ([1871] 1909: 950). Mill set himself apart from his classical forebears in his assessment of the limits of the system of natural liberty, but he demonstrated an important continuity with them in his insistence that the burden of proof should fall "on those who recommend, government interference." Mill's summary version of his view of the matter is unmistakable in its message: "*Laisser-faire*, in short, should be the general practice: every departure from it, unless required by some great good, is a certain evil" ([1871] 1909: 950).

HENRY SIDGWICK AND THE DISMANTLING
OF THE SYSTEM OF NATURAL LIBERTY

Mill's forays into the realm of externality-related problems with the system of natural liberty and the effects of self-interested behavior received further development at the hands of Cambridge philosopher Henry Sidgwick, whose *Methods of Ethics*, originally published in 1874, was a landmark volume in the classical utilitarian tradition of Jeremy Bentham and John Stuart Mill, and whose *Principles of Political Economy* (1901)[41] marked—with a foot in each camp—an important transition in the move from classical to marginalist thinking.[42]

Sidgwick considered self-interest a centerpiece of human motivation, noting in his *Principles of Political Economy* that it works "powerfully and continually" (1901: 402). Because of this, he was a vociferous defender of the self-interest assumption within political economy. Although Sidgwick went to some lengths to rebuff the critics who suggested that promoting self-interested action was a *normative goal* of English political economy, he also maintained that self-interested behavior—for example, in the way of attempting to sell for the highest price that the market will bear or attempting

---

[40] Mill continues by saying that to rise above mediocrity requires following the lead of "One or Few" possessed of great wisdom ([1859] 1992: 119)—a sentiment that parallels the positions of Plato and the Physiocrats.

[41] Sidgwick's *Principles* was originally published in 1883. References given here are to the third edition, which was published in 1901, and which is identical to the second edition of 1887.

[42] Bart Schultz (2004) has authored an excellent, highly detailed biography of Sidgwick.

to buy at the lowest possible price—is not "blameworthy" ([1885] 1904: 183). In fact, Sidgwick believed that self-interest had tremendous utility in the economic sphere, to the point where "the difficulty of finding any adequate substitute for it, either as an impulsive or as a regulating force, is an almost invincible obstacle in the way of reconstructing society on any but its present individualistic basis" (1901: 402).

Even so, Sidgwick did not consider the results of the operation of self-interest to be anything like wholly good, nor did he find any evidence of claims to that effect within classical political economy—at least that of the nonvulgar variety. He was well aware, though, that extreme laissez-faire views were often on display in the newspapers, in politics,[43] and in popular discourse throughout the Victorian period: "There is indeed," he said,

> a kind of political economy which flourishes in proud independence of facts; and undertakes to settle all practical problems of Governmental interference or private philanthropy by simple deduction from one or two general assumptions—of which the chief is the assumption of the universally beneficent and harmonious operation of self-interest well let alone. ([1885] 1904: 171)

Sidgwick had little use for this brand of political economy, suggesting that it should be "banished to the remotest available planet" as soon as possible ([1885] 1904: 171). He was quick to point out, though, that the roots of this vulgarity cannot be found in Smith, whose "advocacy of natural liberty in no way binds him to the perpetual and complex opposition and conflict of economic interests involved in the unfettered efforts of individuals to get rich" (1885 [1904]: 172).[44] He did, however, lay some of the responsibility at the feet of David Ricardo (1817) and his "more abstract and purely deductive method" (1885 [1904]: 173), a method in many ways at odds with what Sidgwick considered his own more empirically oriented approach.

While Sidgwick believed that self-interest has tremendous utility in the economic sphere, he did not go so far as to suggest that the system of natural liberty functions optimally at all times and in all places. Even if one grants that individuals *are* the best judges of their own interests, he said, it does not follow that a group of people, each engaged in the intelligent pursuit of his self-interest, will, if only minimally restrained, realize the greatest possible happiness for the group (1897: 144–45). Sidgwick identified two general categories of divergence between private and social interests:

[43] Robert Peel and William Gladstone are prime examples here. See, for example, Hilton (1979).

[44] Indeed, in Sidgwick's view, to suggest that Smith proffers "a dogmatic theory of the natural right of the individual to absolute industrial independence ... is to construct the history of economic doctrines from one's inner consciousness" ([1885] 1904: 173).

those where laissez-faire's wealth-maximizing results are not in society's best interest because there is more to life than wealth, and those where laissez-faire does not even generate the wealth-maximizing result.

In the former case, Sidgwick observed that "the universal practice of modern civilized societies has admitted numerous exceptions to the broad rule of *laisser-faire*." These exceptions included (1) the protection of those who cannot see to their own self-interest, such as the mentally infirm and children, with the result that we have, for example, regulations regarding children's education and employment;[45] (2) measures that deal with issues of physical or moral well-being, such as "sanitary regulations, restrictions on the sale of opium, brandy, and other intoxicants; prohibitions of lotteries; regulation of places of amusement; and similar measures" ([1886] 1904: 203); and (3) policies designed to rectify problems with the distribution of income ([1886] 1904: 202–5).[46]

Sidgwick also pointed to a number of situations where laissez-faire is *not* wealth maximizing. The problem here, according to Sidgwick, is that the underlying conditions necessary for the system of natural liberty to work the wealth-maximizing magic so often attributed to it do not correspond, in many instances, to actual economic circumstances. The result is that "even in a society composed—solely or mainly—of 'economic men,' the system of natural liberty would have, in certain respects and under certain conditions, no tendency to realize the beneficent results claimed for it" (1901: 402–3). For example, one party's actions may well interfere with the freedom of other parties—such as in the realm of property, where "use" can often give rise to negative spillover effects. Freedom of contract, too, may result in harmful effects to third parties—individuals or society as a whole—and may also violate other existing laws, or even lead to voluntary slavery, which, he argued, is not in society's economic best interests (1897: 90; 1901: 405–6). Problems also arise owing to monopoly, where Sidgwick's concern was not just that monopoly reduces output and increases price, as compared with a competitive market, but also that the monopolist, by virtue of his privileged position, may not have any incentive to invest in the development of more economical production techniques.

One particularly prominent and instructive set of examples cited by Sidgwick to illustrate the divergence between private and social interests dealt with the use of natural resources, including the potential depletion of mines, fisheries, and plant species, and the diversion of waterways necessary for irrigation and "the supply of motive power."[47] Sidgwick began this discussion by pointing out that in a "*perfectly ideal* community of economic men all

---

[45] See also Sidgwick (1901: 425).
[46] This and related issues are discussed in Backhouse (2006).
[47] See Sidgwick (1897: 147; 1901: 409–13).

persons concerned would doubtless voluntarily agree to take the measures required to ward off such common dangers." He went on to qualify this, though, noting that, in reality, "the efforts and sacrifices of a great majority are liable to be rendered almost useless by the neglect of one or two individuals" (1901: 409–410, emphasis added).[48] Sidgwick illustrated the resulting problem by applying the then-emerging marginal analysis to the common-pool fisheries situation (1901: 410):

> Take, for instance, the case of certain fisheries, where it is clearly for the general interest that the fish should not be caught at certain times, or in certain places, or with certain instruments, because the increase of actual supply obtained by such captures is overbalanced by the detriment it causes to the prospective supply. Here—however clear the common interest might be—it would be palpably rash to trust to voluntary association for the observance of the required rules of abstinence; since the larger the number that voluntarily abstain, the stronger becomes the inducement offered to those who remain outside the association to pursue their fishing in the objectionable times, places, and ways, so long as they are not prevented by legal coercion.

This issue of "overusing" natural resources is one facet of two larger issues that Sidgwick saw as potentially serious sources of problems with laissez-faire.[49]

The first of these is the failure to account properly for the interests and needs of future generations, because self-interested economic agents do not take account of the full social impact—positive or negative—of their activities (1901: 412–13, 475–76),[50] a problem that had been noted previously by Mill.[51] For example, a project involving a large present outlay but with benefits (in excess of costs) that accrue only in the distant future may not be undertaken because those who wish to undertake the project lack sufficient capital, while those possessing such capital would refuse to lend or invest because they could not themselves appropriate a sufficient share of the resulting long-term gain. Sidgwick applied a similar line of reasoning to parents, some of whom are unable to see what is in the

[48] See also Sidgwick ([1886] 1904: 207). The parallel to Coase (1960) should not be lost on the reader. See chapter 5, infra.

[49] The reader will note that there are commonalities between this analysis by Sidgwick and Mill's discussion of "over-ownership" of lands during the colonization process, discussed earlier.

[50] Sidgwick repeatedly emphasized that the scope of the general happiness, good, or welfare encompasses the interests of both present and future generations, and he also argues that this interpretation is held by "the great majority of persons" (1897: 38).

[51] The general issue was recognized by Mill in his *Principles* and in his defense of the religion of humanity ([1865] 1969), but it received a far more detailed and analytical treatment, and was ascribed a significantly more expansive domain, in Sidgwick's discussion.

long-run best interests of their children and thus will be inclined to under-invest in their education.

A second problem highlighted by the common-pool example is the "incentive to cheat," which can manifest itself in a variety of ways in the context of voluntary association, including through the overuse and free-rider problems. The power of this incentive is sufficiently large that Sidgwick considered it "dangerous" to trust voluntary agreement or association for the accomplishment of functions of public importance. This included functions of a traditional public goods variety or more nontraditional (but no less important) tasks such as flood protection for low-lying areas or the protection of animals and plants against disease (1897: 150).

Sidgwick also discussed a number situations in which he believed private enterprise would not provide goods and services in the necessary amounts because of the inability to appropriate returns sufficient to justify the investment. The provision of lighthouses, forests (with "their beneficial effects in moderating and equalising rainfall"), worker training, scientific discoveries, and inventions—some of which had been noted by Mill[52]—constitute one such class of activities (1901: 406; 1897: 148). A similar line of reasoning underlies Sidgwick's defense of and expansion upon Mill's case for temporary infant-industry protection: long-run gains may exist from the development of domestic industry, but short-run competitive disadvantage leaves private interests unwilling to enter without some form of protection (1901: 488–91).

What, then, are the implications of all of this for the role of the state within the economic system? One possible answer, and the one much in evidence in the classical literature, is the adoption of a laissez-faire approach, which Sidgwick defined as "the rule of 'letting people manage their own affairs in their own way, so long as they do not cause mischief to others without the consent of those others'" (1897: 137n). Here, the limits of government activity involve satisfying the "individualistic minimum," which consists of security of person, property, and contract, and ensuring noninterference among persons absent compensation (1897: 42, 79).

This individualistic minimum contrasts with a second approach, which Sidgwick referred to as "socialistic" interference. Not to be confused with social*ism* or collectivism, which was the subject of widespread concern and discussion throughout this period, socialistic interference consists simply of "any limitation on the freedom of action of individuals in the interest of the community at large, that is not required to prevent interference with other

---

[52] We see here, as in Mill, a mention of the lighthouse as a good that cannot be provided through the private sector. The empirical validity of this assertion was challenged by Coase (1974a), whose interpretation of the facts was later challenged by David Van Zandt (1993) and Elodie Bertrand (2006). See also Medema (1994, ch. 5) and O'Brien (1998: 31–33). Richard Musgrave (1985: 2–15) provides a useful overview of the history of public goods theory.

individuals or for the protection of the community against the aggression of foreigners" (1897: 42–43). Such actions have the effect of narrowing "the sphere of private property and private enterprise by the retention of resources and functions in the hands—or under the regulation—of Government as representing the community" (1897: 153). The problem, as Sidgwick went to some lengths to point out, is that teasing out the meaning of and content that society should give to these categories is no mean feat. For example, while arguing that infliction of avoidable damage on another party presents a prima facie case for government enforcement of compensation, Sidgwick called attention to the difficulty of making such judgments owing to the reciprocal nature of these external effects: preventing harm to one party restricts the freedom of action of another party. Not surprisingly, given his utilitarian approach to these issues, Sidgwick concluded that the extent to which one party should be free from interference by the other "can only be settled by a careful balance of *conflicting inconveniences*" (1897: 69, emphasis added).[53]

Sidgwick's concerns about the less-than-clear-cut nature of the individualistic-socialistic distinction can be further illustrated by examining the issue of fraud prevention—a task which, as he points out, clearly seems to fit within the individualistic minimum. On the one hand, society has any number of fraud prevention rules in place (1897: 135):

> To prevent the flesh of diseased animals from being disguised as the flesh of healthy animals; to prevent would-be surgeons or apothecaries from pretending to have obtained certificates of qualification which they have not really obtained; to oblige employers who may have contracted to pay wages in goods to supply such goods in strict accordance with contract as regards quality and price.

Sidgwick believed that all of this was "clearly and directly individualistic" (1897: 135). Yet, he continued, there are forms of fraud prevention that would be seen as violations of the individualistic minimum—such as if the government "absolutely prohibits the purchase of food it deems unhealthy, the consultation of a physician it deems unqualified, the adoption of methods of payment it deems unfit." In these cases, Sidgwick argued, the state's actions fall squarely within the realm of the "paternal" (1897: 135).

There are, however, other alternatives for dealing with these types of information problems—ones in which, as Sidgwick noted, government can take steps to prevent deception without incurring charges of paternalistic interference. For example, he said, the government could provide

---

[53] Recall that Mill seems not to have recognized this reciprocity. Once again, the commonality with Coase (1960) is worth noting. These remedies, Sidgwick said, should be sufficient both to compensate fully for harm done and, following Bentham, to prevent these harms in the future (1897: 110).

consumers with information regarding "the dangerous qualities of com-
modities offered for purchase," or provide workers with information about
"the dangerous nature of the instruments which their employers require
them to use," and all of this could be done without forcing anyone to act on
this information (1897: 135–36). This, of course, parallels Mill's category
of nonauthoritative interference, discussed earlier. For Sidgwick, whether
the government's actions are considered to be individualistic or socialistic
thus comes down to the method that it employs in its attempt to prevent
the harm. By employing "measures to remove ignorance," the government
fulfills the task of protecting individuals from harm caused by the actions
of others, but still allows these individuals to assume the relevant risks if
they so choose. Prohibitions, by way of contrast, involve the government
making people's choices for them. For example, by restricting the depletion of natural resources, government fulfills its duty of "representing the
community [present and future] to prevent the bounties of nature from
being wasted by the unrestricted pursuit of private interest" (1897: 147).[54]
The determination of the extent and limits of this, including the scope of
private versus common property, was something that Sidgwick believed had
to be "settled by the aid of special experience on a balance of conflicting
considerations" (1897: 77).

Whatever commentators might have said in former times, however, it is,
according to Sidgwick, "an anachronism to not recognize fully and frankly
the existence of cases in which the industrial intervention of Government is
desirable, even with a view to the most economical production of wealth"
([1885] 1904: 175).[55] Yet, the fact that market outcomes are not always
wealth-maximizing or otherwise in society's best interests did not mean,
for Sidgwick, that government intervention is the best course of action.
"[I]n human affairs," he said, "we have often only a choice of evils, and
even where private industry fails to bring about a satisfactory result, it is
possible that governmental interference might on the whole make matters worse" ([1886] 1904: 206).[56] In support of this, Sidgwick pointed

[54] See also Sidgwick (1901: 475–76).

[55] Sidgwick argued that the shortcomings of private enterprise justify government interference with the provision of goods that he categorizes under the heading "machinery of
transfer" (things that facilitate transactions and exchange). Here, Sidgwick made a more
sophisticated case than that extant in the literature for governmental provision of traditional
public works, including roads, canals and railways, telegraph and postal services, and light and
water, as well as the provision of currency, banking and insurance services for the poor, and
the collection and dissemination of statistical information. Not only is government, according to Sidgwick, "peculiarly adapted to provide" these services; in doing so, it becomes the
facilitator of commerce and the market rather than an impediment to it (1901: 438–39).

[56] Sidgwick expressed a similar sentiment in his *Principles:* "It does not of course follow
that wherever laisser-faire falls short governmental interference is expedient; since the inevitable drawbacks and disadvantages of the latter may, in any particular case, be worse than the
shortcomings of private enterprise" (1901: 414).

out several "drawbacks and disadvantages" associated with government intervention: (1) government using its power for corrupt purposes; (2) the desire to please special interest groups; (3) "wasteful expenditures under the influence of popular sentiment" that arise because "the mass of a people, however impatient of taxation, are liable to be insufficiently conscious of the importance of thrift in all the details of national expenditure"; (4) the supervisory problems with the expansion of the range of government activities; (5) the cost of the of taxes associated with these operations of government; and (6) the lack of incentives for government workers to carry out properly the functions assigned to them (1901: 414–15; 1897: 167–68). Many of these same concerns had preoccupied Smith. In Sidgwick's case, though, it all came down to utilitarian calculations: He believed that these "costs" must be weighed against the benefits to determine the appropriateness of government intervention. Even when these calculations suggested that intervention *is* in the public interest, however, Sidgwick believed that the interference should be as mild and as narrowly drawn as possible while still accomplishing the desired goal.

Even allowing for all of the potential drawbacks associated with state action, Sidgwick nonetheless felt that the extent of the failure of public and social interests to coincide was such that governmental interference should be regarded "as not merely a temporary resource, but not improbably a normal element of the organization of industry" (1901: 414). In these cases, he said, "the general economic presumption in favor of leaving social needs to be supplied by private enterprise is absent, or is balanced by strictly economic considerations on the opposite side" ([1886] 1904: 206). Yet reflecting his belief that self-interest channeled through markets remained the best single system society had yet been able to devise, he went on to insist that the interference he was recommending should be seen only as "a supplementary and subordinate element" (1897: 146).[57]

In spite of the various negatives that Sidgwick associated with state action, he did not share the degree of pessimism exhibited by Mill and the larger classical tradition toward the possibilities of government intervention. In fact, Sidgwick suggested optimism—that in the long run "moral and political progress [in society] may be expected to *diminish*" the extent and severity of the shortcomings associated with government intervention (1901: 416, emphasis added). This, he said, will increase over

[57] A further issue identified by Sidgwick is that, in many cases, the "*economic* considerations" at stake are inconsequential. As a result, "the final decision" as to the expediency of many regulatio ns "does not fall within the sphere of political economy and cannot be arrived at by strictly economic methods" because "life and death are goods which it is not possible to estimate at a definite pecuniary value" (1901: 424). Interestingly, though, Sidgwick did allow that "all reasonable persons would admit that at a certain point the machinery for saving even life and health may become too costly," and thus "the practical necessity of balancing these goods in some way against wealth cannot be avoided" (1901: 424, n.1).

time the range of activities that government can carry out in a manner superior to market forces. Sidgwick's long-run optimism is most strikingly expressed in his assessment of socialism. While of the mind that collectivism would, at the time of his writing in the late nineteenth century, "arrest industrial progress" and bring about "equality in poverty," he saw something potentially quite different for the future (1897: 159):

> It is, I think, quite conceivable that, through improvements in the organization and working of governmental departments, aided by watchful and intelligent public criticism—together with a rise in the general level of public spirit throughout society—the results of the comparison [between individualism and collectivism] will at some future time be more favourable to governmental management than they hitherto have been.

The question of the accuracy of this prognostication, which reflects sentiments not unlike those found in Smith,[58] is less important for present purposes than its contrast with the classical view and its subsequent influence on the Cambridge welfare tradition, as evidenced by its repetition in the writings of Alfred Marshall and A. C. Pigou.[59]

UTILITARIANISM, OPTIMISM, AND THE FLIGHT FROM NATURAL LIBERTY

As we move through the second half of the nineteenth century, we witness a gradual evolution of the relationship between self-interest, market, and state. In Mill we see continuity with the classical tradition in his discussion of the state and, especially, his dim view of the prospects for government intervention.[60] We also find in Mill, however, a more expansive view of the failings of the system of natural liberty than could be found to that point in classical political economy. In the transition from Mill to Sidgwick, we have added to this a view of the state that represented a major departure from the classical perspective. Via this two-stage process, then, we arrive, by the late nineteenth century, with a view of the respective efficacies of natural liberty and the state that is in some sense 180 degrees opposed to the perspective that was dominant during the classical period.[61]

---

[58] See ch. 1.

[59] See, for example, Marshall ([1907] 1925: 336; 1926: 395) and Pigou (1912: 250; 1932: 333–35), as well as the discussion in ch. 3, infra. It is interesting to contrast Sidgwick's optimism here with his stated empirical approach to these issues.

[60] In this sense, Mill's perspective was more of a piece with the nonutilitarian branch of classicism than with that of his father and Bentham.

[61] I qualify this with "in some sense" to emphasize that the transition was not anything like so great as to be labeled "socialist." We had, however, moved back to a preclassical view in

Mill's theory of market failure and accompanying view of the role of the state was heavily grounded in his utilitarianism. This allowed him to move the debate beyond the "handy rule of thumb" pragmatism that characterized much of classical political economy to a grounded criterion for government intervention. That having been said, his was not a full-blown utilitarianism. Liberty absent negative spillovers is inviolable for Mill, and utilitarian demonstrations that government could enhance welfare by violating individual liberty, regardless of extent, are not sufficient to justify government intervention. For Mill, there was a universal rule for *noninterference*, but not for *interference*: utilitarianism comes in, and only comes in, in the presence of harmful spillover effects.

Mill's belief that utility is "the ultimate appeal on all ethical questions" ([1859] 1992: 24) tells us that he placed individual liberty on a plane above ethical debates and beyond subjection to the utilitarian calculus. Such was not the case for economic activity, however. Trade fit into the utilitarian category because it is "a social act": "Whoever undertakes to sell any description of goods to the public, does what affects the interest of other persons, and of society in general; and thus his conduct, in principle, comes within the jurisdiction of society" ([1859] 1992: 170). As Mill pointed out, the social nature of economic activity had long been recognized, and had functioned as the rationale for the extensive regulation of economic activity throughout the ages.[62] Only "after a long struggle," he said, did the benefits of free trade become more clear and cause a fairly dramatic change in thinking on this matter—as worked out in classical free-trade doctrine.[63]

What we have in Sidgwick is a well-developed view—one that he considered empirically based[64]—both of the limitations of self-interested action operating through the market and of governmental attempts to improve on these outcomes. Here, simplistic and a priori approaches to questions of the role of the state give way to a thorough-going utilitarianism—one in which "the ultimate criterion of the goodness of law, and of the action of government generally, is their tendency to increase the general happiness" (1897: 39). In terms of figure 2.1, there is no region in which government intervention is inappropriate or off limits in an a priori sense. In Mill's system, by way of contrast, for government to intervene for a person's own good, "either physical or moral," is completely out of bounds. Sidgwick

---

the sense that the state was seen as a more overtly necessary player in the process of reining in the base effects of self-interest.

[62] See, e.g., Gordon (1975).

[63] Mill's characterization of trade as a social act means that the justification for the doctrine of free trade derives from its social utility, rather than from individual liberty. As Mill ([1859] 1992: 170–71) notes, though, the social utility and individual liberty arguments are often compatible with one another.

[64] See, however, O'Brien (1998).

argued that while individualism is often consistent with utilitarianism, it is utilitarian concerns that are paramount. Furthermore, he said, from a utilitarian perspective larger societal interests sometimes trump the dictates of individualism.[65] The fact that people are at times unable to see their own best interests or to take adequate care of themselves justifies, in his view, certain paternalistic actions on the part of government—hence the need for health regulations on foodstuffs, the licensing of physicians and other occupations, workplace safety regulations, and so on (1901: 425). Sidgwick thus showed a much greater consistency in his utilitarianism than did Mill.[66] In part because of this, but also because of his less negative view of government agents, Sidgwick was willing to allow for a much more expansive role for the state than was Mill.

The source of Sidgwick's critical attitude toward the a priori and abstract deductive approaches to examining the working of the system of natural liberty and the potential for improvements via the policy process lies his utilitarianism,[67] and it is thus not surprising that Sidgwick would suggest that political economy was beginning to move in a better direction with the development of a more empirically grounded approach to policy issues. He felt that the empirical turn was best exemplified in the work of Mill, who made things "more balanced, qualified, and empirical," and more in tune with modern science ([1885] 1904: 174). Sidgwick also found empirical support for his position in the general mood of the day, where, he said, the "drift of opinion and practice is in the direction of increasing the range and volume of the interference of government in the affairs of individuals" (1897: 143).[68]

In spite of his negative assessment of Ricardo's abstraction and his own belief that he could not himself be charged with "overrating the value of abstract reasoning on economic subjects, or regarding it as a substitute for an accurate investigation of facts" ([1885] 1904: 171), Sidgwick did not deny that there *is* a role for abstract theory in policy analysis. While the appropriateness of government interference in any particular case requires an examination of the various facets of the actual problem as it arises and cannot be resolved by appeals to abstract theory, abstraction, he said, can provide a framework for thought and analysis. It may "supply a systematic view of the general occasions for Governmental interference, the differ-

---

[65] See Sidgwick ([1874] 1981: 444–45).

[66] John Rawls speaks to the greater consistency in the utilitarianism of Sidgwick as against Mill in the "Foreword" to the 1981 reprinting of Sidgwick's *Methods of Ethics* ([1874] 1907).

[67] At one point, Sidgwick described himself as a "mere empirical utilitarian" (Sidgwick [1886] 1904: 211).

[68] He does note, however, that much of this expansion has to do with the protection of individuals from the effects of the actions of others, and to that extent can be seen as consistent with individualism (1897: 143).

ent possible modes of such interference, and the general reasons for and against each of them, which may aid practical men both in finding and in estimating the decisive considerations in particular cases" ([1885] 1904: 176). It can show when the "drawbacks" referred to earlier are likely to be least, and how they might be minimized, as well as when returns to private provision are not sufficiently large or where private and public interests are likely to collide.

In fact, Sidgwick suggested that abstract reasoning, far from supporting the laissez-faire orthodoxy, points in the same direction as his own approach: "The general presumption derived from abstract economic reasoning," he said, "is not in favour of leaving industry altogether to private enterprise ... but is on the contrary in favour of supplementing and controlling such enterprise in various ways by the collective action of the community" (1901: 417). It shows that the flaws in the system of natural liberty mean that "various kinds of interference with industry ... may be necessary or expedient" for dealing with industry issues such as cartels and monopolies, as well as for protecting the "life, health, physical comfort, freedom, and reputation of individuals" from intentional or unintentional harms inflicted by other individuals (1901: 423).

CONCLUSION

Mill and Sidgwick both came at the question of the economic role of government from a utilitarian perspective and, in doing so, took the pragmatic view well (and increasingly) beyond that of the classical economists of the first half of the nineteenth century. Mill set himself apart from his classical forebears in attributing a much more expansive set of limitations to the system of natural liberty, but he shared with them a dim view of government agents and a resulting pessimistic view of the ability of government to improve on market performance—to the extent that the case for the "expediency" of intervention had to be *strong*. Sidgwick ascribed an even greater set of failings to the system of natural liberty than did Mill. While Mill refused to subject individual liberty absent negative spillovers to the same utilitarian analysis that he advocated for situations when spillovers are present, Sidgwick, in marked contrast, went all the way with utilitarianism and expressed a great deal more optimism about the efficacy of government intervention. The import of this transition for subsequent economic thinking flows from the significant influence that Sidgwick had on A. C. Pigou, who, not long thereafter, took all of this a step further, grafting the analysis of the potential for market failure found in Sidgwick to the emerging technical toolkit of marginal analysis and, in the process, established the approach that was to dominate the analysis of market failure for much of the twentieth century.

CHAPTER THREE

Marginalizing the Market

MARSHALL, PIGOU, AND THE PIGOVIAN TRADITION

SIDGWICK'S ANALYSIS marked the beginning of what came to be known as the Cambridge tradition of welfare economics, which worked its way through Alfred Marshall on the way to its far more elaborate, and yet more narrow or pointed, development at the hands of A. C. Pigou. Marshall, who occupied the chair in political economy at Cambridge from 1885 to 1908 was the driving force behind the professionalization of economics in Great Britain around the turn of the century.[1] His *Principles of Economics*, first published in 1890, was perhaps the most influential text of the marginal revolution.[2] Though Marshall considered his analysis to be a straightforward extension of the classical position, it contained a number of elements that marked important departures from the classical tradition, including what some would argue was his most signal contribution—the notion of substitution at the margin, which underpinned his model of demand and supply—and an attempt to develop what he considered an improved measure of economic welfare. Influenced by Sidgwick's philosophical perspective and armed with Marshall's theoretical toolkit, Pigou, Marshall's student and successor in the chair of political economy at Cambridge, proceeded to construct a marginalist analytical framework that shed new light on the problems of market failure and the economic role of government.

MARSHALL'S FIRST STEPS

In contrast to Sidgwick and Pigou, Marshall did not devote a great deal of attention to the theory of economic policy, and the remarks that he did make were often in response to concrete issues of policy on which he decided to comment or offer advice. As trade was the hot-button policy issue of the day, and socialism was gaining supporters at a rapid clip during Marshall's professional life, it is perhaps not surprising that much of his commentary on the role of the state took place against these backdrops.

---

[1] On Marshall, see Groenewegen (1995), Cook (2009), Maloney (1985), and Raffaelli, Becattini, and Dardi (2006).

[2] The other contenders would be W. S. Jevons's *Theory of Political Economy* (1871), Carl Menger's *Principles of Economics* (1871), and Léon Walras's *Elements of Pure Economics* (1874), the last of which, along with Marshall's *Principles*, has the most significant legacy today.

Marshall believed that the preceding centuries had brought significant progress in the "individual liberty," "independent thought," "mental capacity" and "moral strength" of the population. One effect of this progress was to stimulate industry and trade, and this economic progress, according to Marshall, put the common people in a position where they were "not very far inferior in shrewdness, and constructive ability to the ruling classes" (1923: 42). The practical import of this development was that the advantage that the common man had over government officials, because of "the more intimate knowledge possessed by each of his own circumstances, and the technical problems of his own work," was only increasing. This, said Marshall, made it likely that industry and trade would develop most advantageously if left to take their own course (1923: 42).

Though well aware of the benefits flowing from private activity and very much preoccupied with establishing the essential continuity between his own work and the classical tradition, Marshall, like Sidgwick, was concerned about avoiding what he considered the naïve laissez-faire views often associated with the classical school, noting in the preface to *Industry and Trade*, "the limited tendencies of self-interest to direct each individual's actions on those lines, in which it will be most beneficial to others" (1923: viii). To do this as part of an "economic science," however, required some means by which to assess economic welfare across alternative states of the world. National wealth, the measure favored by many of the classical economists, was quantifiable, but it missed out on those factors that might cause individual satisfaction to diverge from national income. Sidgwick was unable to come up with such a measure. Marshall, however, did, in the form of consumer surplus—a static, reasonably operational concept that had its roots in the utilitarian tradition (or at least that strand of it that ran through J. S. Mill and Henry Sidgwick) and was consistent with Marshall's general approach to constructing an economic toolkit.[3]

Marshall applied consumer surplus analysis to areas including tax policy, monopoly, and, perhaps most significantly, the analysis of demand and supply under constant, increasing, and decreasing returns. The last of these went to the root of the theory of competitive markets and the oft-stated normative justification for a competitive market system: "[T]he general doctrine that a position of (stable) equilibrium of demand and supply is a position also of *maximum satisfaction*" (Marshall 1920: 470). It was here that Marshall made the controversial argument that economic welfare may be enhanced through measures that expand output levels in industries characterized by increasing returns and restrict the output levels in industries characterized

---

[3] Consumer surplus is the difference between the amount that consumers are willing to pay for a good and the price that they actually pay for it. See Marshall (1920: 124–34).

by decreasing returns (1920: 472ff).[4] This could be accomplished by levying a tax on those goods whose production was subject to diminishing returns and using the resulting revenue to provide a subsidy for goods produced under conditions of increasing returns. In employing such a scheme, he says, the government may confer "a great economic benefit on the nation as a whole" (Whitaker 1975, 2: 232). This exposition of the potential limits of laissez-faire as a source of maximum satisfaction, albeit not extensive, was sufficient to cause Keynes to conclude that Marshall's "proof that *laissez-faire* breaks down in certain conditions *theoretically*, and not merely practically, regarded as a principle of maximum social advantage, was of great philosophical importance" (Keynes, in Pigou 1925: 44). Marshall had revealed a chink in the theoretical armor of laissez-faire under the sort of highly competitive conditions thought to be most favorable to its welfare-promoting properties. In the process, he also set the stage for Pigou's much more extensive analysis in the coming decades.

Having established the theoretical case for certain classes of market failure and associated government corrective measures, Marshall did not take the next step and advocate for a wide-ranging set of policies to address market failures. Although cognizant of the benefits that would flow from such policies, Marshall, like Mill and Sidgwick before him, was particularly concerned about the costs associated with the political and bureaucratic processes necessary to implement and carry out these schemes.[5]

In his wide-ranging treatise on *Industry and Trade*, Marshall claimed that "[a]lmost every extension of Government activity brings with it good and evil, both economic and political" (1923: 496). The chief problem that Marshall saw arising from the interplay of economic and political forces was the incentive for corruption. Corruption was a recurring theme in Marshall's discussion of the political process, as it had been for Smith, and Marshall seems to have considered it particularly endemic to trade policy. Rent seeking was certainly a culprit, as those who stood to gain from such policies tried to manipulate the policy-making process to their benefit. These policies, however, also impacted the officials who administered them by "increas[ing] their temptations to use public authority for the purposes of private gain" (1923: 43). Such was the power of special interests at the voting booth, he said, that "political considerations" often ended up governing decisions that ought instead to be made on "technical grounds." As a result, Marshall felt that the interests of the population as a whole were

---

[4] See, for example, Clapham (1922), Knight (1924), Sraffa (1926), and Young (1928). Several of the articles from this literature are reprinted in Stigler and Boulding (1952).

[5] See, for example, Whitaker (1975, 2: 232) and Marshall (1920: 473). As we shall see, Pigou was not quite so circumspect when he dealt with these themes a few years later.

often (and incorrectly) being sacrificed to the particular interests of one segment of the population (1923: 494).

Marshall was happy to spread the blame for these problems. He considered the political motivations of legislators an impediment to sound policy and thought that special interest groups looked at the electoral process as an opportunity to advance their particular sectional interests. The result, he said, was that "the nation as a whole [would] become less noble, weaker and ultimately poorer" (1923: 495). Nor were his concerns about government limited to the actions of politicians and legislators; he also expressed significant qualms about the operation of bureaucracies, identifying several reasons why government bureaucracies produce undesirable outcomes. He believed that the ministers charged with overseeing the bureaus, and upon whom final decision-making power rested, lacked sufficient knowledge of their departments. This problem was compounded because the rank of the bureaucrats—the subordinates on whose advice the ministers relied—was determined largely by seniority rather than ability. Furthermore, political control over bureaucracies and the ability to monitor bureaucratic activities effectively was often weak, and even when politicians did attempt to exercise some measure of oversight, their motives, and thus the results, were something less than optimal.

Given Marshall's concerns about politician behavior and bureaucratic functioning, it is hardly surprising that he considered government action inimical to progress. Marshall emphasized that it was private enterprise, not government, that had been responsible for rising productivity ([1907] 1925: 338):

> Government creates scarcely anything. If Governmental control had supplanted that of private enterprise a hundred years ago, there is good reason to suppose that our methods of manufacture now would be about as effective as they were fifty years ago, instead of being perhaps four or even six times as efficient as they were then.

This statement may help us to understand why Marshall, who was broadly sympathetic toward measures that would increase the wealth of the lower classes, found himself attracted to socialism with his heart but not his head.[6] Marshall did believe that the vast expansion of economic activity over the preceding centuries had dramatically increased the "*possible* functions of Government" ([1907] 1925: 338), but that the magnitude of the "increase in the complexity of the problems of industry" combined with the small "increase in the mental capacity of Government for dealing with" such

---

[6] On the latter, see, for example, Marshall's letter to Lord Reay of November 12, 1909 (in Pigou 1925: 461–65).

problems meant that there was not—"for the time at least"—a proportionate expansion in the "*appropriate* functions" of government (1923: 42).

This last bit is crucial, as Marshall, like Sidgwick, saw cause for optimism about the future prospects for government. The positive economic effects that he associated with individual progress had also brought about benefits on the political front via "a slow increase in the power of the people to govern the Government that governed them" and thus to provide some degree of check on state action (1923: 42–43). Marshall believed that such a check had been largely absent in Smith's day, and that the pervasiveness of corruption played a major role in Smith's suspicions regarding state action. Marshall spoke very directly about the low moral state of government in Smith's time, but argued that Smith "had no means of anticipating the vast increase in the resources of Government, and in the honesty of public officials which began in the nineteenth century" (1923: 45).[7] Marshall attributed these improvements to parliamentary reform, the spread of religious zeal, the improvement and spread of literature, and even the rise of cooperation, the effect of which was that, during Mill's lifetime, "the probity, the strength, the unselfishness and the resources" of government increased (1923: 335), enabling it to do more.

The ability of government to intervene beneficially increased at an even more rapid clip after Mill's death, in Marshall's estimation. In addition to the spread of general education and "a general surplus of energy over that required for earning a living" ([1907] 1925: 336), Marshall pointed to technological factors such as "shorthand reporting, the electric telegraph, and the improved printing press," which, he said, "have given strength to the general movement towards higher ethical standards." This, in turn, "has been steadily cleansing Parliament, and invigorating Governmental departments" (Marshall 1926: 395). Thus, said Marshall, society had arrived at a point where the expansion in ability of the people to govern their government had allowed many tasks to "reasonably be entrusted to Government in the twentieth century which would have been grossly mismanaged in the first half of the nineteenth." The result was the gradual development of "a certain new tendency" to widen the group of functions considered appropriate for government (1923: 42–43). The problem, according to Marshall, was that, though the potential for government had increased, the complexity of the tasks facing it had increased even further. Moreover, even with all of the gains that had been made, Marshall (1923: 672) felt that

---

[7] Marshall goes so far as to suggest that "Adam Smith's doctrine, carefully interpreted, supports [government's] active intervention in many affairs in an age in which it has acquired the power and the will to govern the people wisely; and the people have acquired the power and the will to govern their Government with knowledge, discretion and restraint" (1923: 719).

it seems to remain almost as true now, as in former times, that the heavy hand of Government tends to slacken progress in whatever matter it touches; and ... that "business influences are apt to corrupt politics; and political influences are apt to corrupt business."

Even using expert committees would not guarantee the best results, he said, as these committees would take outside advice, and this advice often reflects biases and vested interests (1923: 671). In sum, all of the advances in governance methods and Marshall's optimistic view of the possibilities offered by them did not seem sufficient to overcome the corruption issues that seemed to Marshall almost inherent in the operation of government.

PIGOU'S "PRIMA FACIE CASE": MARKET FAILURE IN THEORY AND PRACTICE

When Pigou succeeded Marshall as Professor of Political Economy at Cambridge in 1908, it was his mission to develop further the economics of his mentor.[8] This, however, was a difficult task, as Marshall had analyzed a wide range of problems in both static and dynamic contexts. For new and nontrivial contributions, Pigou turned to areas suggested by Sidgwick, whose work had influenced his views on both ethics and economics,[9] and, in particular, to the question of how far it was "desirable that the action of free competition should be restrained or modified" (Sidgwick 1901: 23).

The result was the construction of a system of welfare economics, a subject which, for Pigou, consisted in the study of the "many obstacles that prevent a community's resources from being distributed among different uses or occupations in the most effective way"—that is, the study of market failures. The purpose of his welfare analysis, in turn, was "to bring into clearer light some of the ways in which it now is, or eventually may become, feasible for governments to control the play of economic forces in such ways as to promote the economic welfare, and, through that, the total welfare, of their citizens as a whole" (Pigou 1932: 129–30). While Pigou claimed to build his welfare economics on Marshall—and Marshall had certainly opened up a couple of important lines of inquiry on this front—the line of descent actually runs more strongly from Sidgwick to Pigou. Pigou's welfare measure has content far broader than Marshall's consumer surplus,

---

[8] Collard (1999) and Aslanbeigui (2008) contain overviews of Pigou's life and career.
[9] See O'Donnell (1979), Aslanbeigui (1995), and Backhouse (2006).

and the breadth and scope of Pigou's analysis corresponds far more to that of Sidgwick than to Marshall's. In fact, the most accurate characterization of Pigou's work here would be to say that he put Sidgwick's ideas into a Marshallian theoretical framework.

Market Failure in Theory

Pigou, like Sidgwick before him, was critical of what he saw as a tendency among classical economists and their followers to ascribe to the free play of self-interest a maximum of economic welfare. Pigou saw the problems of laissez-faire as rooted in certain base effects of self-interested behavior, effects that the system of natural liberty could not overcome. Writing in 1913, London School of Economics economist Edwin Cannan (1913: 333) said that "the working of self-interest is generally beneficent, not because of some natural coincidence between the self-interest and each and the good of all, but because human institutions are arranged so as to compel self-interest to work in directions in which it will be beneficent." Pigou seems to have concurred with Cannan's assessment and quoted him approvingly. He went on to say, however, that in spite of all of the efforts made to create institutions that would channel self-interest toward the larger social interest, there remain "failures and imperfections," even in the most advanced of nations (Pigou 1932: 129).

Pigou rejected Marshall's consumer surplus as a means for measuring that magnitude of these failures and imperfections, choosing instead to focus on what he called the "national dividend": "that part of the objective income of the community ... which can be measured in money" (Pigou 1932: 31).[10] This national dividend, then, was the social product or the value of output—the same measure used by many of the classical economists.[11] It was to be Pigou's measuring stick—the criterion based upon which he assessed economic outcomes. The task that he set for himself was to examine, in part, "how far the free play of self-interest, acting under the existing legal system, tends to distribute the country's resources in the way most

[10] Pigou also used a broader measure, "economic welfare," which included the dividend but accounted for distributional effects as well. For example, in Pigou's system, an increase in the national dividend will increase economic welfare, all else being equal, if the portion of the dividend accruing to the poor is not reduced in the process (1932: 82). This broader notion of economic welfare was soundly thrashed by Robbins (1932) and the Paretians, though the Paretian measure, for all its theoretical elegance was, too, found untenable.

[11] Malthus (1798) was an exception here. He argued that increases in national output that did not result in an increase in the means of subsistence (particularly the food supply) could not necessarily be considered wealth-enhancing, given the importance of the food supply vis-à-vis population pressures.

favourable to the production of a large national dividend, and how far it is feasible for State action to improve upon 'natural' tendencies" (1932: xii). To get at these issues, Pigou utilized the concept of the margin, which was so central to the Marshallian analytical system, and which enabled Pigou to put his analysis in a marginal benefit–marginal cost framework. The two key analytical constructs here were marginal social net product and marginal private net product. Pigou defined the former as "the total net product of physical things or objective services due to the marginal increment of resources in any given use or place, no matter to whom any part of this product may accrue" (1932: 134). The marginal private net product is similar, but consists of the portion that "accrues in the first instance ... to the person responsible for investing resources" in the process or activity in question (1932: 134–35). Each of these constructs measures net benefits, with these net benefits accruing to society as a whole in the one case and to the resource owner alone in the other. They are also simply the physical measures; the *value* of these net products is the amount of money that they are worth in the market (1932: 135).

As Marshall, Jevons, and others had shown, self-interested behavior on the part of economic agents brings about the equality of *private* net products. Pigou, however, pointed out that the national dividend is maximized only when marginal *social* net products are equalized across the various uses of society's resources (1932: 136). The implication of these two conditions is that the national dividend will be maximized—self-interest and social interest will coincide—only when marginal private net products are equal to marginal social net products. This, then, led Pigou to examine the extent to which market forces generate these coincidences and the circumstances that determine whether and to what extent private and social net products diverge. It is when such divergences arise, said Pigou, that a potential role for government corrective action arises, as "certain specific acts of interference with normal economic processes may be expected not to diminish, but to increase the dividend" (1932: 172).

The first class of divergences between private and social net products pointed to by Pigou are those where agents with the potential to invest in socially beneficial capital improvements fail to do so in optimal amounts because there is some positive probability that they will not be able to recoup the necessary share of associated benefits (1932: 174–83). This type of situation can arise in agricultural tenancy relationships, where tenants will have little incentive to invest in improving the land if there is a strong probability that they will not be able to recoup this investment when the tenancy arrangement comes to an end. Likewise, when private firms are given concessions to operate "public utilities," the incentive for them to make capital improvements is reduced in proportion to the probability that the plant may, at the expiration of the concession contract, pass into the hands of government without compensation. Pigou noted that the resultant underinvestment problem can be mitigated to some extent via negotiation—that contractual terms can be specified to mandate compensation. In reality, though, Pigou found these private measures less than adequate to ensure the optimal level of investment and suggested that a more adequate adjustment could come via laws that mandate compensation for capital improvements made, whether between government and concessionaire or between landlord and tenant.

The second class of divergences that Pigou examined was perhaps the most important in terms of long-run impact on the literature—the existence of spillovers. These divergences arise in situations where

> one person A, in the course of rendering some service, for which payment is made, to a second person B, incidentally also render services or disservices to other persons (not producers of like services), of such a sort that payment cannot be exacted from the benefited parties or compensation enforced on behalf of the injured parties. (1932: 183)

This, of course, is the classic situation of externality, and Pigou distinguishes between two general types. The first, now commonly referred to as positive externalities, involves situations where marginal private net product is less than social net product, "because incidental services are performed to third parties from whom it is technically difficult to exact payment" (1932: 183–84). Pigou lists a number of examples, including lighthouses, parks, roads and tramways, afforestation, street lighting, pollution abatement, and scientific research. Each of these provides benefits to society beyond those to the agent directly engaged in providing the good or service, thereby generating a social net product in excess of the private one and causing an underproduction of those goods and activities through the market. The second category is negative externalities, where, "owing to the technical difficulty of enforcing compensation for incidental disservices," marginal private net product exceeds marginal social net product (1932: 185). Here Pigou includes the effects of such things as congestion and destruction of amenity from new factories and from new buildings erected in crowded city centers, the damage to roads from automobiles, the production and sale of alcohol, and the health effects on children from factory labor of women. These activities generate costs to society beyond those incurred by the individuals directly involved, and thereby cause the private net products to exceed the social. The market, then, will tend to overproduce these goods and activities.[12]

---

[12] The emerging recognition that there was something between perfect competition and monopoly—namely, monopolistic competition—led Pigou to suggest further sources of market failure tied to this type of market structure. One of these is advertising, which would have no value in a highly competitive system. Because, in his view, advertising often serves

Pigou allowed that the divergences between private and social products that arise between contracting parties—as in the case of the principal-agent problems that result from tenancy situations—may be amenable to resolution by negotiation, but he did not believe that this was possible in situations of third-party effects. He said, however, that it is possible for *the state* to step in "to remove the divergence in any field by 'extraordinary encouragements' or 'extraordinary restraints'," the "most obvious" forms of which are "bounties and taxes" (1932: 192). Thus, one could levy taxes on establishments that serve alcohol, tax petrol, or impose a car license fee, the funds from which could be used to improve roads, tax advertisements, and subsidize scientific research.[13] In certain cases, "when the interrelations of the various private persons affected are highly complex," bounties and taxes may not be sufficient, and regulations—such as zoning ordinances and other forms of local planning—may be in order (1932: 194).

Pigou was convinced that the interactions of large numbers of people would often generate spillovers and that these wide-spread external effects invalidated the claims made by certain earlier commentators regarding the beneficial workings of the system of natural liberty. The growth of cities provided a signal illustration of the problems posed:

> It is as idle to expect a well-planned town to result from the independent activities of isolated speculators as it would be to expect a satisfactory picture to result if each separate square inch were painted by an independent artist. No "invisible hand" can be relied on to produce a good arrangement of the whole from a combination of separate treatments of the parts. (1932: 195)

Because of this, Pigou thought it necessary that "an authority of wider reach" should step in and "tackle the collective problems of beauty, of air and of light," just as had been done for public utilities such as gas and water (1932: 195).

While the analysis of externalities had the most significant long-run impact on the literature, it was the third situation of divergence between private and social interests identified by Pigou—the presence of increasing or decreasing returns in production—that was the most controversial at the time of his writing. We have already seen that this problem was first probed by Marshall in his elaboration of the idea of consumers' surplus. The issue, of course, is that investments in industries characterized by

---

merely as an attempt to transfer business from one seller to another, it generates a social net product lower than the private one. A second problem arises because imperfect competition allows for the possibility of fraudulent business practices, which would not be possible in a highly competitive system (1932: 196–203).

[13] Marshall had argued likewise, advocating, for example, taxes on those who build houses in highly populated areas to finance the construction of playgrounds.

decreasing returns will raise costs, and thus prices, for all, thereby yielding a social net product that is less than the private one. Conversely, investments in industries that exhibit increasing returns will generate lower costs, and thus prices, for all, meaning that the social net product of such investments exceeds the private one. While Marshall offered a tentative, or provisional, analysis of conditions under which taxes on industries subject to decreasing returns and subsidies to those exhibiting increasing returns could increase national welfare, Pigou's discussion exhibited no such hesitance. In *Wealth and Welfare* (1912: 178–79), Pigou advocated for taxes on all industries subject to decreasing returns and subsidies to all industries exhibiting increasing returns, doing so on the grounds that only then could a nation approximate ideal output in the absence of constant returns.[14]

The cumulative effect of this discussion was a strong sense that market failure is a rather pervasive problem and that governmental measures are necessary to deal with the situation. As Pigou put it in his *Economics of Welfare* (1932: 331),

> In any industry, where there is reason to believe that the free play of self-interest will cause an amount of resources to be invested different from the amount that is required in the best interest of the national dividend, there is a *prima facie* case for public intervention.

As we shall see later on, this became the mantra for much of the analysis of market failure that was to follow in the coming decades. The question for Pigou, though, was how this prima facie theoretical case should work itself out in the realm of economic policy. Here, his *Economics of Welfare* is of comparatively little use, since its purpose was simply "to study certain important groups of causes that affect economic welfare (1932: 11) rather than to solve potential problems.[15] We thus must look elsewhere for Pigou's prescription—specifically, to his relatively unknown 1935 essay on

---

[14] See also Pigou (1932: 213–28). Pigou's discussion on this score was criticized by Marshall, both on certain technical points and because certain things that Marshall considered provisional and qualified were set out in far more concrete terms by Pigou. See the discussion of Marshall's notes on *Wealth and Welfare* in Bharadwaj (1972). Pigou's work in this vein was, of course, part of the running controversy over the treatment of the problems of increasing and decreasing returns, a discussion that included articles by Clapham (1922), Knight (1924), Sraffa (1926), Young (1928), and Ellis and Fellner (1943). Several of the pieces from this controversy are reprinted in Stigler and Boulding (1952).

[15] "[T]he type of science that the economist will endeavor to develop must be one adapted to form the basis of an art. It will not, indeed, itself be an art, or directly enunciate the precepts of government. It is a positive science of what is and tends to be, not a normative science of what ought to be" (1932: 5). See also Pigou's "Economic Science in Relation to Practice" (1908).

"State Action and Laisser-Faire," published in a slim volume on *Economics in Practice*.

Market Failure in Practice

The subject of Pigou's 1935 essay, which is the published text of a lecture given in Cambridge, is "the attitude of economists towards state action" (1935d: 107). Pigou comes right out of the gate with a philosophical argument—not protesting *against* laissez-faire, but stating that it is "unreal and misleading" to make a sharp distinction between state action and laissez-faire (1935d: 109):

> No defender of so-called laisser-faire desires that the State should do absolutely nothing in matters relevant to economic life. The most ardent believer in the economic harmonies, that are supposed to flow from the unimpeded pursuit by individuals of their private interests, argues that these harmonies will not emerge unless robbery at arms is restrained by law, fraud repressed, and contracts which have been formally accepted enforced.

This, of course, is completely consistent with Adam Smith's discussion in *The Wealth of Nations* (1776), and, as Pigou pointed out, it is also reflected in the sentiment of Cannan—who was no friend of the Pigovian-Cambridge tradition—that it tends to be man-made institutions, rather than natural forces, that channel self-interest in beneficial directions.[16] Pigou listed institutions such as family, property and contract law, prohibition of fraud, and the police as obvious and almost universally unobjectionable components of the societal structure in the West that help to channel the operation of self-interest to the benefit of society (1935d: 110).

Acceptance of this basic idea about the relationship between government and economy changes the entire character of one's thinking about market and state. The "real question," said Pigou, "is not whether the State should act or not, but on what principles, in what degree and over what departments of economic life its action should be carried on." Nor did he find the answers to this question at all obvious: "The issue is not one of yes or no," he said, "but of more or less; of delimiting an uncertain frontier; of weighing, in different departments, conflicting advantages, the balance of which sometimes tips to one side, sometimes to the other" (1935d: 110).

This highly pragmatic sentiment might seem to leave rather little room for the sort of theoretical approach set out in *The Economics of Welfare*. Indeed, given the theoretical nature of that book, it may come as a surprise—at least if one neglects his strong links to Marshall—to note that,

---

[16] See the full quotation from Cannan on p. 60.

in another of these lectures on economics in practice, Pigou called economics "a tradesman among the sciences" (1935a: 2). But Pigou was very
much a product of the Cambridge tradition, and so he believed that while
the elegant systems of equations set out by continental scholars such as
Léon Walras in his *Elements of Pure Economics* (1874) and Vilfredo Pareto in his *Manual of Political Economy* (1906) had a certain "aesthetic
appeal," the complexity of the actual economic environment "does not
lend itself to triumphs of pure reasoning" (1935a: 3–4). The emphasis,
he said, should be on the discovery of "practically useful results," for it is
here that economics finds its reason for being—"its promise of fruit rather
than ... its promise of light" (1935a: 4–5).

This did not mean, however, that Pigou was willing to write off theorizing or suggest that economists should study only practical problems, as
we can see from his strong defense of economic theorizing in the "empty
boxes" debate.[17] There, Pigou cited Clerk Maxwell's work as an important
instance of high theory leading to significant practical application in the area
of wireless telegraphy. When it came to finding a proper balance between
high theory and more practical analysis, Pigou suggested that economics
could learn from the natural sciences, where results sometimes flow from
highly practical experiments, but where, in other instances, "[r]emoter,
more fundamental, so to speak more theoretical, investigations sometimes
in the end yield the largest harvests" (1935a: 6).

Pigou was well aware, though, that the policy realm introduces a number
of complications, the most fundamental of which is that one cannot determine
which particular course of action is desirable absent some normative criterion
for judging between them (1935b: 132). Many policies are widespread in
their effects. On which people, he asks, are the effects to be measured? Do
we look at the effects on domestic society? On some subset of society? If the
latter, which subset? On the whole world? The answers to questions of this
nature, Pigou contends, take us outside the boundaries of economics; they
are instead "for the student of Ethics, not for economists" (1935b: 133).

Here, Pigou's perspective, while thoroughly Marshallian in orientation,
also supports the controversial position taken by Lionel Robbins in his
Essay on the Nature and Significance of Economic Science (1932). Robbins
contended forcefully that value judgments have no place in economic science, belonging instead to the realm that he labeled "political economy."[18]
This line of thinking is much in evidence in Pigou's (1935d: 107) contention that

> in economics proper the word *ought* has no place. Its business is to study
> what *tends* to happen, to trace the connection between causes and effects,

[17] See, for example, Clapham (1922) and Pigou (1922).
[18] See also Robbins (1981) and Colander (2009).

to analyse the interplay of conflicting forces. It is a positive science, not a normative science. It is concerned, like physiology, to discover what effects various drugs will produce, not, like medicine, to prescribe what drugs ought to be taken.[19]

In both its tendency statement orientation and conscious distancing of economics from normative prescription, Pigou's statement here leaves him at odds with the approach to market failure that was developed by the next generation of scholars, who based their views upon his *Economics of Welfare*.

Confining the analysis to the positive side does not render it problem free, however. In particular, Pigou acknowledged that it is very difficult to gauge the effects of many proposals beyond what he called "vague judgments." The problem, he said, is that while economics is very successful at qualitative analysis, it has severe limitations on the quantitative analysis side. The result is that prediction amounts, at best, to "instructed guesswork," although he held out hope that the progress of economics might lead to some advances on this front (1935d: 109).

How does all of this apply to Pigou's discussion of market failure? In attempting to discern the appropriate scope of state action, Pigou argued that the market system leads to two forms of "evils and wastes" (1935d: 113).[20] The first of these arises from the incompetence of individual agents in pursuing their chosen ends. Problems of this nature usually arise from failure of private agents to forecast properly the market for their products and, in Pigou's time, this tendency led to calls for central planning. Nevertheless, said Pigou, the case for state action (central planning) here comes down to one's willingness to assume that the state can do a better job of forecasting demands than can private enterprise—a proposition that Pigou found rather dubious (1935d: 114–15):

It is easy for a public servant, looking back when he knows the course that demand has taken, to point out the mistakes of those who tried to forecast it. But it is a very different thing for that public servant to make a forecast. The fundamental assumption, on which the whole case for this sort of planning rests, is that public servants will prove specially skilled at this.

That Pigou found this assumption "at least a doubtful one" (1935d: 115) is not surprising in light of his views on the problems with the bureaucratic process, which we will discuss momentarily.

This issue takes on a somewhat different cast, however, when Pigou turned his attention to the other form of "evils and wastes," when the

---

[19] When he said "economics proper," Pigou was referring to his conception of economic science. Marshall used this expression in a similar way. See Coase (1975).

[20] A more extensive discussion of Pigou's conception of waste can be found in his essay on "Economy and Waste" (1935c).

pursuit of private interests runs counter to the *social* interest. This, said Pigou, justifies state action "in principle" unless one believes that private and social interests are always perfectly compatible. Pigou, of course, rejected the idea of universal compatibility, pointing out that, contrary to what "invisible hand" explanations might imply, institutions are not always structured in such a way as to channel private interests to the best interests of society as a whole (1935d: 115). The theoretical demonstration of this had been one of the major contributions of his *Economics of Welfare*. Nor was this a uniquely Cambridge insight, as Pigou was quick to point out: "[T]he doctrine of the invisible hand evolving social benefit out of private selfishness has never been held by economists—certainly it was not held by Adam Smith—in that absolute and rigid form in which the popular writers conceive it." Rather, he says, "All are agreed that many times the hand falters in its aim" (1935d: 115).

Pigou broke down the resulting disharmonies into three general categories. The first was disharmonies in production, under which he included instances where firms are able to garner for themselves substantial monopoly power, situations of negative or positive externality, and excessive discounting of the future, the last of which gives rise to problems such as underinvestment and premature depletion of natural resources. The second type of disharmony that he identified is in the distribution of income, where substantial inequalities give rise to social losses.[21] Finally, there is a third manifestation of disharmony in the various problems associated with industrial fluctuations, including in levels of production, consumer demands, and the expansion and contraction of credit (1935d: 116–24). What we have here are, in modern language, allocation failure, distribution failure, and stability failure, respectively—"failures" in the sense that, in each instance, the market fails to generate the best possible result for society.[22] When such market failures arise—that is, when "private self-interest, acting freely, subject only to the ordinary forms of law, does not lead to the best results from a general social point of view"—there is, says Pigou, "a *prima facie* case for State action" (1935d: 124).[23]

---

[21] Here Pigou explicitly invokes the assumption of diminishing marginal utility of income and does so in an almost sarcastic way, noting that, "[t]he ninth course of the plutocrat's dinner, despite the indirect benefit that it may confer on his doctor, yields much less satisfaction on the whole than the milk which the cost of it might have secured for a poor man's child" (1935d: 121). Pigou also finds this distributional disharmony in the wage bargain, absent employee unions.

[22] Our focus, of course, is allocation failure, although certain aspects of the discussion generalize.

[23] Recall that Pigou makes the same argument in his *Economics of Welfare* (1932: 331). See also p. 64.

To this point, the story sounds remarkably like that in *The Economics of Welfare* and should be familiar to those acquainted with the postwar neoclassical theory of market failure. Where, however, does the prima facie case actually take Pigou? Specifically, what does this actually imply for policy? Pigou speaks briefly to this topic in both *Wealth and Welfare* and *The Economics of Welfare*, noting that "[t]he case ... cannot be more than a *prima facie* one, until we have considered the qualifications, which governmental agencies maybe expected to possess for intervening advantageously." Here, he gets specifically to the theory-practice distinction, although not characterizing it as such, when he says, "It is not sufficient to contrast the imperfect adjustments of unfettered private enterprise with the best adjustment that economists in their studies can imagine. For we cannot expect that any public authority will attain, or will even wholeheartedly seek, that ideal" because of information problems faced by, and the pressures brought to bear on, governmental agents (1912: 247–48; 1932: 331–32). One can hear in this echoes of his predecessors' qualms regarding the ability of government to get things right.

In "State Action and Laisser-Faire," Pigou provides a more elaborate answer, albeit again not the answer one might expect based on the direction taken by modern Pigovian economics and ascribed to it, and to Pigou himself, by the critics. The prima facie case, Pigou says, "only takes us a little way"; in deciding on the practical desirability of state action, "it is not enough to know that a form and degree of it can be conceived, which, if carried through effectively, would benefit the community." He had already shown in his *Economics of Welfare* that it was possible to design such a scheme in theory. When it comes to moving from theory to practical application, however, things get more complicated (1935d: 124):

> We have further to inquire how far, in the particular country in which we are interested and the particular time that concerns us, the government is qualified to select the right form and degree of State action and to carry it through effectively.

Ascertaining the qualifications of government, in turn, has several components. First, the attitude of the citizens toward government action is of great import, as any actions are more likely to be effectively implemented and carried out if they have substantial public support. Second, there is the issue of the "quality" of the decision-making body that will be determining the form and extent of state action. Pigou (1935d: 125) says that the quality of this body will be a function of

> the intellectual competence of the persons who constitute it, the efficacy of the organisation through which their decisions are executed, their personal integrity in the face of bribery and blackmail, their freedom from domina-

tion by a privileged class, [and] their ability to resist the pressure of powerful interests or of uninstructed opinion.

The basic problem, according to Pigou, is that "[e]very public official is a potential opportunity for some form of self-interest arrayed against the common interest" (1912: 248), a sentiment strikingly like what one finds in Smith, as well as in Sidgwick and Marshall. The financial stakes that accompany many policy proposals are incredibly high and make "[l]ogrolling and lobbying ... powerful forces" that "are certain to be called into play" (1935d: 126). Because of this, politicians are "subject to great pressure from persons who can control votes," a problem that is made all the more difficult by lobbying groups also being the sources of politicians' campaign funds (1912: 248). Moreover, the growth of government enterprises generates substantial new bureaucracies and "the employment of tens of thousands of additional public servants," which, in turn, means increased patronage for party leaders (1912: 248). All of this makes the quality of the individuals who make up the governing body of the utmost import for sound policy. Unfortunately, said Pigou, the unseemly aspects of interest-group pressure tend to deter upright people from entering politics, which serves only to further loose the forces of corruption. The results of the political process thus will likely be skewed, in that the efforts of the state are "most likely to be invoked successfully by the strong," regardless of what is actually in society's best interests (1935d: 126). For Pigou, it is these practical concerns of a political nature, rather than "any abstract plea for laisser-faire in matters of trade," that speak most loudly against government interference.

Pigou followed Marshall in believing that, although government in Adam Smith's day was corrupt, inefficient, and capable of achieving little, during the 150 years since Smith there had been a rise of "governing authorities ... enormously better equipped for successful action" (1935d: 126). Referencing Marshall's "Economic Chivalry" essay, Pigou attributed this in part to increased levels of education and the "surplus energy" that was made possible by increases in the technology of production. He praised the civil service for its "high capacity and unquestioned public spirit" and the politicians for their absence of personal corruption (1935d: 126).[24]

Yet, while the quality of the individuals serving on the political front was improving, Pigou was not so naïve as to suggest that governing bodies had reached anything like perfection. In particular, he pointed to four shortcomings that he felt characterized representative assemblies. First, elected officials are chosen for a host of reasons unrelated to economic regulation, and there is thus little reason to expect that they have any particular

---

[24] See also Pigou (1912: 249).

competence for intervening in industry. Second, the makeup of these assemblies tends to fluctuate a great deal over time, depriving society of the benefits of experience and, with that, what may be more desirable levels of policy continuity. Third, municipal size and appropriate economic size may be vastly different, which means that attempting to set up a public enterprise on the same scale as the municipality may lead to major inefficiencies. Finally, these assemblies are political in nature and thus subject to "injurious forms of electoral pressure" of the types we have mentioned earlier (1912: 249–50).

While the legislative option was problematic, Pigou argued repeatedly that recent advances in governance structures presented a possible solution.[25] Specifically, he believed that quasi-governmental entities—he mentions Public Service Boards and Commissions—not directly subject to political control offered a means of avoiding some of these problems that had not been available in times past. While members of general governmental bodies were elected for a host of reasons often unrelated to the regulation of industry, the specialized boards and commissions could appoint members whose abilities were well suited to the regulation of industry. The continuity problem and the influence of electoral whims could be resolved by appointing these individuals for longer terms of service than were standard for elected officials. This would have the further beneficial effect of insulating them from electoral pressures (1932: 333–35; 1935d: 127). Pigou thought that this would increase the likelihood of government interference proving beneficial in any given situation, as compared with former times (1912: 249).

The overarching point, for Pigou, was not that state action is the appropriate response to market failure, but rather that there is no definitive answer that one can give, a priori, about the magnitude of the problems associated with state intervention. At times their effects will be "trifling," while at other times they will be "dominant" (1935d: 127). Thus, he said, whether one comes at this from a predisposition toward laissez-faire or toward state action, one is led to a single conclusion (1935d: 127):

> Inquiring how far the free play of private self-interest makes for social advantage, we find that it frequently fails to do this, but that there are many different forms and many different degrees in its failure. Inquiring how far Government is fitted to take action against these failures, we find that its fitness to do this varies, not only in different places and different times, but also as between interventions directed against different kinds of failure.

The larger lesson that Pigou drew from this was that generalizations are of little or no help in dealing with the difficult issues of economic policy.

[25] See Pigou (1912: 250; 1932: 333–35; 1935d: 127).

In particular, he said, "The issue about which popular writers argue—the principle of laisser-faire *versus* the principle of State action—is not an issue at all. There is no principle involved on either side." Instead of appealing to so-called principle, Pigou argued, "Each particular case must be considered on its merits in all the detail of its concrete circumstance" (1935d: 127–28).

It is interesting to compare Pigou's position here with that of Sidgwick, who, like Pigou, worked out the analytics of market failure and governmental response in a quasi-marginalist framework. As we saw in chapter 2, Sidgwick (1901: 417) concluded that

> the general presumption derived from abstract economic reasoning is not in favor of leaving industry altogether to private enterprise ... ; but is on the contrary in favour of supplementing and controlling such enterprise in various ways by the collective action of the community.

But, he said, abstract deductive analysis cannot provide detailed practical information for policy-making: the particular conditions of time and place render sweeping generalizations inappropriate. Sidgwick concluded that, in moving "from abstract principles to their concrete applications ... it seems best to adopt a more empirical treatment" (1901: 417–18), one that recognizes the potential drawbacks that may be associated with government interference and weighs these against the "evils" that this intervention is designed to remedy. In juxtaposing Pigou's position with the these sentiments of Sidgwick, as well as the position of Marshall, which was discussed earlier, we get a clear sense that Pigou's practical approach falls squarely within the larger Cambridge tradition.

THE PIGOVIAN LEGACY

Pigou's analysis of private and social net products, first in *Wealth and Welfare* and then, more expansively, in his *Economics of Welfare,* marked the culmination of the first stage in the analysis of market failure and simultaneously laid the foundation for the second: the development of the neoclassical theory of market failure in the middle third of the twentieth century.

The three decades following the publication of *Economics of Welfare* saw the fleshing out of Pigou's theoretical analysis, as those working in the burgeoning field of welfare economics were able to demonstrate, with increasing analytical rigor, the conditions necessary for market optimum, the factors and forces that would cause market outcomes to diverge from the optimum, and the means by which governmental action could correct those market failures.[26] While Pigou had demonstrated the existence of market

---

[26] See Mishan (1971) for a survey.

failure where private and social interests diverge, his attempts to show that phenomena such as positive or negative third-party effects *cause* market failure relied on logical argument, and his assertions that government could remove these divergences with appropriate policy measures were simply statements of possibility or potential, rather than demonstrations on an analytical par with analysis of market failures themselves. The groundwork had been laid, however, and it was not long before economists were employing their burgeoning mathematical toolkit to hammer down the necessary conditions for optimality[27]—demonstrating both that externalities did indeed cause departures from the social optimum and that taxes, subsidies, and regulations could be implemented that would cause the actions of private agents to harmonize with the social interest. This perspective came to dominate both the professional literature and the textbook treatments of public goods and externalities in the last half of the twentieth century.

James Meade's 1952 article, "External Economies and Diseconomies in a Competitive Situation," is a classic rendering of the neoclassical take on Pigou's analysis. Meade instances the case of apple growers and bee-keepers operating in close proximity. The bees get food from the apple trees, but the farmer receives no income from this service and the bee-keeper incurs no cost. The farmer is thus paid an amount less than the value of his marginal social net product, whereas the bee-keeper receives payments in excess of his marginal social net product. Meade demonstrated, using extensive and precise mathematical detail, the conditions for optimality here, as well as the tax on bee-keepers and the subsidy to apple farmers required to correct the market failure—that is, that would bring their compensation into line with marginal social net product (1952: 188–91).[28] This analysis led

---

[27] See, for example, Bergson (1938), Lange (1942), and Debreu (1954).

[28] Meade's basic points can be captured in a simple model. (This model, which is much simpler than that used by Meade, owes to Bator [1958].) Assume that the production functions for apples (A) and honey (H) are given by

$$q_A = f(L_A), \tag{1}$$

$$q_H = f(L_H, A(L_A)), \tag{2}$$

where L_i is the quantity of labor used to produce good i. The apple farmers' trees provide food for the bees, and thus enter the production function for honey. Meade, however, assumes that the farmer receives no compensation for the services rendered by his orchard. (See, however, Cheung [1973], who describes the routine nature of contracting between bee-keepers and apple farmers in the United States.) Profit-maximization leads each producer to pay a wage equal to the worker's value of marginal product:

$$P_A \frac{dq_A}{dL_A} = w \tag{3}$$

and

$$P_H \frac{dq_H}{dL_H} = w. \tag{4}$$

Meade to conclude that "Capitalists in apple farming *should be subsidised* because the unpaid benefits which they confer upon the bee-keepers more than outweigh the unpaid benefits which they receive from the labour and capital employed in bee-keeping" (1952: 191–92, emphasis added).[29]

The normative leap here is important. Meade took his mathematical demonstration that, under certain conditions, a subsidy equal to marginal external cost will generate optimality and moved from there to an assertion that a subsidy should be paid. Of course, his results implied no such thing. Through all of Meade's analysis, we see great concern for mathematical detail, even extending to the relationship between externalities and the homogeneity of the production function. Yet, he made no mention of any potential problems with the ability of government to ascertain the appro-

---

(We assume, for simplicity, that wages are identical across markets.) Optimality, however, requires that the marginal social net product equal the wage, which implies that, for labor in the apples sector,

$$P_A \frac{d q_A}{d L_A} + P_H \frac{\partial H}{\partial A} \cdot \frac{d A}{d L_A} = w. \tag{5}$$

The second term on the left-hand side of (5),

$$P_H \frac{\partial H}{\partial A} \cdot \frac{d A}{d L_A}, \tag{6}$$

denotes the marginal value of the externality, the value of honey produced as the result of an additional unit of labor employed by the apple farmer. Because the apple farmer does not capture the return from this, he will employ an amount of labor that is less than what is socially optimal. As Meade went on to demonstrate, however, the apple farmer can be induced to employ the socially optimal amount of labor if paid a per-worker subsidy equal to the marginal value of the externality:

$$s = P_H \frac{\partial H}{\partial A} \cdot \frac{d A}{d L_A}. \tag{7}$$

This makes the marginal value of hiring another worker equal to

$$P_A \frac{d q_A}{d L_A} + s = P_A \frac{d q_A}{d L_A} + P_H \frac{\partial H}{\partial A} \cdot \frac{d A}{d L_A}, \tag{8}$$

and the apple farmer will hire additional workers until this marginal value is equal to the wage. It was later shown that optimality requires that a tax or subsidy be equal to the marginal value of the externality at the efficient level of output. See, for example, Baumol (1972).

[29] This statement follows from the fact that bees may provide useful services to the apple farmer by fertilizing the apple trees.

Meade went on to analyze spillovers that are more general in nature, such as where afforestation measures increase rainfall, which provides a benefit to wheat farmers in the area. Here again, Meade derives the conditions for optimality and shows that the market will generate levels of factor compensation in the timber industry that are less than the marginal social net product of those factors. To achieve optimality, either the earnings of factors of production in that industry, or the price of timber, must be subsidized at the appropriate rate.

priate level of taxes or subsidies, or to otherwise accomplish the efficient resolution of externality problems. What was simply a prima facie case for Pigou is the definitive case for Meade.

In adopting this perspective, Meade was representative rather than an outlier. So analytics-driven was this analysis that even the definitions given to externalities were being stated in mathematical terms. J. de V. Graaf offered the following definitions in his slim classic on *Theoretical Welfare Economics*:

> External effects exist in consumption whenever the shape or position of a man's indifference curve depends on the consumption of another man. (1957: 43)

> [External effects] are present whenever a firm's production function depends in some way on the amounts of the inputs or outputs of another firm. (1957: 18)

Buchanan and Stubblebine take a similar tack in their 1962 classic, "Externality": "We define an external effect, *an externality*, to be present when

$$u^A = u^A(X_1, X_2, \ldots, X_m, Y_1).\text{"}[30]$$

In other words, an externality exists when person A's utility is a function of an activity undertaken by person B—here via Y_1, which is the consumption of good 1 by individual B. So conceived, externalities are nothing more than variables that affect the production or utility functions of other agents. From here, it is just a few mathematical manipulations to optimality conditions, and from there to the derivation of tax or subsidy solutions that will generate these optima through the policy process.

The impact of these new tools of analysis for the general acceptance of the market-failure-cum-government-correction approach is exemplified in Kenneth Arrow and Tibor Scitovsky's "General introduction" to a volume of readings on welfare economics (Arrow and Scitovsky 1969: 1), published under the auspices of the American Economic Association in 1969:

> Recently, welfare economics has greatly increased in importance. The increased rigor of modern economics has affected this branch of the discipline most profoundly. Economists want to know exactly what they are after, what is the meaning, the limitations, and the importance of economic efficiency and economic progress. Moreover, the economist's better understanding of the nature of economic processes, his growing desire to control and influence factors once considered God-given or outside the realm of rational calculation, the growth of the public sector, and our ever-greater reliance on policy have also contributed to rendering this branch of economics increasingly important.

---

[30] Buchanan and Stubblebine (1962: 200).

Arrow and Scitovsky's remark is indicative of the focus, within neoclassical welfare analysis, on deriving determinate, optimal solutions to questions of economic theory and policy. In the case of externalities, the shortcomings of the system of natural liberty and the ability of government not just to improve upon the workings of the market but to generate optimal outcomes were "proven." The rhetorical, persuasive force of this analysis should not be underestimated. What this theory demonstrated, in a nutshell, was that perfect markets work perfectly, imperfect markets work imperfectly, and perfect government can cause imperfect markets to also function perfectly. This became the textbook model. The qualms regarding the ability of government actually to accomplish the correction of market failures, so much in evidence in classical economics, and even in the qualifications given by the Cambridge school economists, had all but disappeared. The role of government vis-à-vis the market was no longer an a priori set of assertions nor an opinion based upon casual empiricism; it was demonstrable, in a "scientific" sense.

CHAPTER FOUR

Marginalizing Government I

FROM *LA SCIENZA DELLE FINANZE* TO WICKSELL

WHILE THE CAMBRIDGE SCHOOL was expressing both hesitation and optimism about the ability of government to improve on market failures,
continental scholars were developing models of the political process as an
integral component of the enterprise of public finance. It is not our purpose here to explore the history of public finance, but these continental
models of the political process mark an important moment in the history
of economic ideas. The Cambridge tradition did not neglect the influence
of the political process on economic policy, as we saw in chapter 3, but this
relationship was not woven into the theory proper. The continental scholars, in contrast, brought the political element squarely into the discussion
of public goods provision, to the extent that their work has been hailed as
a precursor of modern public choice theory.[1] The most vibrant strand of
this literature came out of the Italian public finance tradition—*la scienza
delle finanze*—which even today remains relatively unknown outside of
Italy, not least because most of these works are not available in English.[2]
On the rare occasion when the Italian literature was taken note of in the
early part of the twentieth century, the response was not always enthusiastic.
University of Chicago economist Henry Simons (1937: 713, 717), review-
ing Antonio De Viti de Marco's *First Principles of Public Finance* (1936)
in the *American Economic Review*, called the book "a mass of intellectual
confusion and of dangerous half-truths," a "ponderous apology for actual
fiscal practices," and "a model for the kind of writing which has made our
own literature of public finance a disgrace to economics." The publication

---

[1] Public choice theory is the subject of chapter 6, infra.

[2] This is in spite of the efforts of James Buchanan (1960) and Orhan Kayaalp (1985, 1988,
1989) to popularize this literature. Richard Musgrave (1959), John Head (1974), and Alan
Peacock (1992) also touch on the Italian contributions, and Stefano Toso (1992) looks at
Ricardian equivalence in light of the Italian approach. An excellent recent set of treatments
can be found in a symposium on "The Theory of Public Finance in Italy from the Origins
to the 1940s," published in *Il Pensiero Economico Italiano* in 2003. See also Wagner (2003),
Backhaus and Wagner (2005), and Fausto (2006). The lack of translations also limits the
present discussion. The only translations available are those excerpts included in Musgrave
and Peacock (1958) and de Viti's *First Principles of Public Finance* (1936).

by Richard Musgrave and Alan Peacock (1958) of translated excerpts from several of the Italians' seminal works, along with James Buchanan's (1960) classic survey article on the Italian tradition, have given modern scholars a more positive view of the Italian contribution than one finds in Simons's review, but it remains the case that the degree of economists' familiarity with this literature and its impact on mainstream economics has been virtually nil. The same cannot be said of the seminal work of Knut Wicksell, one of the two or three most prominent continental economists at the turn of the century, whose *Finanztheoretische Untersuchungen* (1896a) provided a springboard for modern public choice analysis as developed in the hands of James Buchanan, Gordon Tullock, and others.[3] Wicksell's impact was far from immediate, though, as his work in the area of public finance was all but ignored within the evolving neoclassical literature on this subject until the 1960s.

The Italian approach to the analysis of state action, like the Cambridge theory of market failure, hinged on the developments of the marginal revolution and the precision that marginalism brought to the theorizing process. Just as the Cambridge tradition used these tools to expose questions about the optimality of markets, so *la scienza delle finanze* raised critical issues about the ability of governments to provide public goods and services in accordance with the dictates of optimality. As we shall see, the conflicting claims regarding the efficiency of government action found among the Italian theories were resolved in the work of Wicksell, who, through a more explicit incorporation of the political process as linked up with individual voter desires, demonstrated the conditions under which the claims made by the disparate elements of the Italian tradition would hold true.[4]

THE ITALIAN TRADITION

The literature of the Italian *la scienza delle finanze* tradition is extensive, with the most seminal contributions coming from Maffeo Pantaleoni (1883), Ugo Mazzola (1890), and Antonio De Viti de Marco (1936).[5] The

---

[3] On this point, see Peacock (1987) and Buchanan (1960). Early examples of Wicksell's influence can be seen in Duncan Black's work on taxation (1955) and Buchanan and Tullock's *The Calculus of Consent* (1962). One can credit Musgrave and Peacock's (1958) collection of translations with drawing attention to and (re)awakening interest in these literatures, as well as the literature of the German school.

[4] A bit of the link between Wicksell and the Italians is noted in the introduction to Musgrave and Peacock (1958: ix–xix), but in a rather different context.

[5] While this literature continued to develop well into the twentieth century, the important foundational elements were set down in the late nineteenth and early twentieth centuries. For example, De Viti de Marco's *First Principles* was derived from lecture notes printed and circulated in 1886–87, where the basic elements of his system were already present. The first

careers of each of these men were a mixture of academic pursuits and public service. Pantaleoni, whose various professorships included a long tenure at the University of Rome, helped to introduce marginalism into Italian economics in his *Principii di economia pura* (1889) and exposed Vilfredo Pareto (perhaps the greatest of all the Italian economists) to this new way of doing economics. Pantaleoni, however, was also active in state and national governance, having at one point served as manager of the finances of d'Annunzio's Free State of Fiume, and he was an ardent proponent of laissez-faire policies and of minimizing the extent of the activities of the state. Mazzola and De Viti, too, were pioneers of the marginalist method in Italy. Mazzola occupied the Chair of Public Finance at the University of Pavia and was an ardent free trader. De Viti was an aristocrat and a classical liberal who, in addition to being a professor of public finance at the University of Rome, was very active in public life, including parliament (Einaudi 1936: 19–21).

The Italian approach to examining the economic role of government, which developed more or less simultaneously with the marginal revolution, is distinguished from the then-extant classical approach in a number of ways. First, the Italian approach, in both its scholarly literature and its educational curriculum, separated the science of public finance from the science of economics. De Viti de Marco (1936: 36) justified the distinction on the grounds that public finance is "concrete," while economics is "abstract"— abstracting, in particular, from historical and political circumstances that serve as complicating factors. The two were thought to require somewhat different methodologies, with the more realistic, factually oriented public finance necessitating a lesser degree of abstraction than economics.

La scienza delle finanze also embodied a more distinctively positive or descriptive component than did the classical theory. In keeping with the spirit of the age, the Italians attempted to locate their analysis in the realm of "science" and to construct a positive economic science that avoided the normative overtones of political economy. De Viti (1936: 37), for example, said that although economics and public finance require different levels of abstraction, both fall into the realm of *science*, which "does not concern itself with giving rules of action" but instead seeks to "establish the reasons why, or the conditions under which, people act in a given way." As is the case in the natural sciences, "the aim is simply to understand, *to know*." The implications of this mindset, as against that of classical political economy, for the study of public finance are clear from De Viti's comments in his 1888 *Carattere teorico dell'economia finanziaria* (*The Theoretical Character of Public Finance*; quoted in De Viti 1936: 49 n):

---

edition of *First Principles* was published in 1928, and an English-language translation of the 1934 edition was published in 1936.

Just as it is not necessary for the economist to discuss which wants man should satisfy and which he should not, so it is unnecessary for the theory of Public Finance to discuss the wants of the State—that is, its functions and the expenditures that it should or should not make. The expenditures are taken as data; since, in actual fact, activity in the field of Public Finance arises in order to meet any expenditure whatever—that is, for the achievement of any goal whatever.

Just as economic science cannot speak for or against things like competition, monopoly, and protectionism, so the science of public finance cannot provide "rules for political action" (De Viti 1936: 37). This, of course, reflects the methodological turn away from normative pronouncements that, as Baumol (1952b: 154) noted, accompanied the marginal revolution in England and on the Continent.[6]

As one might expect, then, the attitudes of Pantaleoni, De Viti de Marco, and Mazzola toward the standard literature of public finance in their era were hardly charitable. This comes out very vividly in Luigi Einaudi's (1936: 22) introduction to De Viti's *First Principles*, where he says that Pantaleoni, De Viti, and Mazzola all

> felt a sense of dissatisfaction as they surveyed that sorry mixture of practical precepts, rambling discussions of philosophic and political themes, comments on legal texts, and loose applications of definitions and economic laws which made up, and still make up, the literature of Public Finance. When one recalls the pages in which were presented a mixture of abstract reasoning and concrete discussion, theoretical schemes and historical examples, deductive reasoning and empirical illustration of legal instances from this or that country, one sees again the master's ironic smile. "This is not science," De Viti would announce as he put the book down quietly. "The fellow's an ass!" Pantaleoni would cry, in brutal condemnation. "He knows no economics and will never learn any!"

Mazzola, though briefly tipping his hat to the potential role for historico-inductive analysis to show how events reflect results derived from pure (abstract, deductive) theory, falls back to the claim that "pure theoretical research must retain its primacy." Of particular importance for present purposes is his belief that a theory which is based on "*the enduring and constant features of human nature*" generates "scientifically accurate results" and constitutes "a safeguard against any all too arbitrary or fanciful interpretation of historical events" ([1890] 1958: 47, emphasis added). This positive, scientific bent played a significant role in motivating the Ital-

---

[6] See chapter 2, p. 27. Indeed, the parallel between the just-quoted extract from De Viti and the Baumol quote is striking.

ians to incorporate the political element into their analysis, in that a "scientifically accurate" explanation of government expenditure and financing processes necessitated coming to grips with the centrality of the political machine within all of this.

Individualism, Self-Interest, and the State

In spite of their attempt to separate public finance from economics, the Italians saw private and public sector activities as complementary, and thus public finance and economics as inextricably linked sciences. This, in turn, is reflected in certain methodological commonalities between the two, as the public finance scholars consciously brought the tools of marginal analysis—including maximization and equilibrium—developed by Jevons and Walras to bear on public sector issues.[7] Thus we find De Viti de Marco saying that the purpose of public finance is to transfer "the principles of the theory of value from Private Economics into the field of Public Economics" (1936: 36). An important piece of this was the generalization of the self-interest model to the public sector, and this had three significant implications for the theory.

First, in spite of the "public" or "collective" aspect of public sector activity, the basic unit of analysis was the individual. The attempt to define the collective as nothing more than the sum of the individuals is nicely illustrated in De Viti's *First Principles* (1936: 34). De Viti said that "the economic activity of the State arises from *collective wants*—that is, from feelings of dissatisfaction on the part of individuals who make up the social organism." The felt need to remedy this dissatisfaction leads individuals to produce the goods that they believe will help to satisfy these collective wants. Public finance, then, is the analysis of this process, investigating

> the conditions to which the productive activity of the State must be subjected in order that the *choice of the public services which are to be produced, the determination of their respective amounts, the distribution of the cost among consumers, etc.*, may take place according to the principles of the theory of value—that is, with the least possible waste of private wealth, in order to attain the greatest satisfaction of collective needs. (1936: 36)

It is important to avoid misapprehending what De Viti means by "collective needs" here. These needs, he says, are "born in a group from the very fact of social life," but they are "*felt* by the individual.... Only the individual can feel pain or pleasure; in this respect, the wants of the group as a whole do not differ from individual wants, since both have their origin

[7] See, for example, Pantaleoni (1883: 16–17) and Mazzola ([1890] 1958: 37).

in the individual (1936: 38). Mazzola, too, insisted that collective wants are derivative of individual preferences,[8] and Giovanni Montemartini was probably most direct of all when he wrote that "there are *no* public, or collective, needs in the strict sense of the word, as opposed to private needs" ([1900] 1958: 151, emphasis added). The methodological implications of this individualism for the study of public finance fall out in straightforward fashion: the theory of public finance "must, as far as possible, break down the State's calculation into the economic calculations of the individuals or groups which represent the constituent elements of the State's calculation" (De Viti 1936: 41).[9]

This raises the question of how individuals and states make these calculations, which takes us to the second and third implications of the Italians' use of the self-interest model. The second is that *la scienza delle finanze* assumed that individuals use the same decision process in thinking about public goods as they do when thinking about private goods.[10] De Viti said that collective action cannot be understood unless one recognizes that man is motivated by hedonism in both contexts. He then proceeded to identify two consequences that flow from this hedonism: people want public goods to be produced in cost-minimizing fashion so as to keep their tax burden as low as possible, and they attempt to consume as much of the public good as possible while contributing as little as possible toward its cost (1936: 35–36).

The third implication is that the decision-making processes of government agents were assumed to be akin to those used by individual producers and consumers in their production and consumption choices.[11] Here, though, the Italians were of two minds on the influence of individual maximization on the political process. One group, led by Pantaleoni, Mazzola, and De Viti de Marco, assumed that it led political agents to attempt to maximize social welfare, and based upon this assumption they constructed what we will call "optimal public equilibrium" models. A second group, which included Amilcare Puviani and Giovanni Montemartini, assumed a more self-centered form of self-interested behavior on the part of political

[8] "If the autonomous individual need remains unsatisfied, so does the public need contained therein. Public goods in themselves afford no satisfaction, and we cannot speak of any satisfaction of public needs" (Mazzola [1890] 1958: 41).

[9] De Viti de Marco's discussion of these calculations of individuals and groups seems to be in terms of adding up the intensities of satisfaction, rather than quantities—giving one an inkling of the Samuelson (1954) public goods model.

[10] This consistency assumption was to become a cornerstone of economics imperialism in the last third of the twentieth century. See, for example, Becker (1976) and Lazear (2000).

[11] As Kayaalp (1989: 155) has pointed out, the individualistic nature of the Italian approach separates it from the other Continental public finance tradition, the German *Staatswirtschaft*. This also explains why the present study does not examine the German literature, excerpts from which can be found in Musgrave and Peacock (1958).

agents, based upon which they generated models of *government* failure not unlike the *market* failure models of the Cambridge school.

Optimal Public Equilibrium: The Good Government Model

The first major foray into optimal public equilibrium analysis was Maffeo Pantaleoni's model of governmental budgeting as a process in which government officials compare the benefits received from public goods and services with the costs of the taxes necessary to finance them. The influence of the emerging marginalist mode of theorizing on this work is evident in Pantaleoni's ([1883] 1958: 19) description of the process of governmental approval of public expenditures:

> We may take it that Parliament sets out to obtain the largest total sum of utility by weighing the country's wishes against its capabilities—by whatever standards both may be measured; clearly the approval or rejection of any expenditure must be based on a judgement which is the resultant of a complex of different elements or propositions. These are obtained by weighing in decreasing order the marginal utilities deriving from the various possible expenditures and then weighing the marginal utilities inherent in every combination of expenditures against the marginal sacrifice caused by the total taxation which each of these combinations would entail.[12]

That this was a novel and even controversial way of discussing questions of public finance was not lost on Pantaleoni, who noted that his approach "may appear somewhat enigmatical to any reader not familiar with the economic theory of degree of utility, developed by the late Jevons and by Léon Walras" ([1883] 1958: 16).

The maximization approach described by Pantaleoni generates two criteria for evaluating public goods. First, the benefits from the public activity must be greater than or equal to costs, where costs measure the sacrifice in terms of private goods foregone; second, the distribution of tax revenues across the public goods and services must be such that the marginal utilities across uses are equated (Pantaleoni [1883] 1958: 16–17).[13] What Pantaleoni

---

[12] Although British public finance continued to be strongly wedded to the ability-to-pay principle, Sidgwick (1901: 545), for one, did bring in the marginal principle, offering that "we must regard both expenditure and supply as having at least a margin within which the restriction or enlargement of either must partly depend on the effects of the corresponding restriction or enlargement of the other; within which, therefore, the gain secured to the public by an additional increment of expenditure has to be carefully weighed against the sacrifices inevitably entailed by the exaction of an additional increment of supply."

[13] This is the public goods equivalent of Gossen's second law (utility is maximized when an individual distributes his money across various uses so that the marginal utility from the

particularly liked about this approach to expenditure and financing was that it highlights the interdependence between the two sides of the budget and makes them, in his words, "perfectly synchronous" ([1883] 1958: 20).[14]

What we have here is a theoretical model that is the antithesis of the classical approach, with the portrait of inept government agents replaced by one of an efficiently operating government made up of rational calculators of social benefits and costs. In keeping with the practical bent that the Italians said must characterize public finance, however, Pantaleoni did not see this as nirvana-esque abstraction. Rather, he claimed that this was a reasonably accurate depiction of the operation of government, that "year by year" governments—in Europe and America, at least—put together budgets "with a fairly considerable degree of perfection" ([1883] 1958: 22). Einaudi (1936: 25), writing a half-century later, defended Pantaleoni's reasoning here, arguing that it was not pie in the sky, but rather was done "with his eyes turned realistically on the Italy of his time, applying Jevons's rules concretely to the budgets presented by contemporary Ministers of Finance." Einaudi is undoubtedly guilty of a significant measure of hyperbole here. Yet, it is interesting to note the similarities between this portrait of nirvana-like results and that of the Pigovian tradition—the distinction being that the latter literature did not incorporate any theory of the governmental/political process to back up its position.[15]

This explanation of the government budgeting process, then, voids casual charges that particular government expenditures are wasteful or inappropriate, given that spending decisions are based on the weighing of relative marginal benefits against the marginal sacrifice associated with their financing. If Pantaleoni's model is accurate, spending decisions cannot be criticized in isolation; effective criticism of state action must consider both the marginal utility to members of society of additional units of the good in question relative to all other possible public goods, and this marginal benefit as compared with the marginal sacrifice associated with the taxation necessary to finance the good (Pantaleoni [1883] 1958: 21).

The question that immediately arises is how individual preferences regarding the marginal benefit of the public goods and the burden of the taxes get transferred into the political realm from the minds of the individuals. Pantaleoni's system gives very little attention to the link between the voter and the legislator, and thus between voter preferences and legislative

---

last unit of money spent on each use is equal), which no doubt came to the attention of the Italians through Jevons (1871).

[14] Of course Pantaleoni is incorrect if one thinks in general equilibrium terms, where labor-supply choices (and thus the determination of income) are made simultaneously with consumption decisions.

[15] This reference to the Pigovian tradition is not meant to refer to Pigou himself, who, as we saw in chapter 3, was not guilty of the nirvana fallacy. On the nirvana fallacy, see Demsetz (1969).

outcomes. The legislative perceptions of marginal utility and marginal sacrifice, he suggests, reflect "the opinion held by the average intelligence comprised in Parliament" [1883] 1958: 16–17)—the average member of parliament occupying the place of the representative producer or consumer in economic theory. In noting that the legislators are legal representatives of the people, Pantaleoni appears to be at least implicitly suggesting that the wise legislator, in applying the marginal calculus to benefits and costs, will form an opinion or ranking of alternatives that is consistent with or reflective of voter preferences.[16] Absent some mechanism for linking up voter preferences with legislative opinions, however, he seems to be assuming that the legislator, in attempting to maximize society's utility,[17] is simply intuiting, to a greater or lesser extent, the popular will rather than responding to the incentives created through the ballot box.

At first glance, Pantaleoni's theory seems to ascribe to legislators a degree of perception that asymptotically approaches omniscience—a far cry from Adam Smith's portrait of the behavior of governmental agents. Nevertheless, having argued that legislative outcomes reflect the result of a marginal balancing exercise, Pantaleoni stepped back and allowed that "these are calculations which require far more time than is available to any Parliament and which far exceed the intellectual capacities of the great majority of mankind" ([1883] 1958: 22). Yet at the same time he argued that "it is *impossible* for Parliament to decide whether a particular expenditure is admissible or not admissible" without ranking the relative marginal utilities ([1883] 1958: 21, emphasis added). How, then, is this marginal balancing exercise accomplished? According to Pantaleoni, it occurs via a budgetary process that had been honed through the ages to make it manageable for the legislators. Pantaleoni did not attempt to minimize the difficulties inherent in making these calculations, and he said, "If practice had not devised numerous and drastic short cuts, the distribution of the revenue amongst even quite a small number of expenditures would be an absolutely insoluble problem for any Parliament" ([1883] 1958: 21).

This process, which has interesting parallels to the modern theory of transaction-cost minimizing responses to problems of bounded rationality,[18] involves the assignment of particular tasks to the various branches of the government bureaucracy, where benefits, costs, and priorities are laid

---

[16] Montemartini's ([1900] 1958: 140–41) criticism of the optimal-equilibrium literature gives force to this interpretation, as we shall later see. Also, while this and the "average intelligence" proposition are vaguely suggestive of the median-voter theory, Pantaleoni's use of means and aggregated preferences indicates that he had nothing this precise in mind here.

[17] Pantaleoni, then, is positing that the legislative body maximizes a strict Benthamite social welfare function.

[18] See, for example, Williamson (1975, 1985) for the development of this idea in the context of the firm, and Weingast and Marshall (1988) for its application to the political process.

out. The process is assisted in that each year's budget process can benefit from the information gleaned from the budgeting processes of previous years, leaving only the need to make revisions from year to year based upon changing circumstances. High-level ministers (in particular, the finance minister) oversee the process to prevent or minimize the bureaucratic propensity to be self-indulgent. The result is that by the time the budget, with its revenue sources and expenditure items, is put before parliament, "the question has to all intents and purposes already been solved, except for details; and the prior work of the administration has already brought every question to the level of the parliamentary average intelligence" ([1883] 1958: 23). Pantaleoni acknowledged that informational and other problems would continue to exist, even at the bureaucratic level, but he nonetheless believed that through this bureaucratic process, "a problem which theoretically would be of the utmost difficulty, namely a value judgement by the Parliament on the marginal utility of a limitless number of combinations of expenditures compared with the sacrifice entailed by various amounts of revenue, is quite well solved by means of a series of administrative devices based on experience" ([1883] 1958: 27).[19] The solution actually has a rather Smithian aspect: "administrative principles and the division of labour render a problem soluble which theoretically presents the greatest difficulties" ([1883] 1958: 25).[20]

These ideas received further development at the hands of Ugo Mazzola, who considered the political organization a special case of the division of labor instituted to facilitate the efficient provision of public goods in an exchange economy ([1890] 1958: 44). This line of thought had been hinted at by Pantaleoni in regard to the bureaucracy, but the idea was generalized by Mazzola in terms of the entire political system. Mazzola also moved the discussion back to the level of the individual demanding agent,[21] where, working from "the tendency of human behavior towards maximizing want

[19] This is not to say that Pantaleoni's explanation does not allow for the potentially negative outcomes that the classical economists envisaged, since he recognized that variations over time in the average intelligence of parliament will affect the perceptions of benefits and costs.

[20] Perhaps this provides us with the key to understanding Einaudi's claim, noted earlier, regarding the high degree of realism underlying Pantaleoni's approach. If one grants Pantaleoni's implicit assumption of welfare maximization, which equates to marginal balancing, the evolution of the bureaucracy provides a way around the calculation problem for the legislators. One can think of the bureaucracy as evolving in part to perform the required calculations—as, in a sense, a transaction-cost minimizing response to the growth of government. Of course, one can still argue, with substantial justification, that these problems of calculation are substantial (and even problematic) at the bureaucratic level as well. See, for example, Coase (1960) and Medema and Samuels (2000).

[21] See also Kayaalp (1988) for an illuminating discussion of Mazzola's public goods theory and its place within the Italian fiscal tradition.

satisfaction at least cost" ([1890] 1958: 46), he developed the idea of the unity of public and private goods consumption while providing an explanation for why prices are formed in one way for private goods and in another way for public goods. Mazzola portrays the provision and acquisition of public goods as an exchange process, and all aspects of consumption and exchange are governed by the principle of utility maximization.[22] Mazzola's view of the demand for public goods and services draws on Carl Menger's (1883) notion of complementarity, which asserts that the utility derived from certain goods depends on the available amounts of other goods. This led Mazzola to the conclusion that "every individual need [contains] some proportion of need for complementary public goods, upon which individual satisfaction is conditional" ([1890] 1958: 40). The share of his resources that the individual will devote to the acquisition of public goods is then determined by the value placed on the complementary utility that the public goods provide ([1890] 1958: 44).

Mazzola next turned his attention to the price-formation process. In a market system, the price of each good adjusts so that the final degree of utility is equal for all goods for each individual. With public goods, however, the establishment of a single market price does not satisfy this condition, owing to nonexcludability. That is, those who cannot or are unwilling to pay the market price cannot be precluded from consuming the goods unless the goods are withdrawn from the market.[23] Therefore, a society that seeks maximum utility at least cost will assign to each individual a tax price equal to his or her final degree of utility from consuming the given amount of the public good (1890: 42). Thus, unlike for private goods, public goods will be purchased at prices that vary across consumers. Mazzola ([1890] 1958: 46) described what he called "the principle of public price formation" thusly:

> In any economy, the tendency towards maximizing utility causes available resources to be so distributed among various uses that the degrees of final utility of all the goods allocated are, after the distribution, equal.
>
> The formation of the prices of public goods comes about in such wise that in any economic unit the degrees of final utility are, after the distribution of public burdens, equal. This price formation is different from that of the

[22] The idea of politics as exchange is central to the work of James Buchanan (e.g., 1989). This grounding in utility maximization, Mazzola said, makes the public goods provision process "a question of economics pure and simple, and not of philosophy or jurisprudence" ([1890] 1958: 39). Here, Mazzola is explicitly rejecting Friedrich von Weiser's (1889) claim that the differentiation between public and private occurs due to their different aims, and that these are matters best left to the realms of jurisprudence and philosophy ([1890] 1958: 39). We thus have another point of departure between the Italian and German approaches to public finance issues.

[23] Here, then, we see an early recognition of the free-rider problem.

market and it rests on the complementary nature of the utility of public goods and on the objective conditions of their consumption.

Only through this process will individuals be able to achieve the maximum satisfaction over their consumption of public and private goods.[24]

It is at this point that the individual valuation scheme of Mazzola links back with Pantaleoni's emphasis on public-sector decision-making. Mazzola pointed out that a violation of the marginal balancing condition across both private and public goods "can arise only from faulty valuation" within the public sector ([1890] 1958: 44). That this principle could be violated is not out of the realm of possibility, but, he said, a violation can occur only when the government agencies doing the valuating "represent the predominating interests of one class or one people" ([1890] 1958: 44). By this criterion, then, under a representative democracy one should observe public good and service provision, and a distribution of the tax burden, that satisfy the dictates of optimality.

This discussion takes on a somewhat more Walrasian cast in the work of De Viti de Marco. As we noted earlier, De Viti believed that the theory of public finance "must, as far as possible, break down the State's calculation into the economic calculations of the individuals or groups which represent the constituent elements of the State's calculation" (1936: 41).The state's calculations, De Viti said, will be a function of the form of government that exists in the state. In nondemocratic societies, the interests served will tend to be those of that narrow group having the *monopoly* on political power—with obvious implications for the public goods and services provided and the distribution of the tax burden. A democratic society, in contrast, is characterized by *competition* for political power, resulting, at any particular time, in a situation in which the group in power is the one that, in the community's judgment, is best suited to provide the public goods and services demanded by the community (1936: 42–43). De Viti posited a *tâtonnement*-like iterative process converging to a political equilibrium in which the governing and the governed are essentially the same: the preferences of the elected officials reflect those of the voters. This was a conclusion that De Viti thought eminently reasonable, since the voters are both the taxpayers and the consumers of the public goods, meaning that there is a "personal identity between producers and consumers" (1936: 43). Operating within all of this is a political exchange in which taxes function as prices for public goods, and thus tax prices and goods quantities are adjusted until an equilibrium is attained.

---

[24] Of course, certain public goods are financed by user fees, as Mazzola ([1890] 1958: 45–46) notes. Here, the market for public goods proceeds like that for private goods, with individuals adjusting their consumption levels to the given (single) price.

While the satisfaction of collective wants plays an important role in determining the economic role of the state, De Viti (1936: 45) was quick to point out that the lines between public and private production to satisfy various types of wants are by no means clear-cut:

> It does not follow logically from what has been said that the State is or must be the exclusive producer of the goods destined to satisfy all collective wants, nor that private enterprise is or should be the exclusive producer of the goods destined to satisfy all individual wants. No such clear-cut division of labour exists in reality, since at times the State produces goods destined to satisfy individual wants, and at times private enterprise produces goods destined to satisfy collective wants. Indeed, it may be pointed out that there scarcely exists a public service the germ of which one does not find in private enterprise, ready to develop, if only as a complementary agency, whenever the State proves itself insufficient....
>
> Even more numerous, however, are the examples ... of public services, ... which are on the way to assuming a permanent place in the business of the State ... ; and still more numerous are those that are found in the group of public services which are at the margin and which, at the present stage in history, are sometimes produced by the State and sometimes by private enterprise.

The conclusion is that "in the absence of disturbing political factors, public enterprise tends to specialize in the production of goods destined to satisfy collective wants, on the condition that, and in so far as, it produces more economically than private enterprise" (De Viti 1936: 48). Furthermore, he noted, this boundary, and thus the source of these goods, will be continually shifting.

While the maximization model has a governmental process implicit in it, what it lacks, or assumes away, De Viti said, is a "political element." This is a factor that, while "more or less influential, almost always plays a part in the concrete phenomena of Public Finance" and tends to cause a divergence of actual results from the outcomes suggested by the maximization model (1936: 49). In particular, the political power of particular economic interests will cause legislative outcomes to deviate from those suggested by the maximization model in certain situations where general welfare and the interests of those in power diverge. As such, argued De Viti, the political element must be taken into account if one is to be able to offer a reasonably accurate explanation of budgetary outcomes (1936: 49–51).

In the work of De Viti de Marco, then, we begin to see cracks in the optimal-equilibrium structure. Mazzola and Pantaleoni had allowed for deviations from optimality as a result of factors such as imperfect information and nondemocratic governance structures, but De Viti argued the case for an additional factor—the pursuit of particular private interests through the political process. This hint of self-interest failing to redound to the public interest—here, as government failure—received much more extensive development in the work of two other Italian scholars, Amilcare Puviani and Giovanni Montemartini.

Government-Failure Models

The contributions of Puviani and Monetemartini illustrate the diversity that existed within the Italian tradition and anticipate to some degree certain insights of modern public choice analysis and its dim view of how self-interest plays out in the operations of the public sector. Puviani's work on fiscal illusion[25] posits a political system dominated by a ruling class rather than based on participatory democracy, and he argued that this ruling class makes political choices with a view to minimizing social friction, rather than in an attempt to promote the general interest (à la Pantaleoni, Mazzola, or De Viti de Marco) or even its own direct self-interest. Puviani suggested that government policy-making proceeds as if government tries simultaneously to magnify in the citizens' eyes the benefits associated with public expenditures and hide the associated burden of taxation.[26] Hence, legislators tend to prefer debt financing to taxation because people—that is, their constituents—improperly discount the future, and certain forms of taxation are preferred to others because they are more politically palatable. The result is a fiscal illusion that serves to minimize popular discontent and thus social friction.

Now Puviani did not claim that governments deliberately resort to such deception in making decisions on expenditures; he thought that it just happened to work out that way. While this claim is certainly open to debate, what *is* quite clear is that his model offers a very different portrait of fiscal activity than do the optimal equilibrium models of Pantaleoni, Mazzola, and De Viti—the major distinction turning on the governance structure (representative or not) assumed and the degrees of information implicitly ascribed to agents by Puviani on the one hand and Pantaleoni et al. on the other.

Aspects of Puviani's ruling-class analysis and the maximization-of-net-returns analysis of De Viti came together in Giovanni Montemartini's discussion of the coercive element within the political process. Montemartini

---

[25] See Puviani (1897, 1903). As Puviani's work has not been translated into English, this discussion draws heavily on Buchanan (1960: 342–46). See also Da Empoli (2002).

[26] Of course this fiscal illusion concept is central to modern public choice theory and its explanation of what is commonly referred to as "pork-barrel politics." For a survey, see Mueller 2003: 221–23, 527–29).

([1900] 1958: 137), who was Professor of Political Economy at the University of Padova, maintained that the theory of public finance requires—but lacks—a theory of the political organization that takes account of both the demand for and supply of public services, and allows the analyst to determine the associated conditions for the equilibrium provision of public goods. In attempting to lay out such a theory, he posited the state as a producer of coercive services and introduced "political entrepreneurs" on the demand side. These entrepreneurs purchase the state's coercive services to get the goods they demand while spreading the costs across all taxpayers. Coercion comes into the picture because the state's power is necessary to distribute the costs associated with the accomplishment of these private goals.

Montemartini said that while individual needs and desires underlie the demand for public goods and services, the fact that people's preferences are not identical means that these needs and desires will differ across individuals. The drive to satisfy these needs and desires gives rise to entrepreneurial activities, as agents seek to secure desired outcomes. Montemartini suggested that these entrepreneurs have three means of attaining any given objective and will select the one that they believe will do so at lowest cost. First, they may work in isolation, independently of one another. Second, they may work in association with one another on a voluntary, cooperative basis. Third, they may act as political entrepreneurs, attempting to distribute the costs (but not the benefits) of their activity over the entire community using the coercive power of the state.[27] These entrepreneurs, being cost-minimizers, will attempt to harness the coercive power of the state to accomplish their goals if that is the least-cost means of doing so. Montemartini noted that the state's coercive power is costly to obtain, making it uneconomical for individuals or small groups.[28] He said, however, that it is much more cost effective for a group of individuals acting in concert, in that such alliances allow members of the group to force those who are not members to contribute through their tax dollars to the cost of producing those goods and services that are in the group's interests ([1900] 1958: 139–40).

Because this process causes people to have costs imposed on them that they would not otherwise willingly assume, the outcomes are unlikely to satisfy the dictates of optimality. This, in turn, implies that the Pantaleoni–De Viti theory, which maintains that the state selects the most productive expenditures and that resources used by the state are used more productively than if they had remained in the private sector, cannot necessarily be sustained. The optimal-equilibrium theories treat the state and its agents as representatives of the community, with the government and the

---

[27] Montemartini calls these, respectively, private enterprise, collective enterprise, and public enterprise ([1900] 1958: 138).

[28] If coercion were not costly to obtain, said Montemartini ([1900] 1958: 141), the political organization would not exist.

community "having common costs and rewards" (Montemartini [1900] 1958: 140). "But in reality," said Montemartini, "the community can never be completely identified with the political enterprise." In fact, he is not even willing to countenance this as a theoretical construct ([1900] 1958: 141):

> We cannot assume even theoretically that the political organization represents a giant cooperative of producers and consumers, as some people like to imagine. The political organization has, in fact, *the purpose* of compelling all the people to bear the costs of specific types of production.

Self-interest and preference differences across persons will preclude agreement about both the public activities that the community should finance and the distribution of the costs, and Montemartini suggested that it is the stronger parties who will determine these outcomes.

WICKSELL, POLITICAL RULE-MAKING, AND GOVERNMENT FAILURE

The positive depictions of a political process operating to maximize net returns and the government-failure models that call these depictions into question are brought together, in a sense, in Knut Wicksell's analysis of and prescription for fiscal decision-making in his *Finanztheoretische Untersuchungen* (1896a). Although, as Lars Pålsson Syll and Bo Sandelin (2001) have pointed out, Wicksell was apparently familiar with the Italian public finance literature, he did not actually deal with it in *Finanztheoretische Untersuchungen*, save for a brief (five-page) discussion of Mazzola, whom Wicksell criticized for not discussing how the marginal balancing exercise is effected. Specifically, Wicksell argued that the agent's marginal utility has far more to do with the willingness of the rest of the citizenry to pay than with the agent's own willingness to pay, and that Mazzola was silent on how all of this would play out in any way that avoids what we now call the free-rider problem. While allowing that Mazzola's theory "contains a core of truth," Wicksell concluded that his balancing condition is "really meaningless" and "leaves much to be desired."[29]

Although the direct influence of the Italians on Wicksell's treatment of state action is minimal, certain of the basic building blocks of his analysis parallel those of the Italians: Wicksell (1896b: 80) applauded the Italians for situating their treatment of tax justice in an economic rather than ethical context, adopted a methodological individualist framework, and employed

---

[29] See Wicksell ([1896b] 1958: 80–82) and the full discussion in Wicksell (1896a: 96–101), as well as Musgrave's commentary (1985: 9–10; 1996: 82).

a similar degree of abstraction in his analysis.[30] Unlike the Italian literature, however, Wicksell's analysis was heavily normative in nature, his goal being to set out a rule for the approval of taxation-and-expenditure packages that he believed would comport with the dictates of justice.

Wicksell could not analyze justice in public sector outcomes apart from the political process that generated them. For example, Wicksell, like the Italians, opposed the equal-sacrifice principle of taxation, but he did so for different reasons. The Italians assumed that a government which maximized utility throughout society would not employ an equal-sacrifice scheme. Wicksell argued two other points. First, he noted that equal sacrifice causes people to pay either more or less for public goods than they receive in benefits, something he considered contrary to justice. Wicksell's methodological individualism comes through clearly in his defense of this position: When the marginal utility that individuals receive from a public good is less than the sacrifice involved in obtaining it (that is, their tax share), they "will, without fail, feel overburdened," he said, and "[i]t will be no consolation to them to be assured that the utility of public services as a whole far exceeds the total value of the individual sacrifices" (1896b: 79). Second, Wicksell pointed out that the apportioning of taxes based upon the equal-sacrifice principle could cause socially beneficial projects to be voted down. Even though benefits may exceed costs by a large amount in the aggregate, the distribution of the tax burden could be such as to cause a majority to vote against the proposal. And noting that legislative bodies tend to be dominated by the upper classes and their interests, he felt that there was a "strong" probability that the lower classes would incur tax costs in excess of benefits received ([1896b] 1958: 77).

This portrait of a divergence between costs incurred and benefits received is emblematic of a larger contrast between Wicksell's analysis and the efficiency claims of the Italian optimal-equilibrium analysis: Wicksell believed that politicians regularly make decisions that are contrary to the will of larger or smaller parts of the population ([1896b] 1958: 87). The dictates of justice can be satisfied, Wicksell argued, only if society implements a rule of *unanimity* for the approval of expenditure and tax policies ([1896b] 1958: 90):

> In the final analysis, unanimity and fully voluntary consent in the making of decisions provide the only certain and palpable guarantee against injustice in

[30] Wicksell was not inclined to apologize for his abstraction, either, noting that "I am ready to admit that some will be inclined to classify much of my discussion as armchair speculation. I accept the charge happily, since it was my purpose above all to construct a complete, comprehensive, and internally coherent system. However much of this—or whether any at all—may be of practical use in the near future, men of affairs may decide" ([1896b] 1958: 73).

the tax distribution. The whole discussion of tax justice remains suspended in mid-air so long as these conditions are not satisfied at least approximately.[31]

The unanimity rule ensures that no one incurs costs in excess of benefits received and also allows for the approval of any public project for which benefits exceed costs, provided that the distribution of the tax burden is done appropriately—that is, according to the benefit principle ([1896b] 1958: 89–90). In doing so, the rule guarantees that self-interested action redounds to the larger interests of society.[32] Wicksell realized that a requirement of absolute unanimity would not be practical in reality, and he discussed the use of supra-majorities—three-fourths, five-sixths, and nine-tenths—that would provide "approximate unanimity," combined with voting on a spectrum of possible alternative tax and spending combinations, as more appropriate for actual implementation.

One of the attractive features of the unanimity rule, as Buchanan and Tullock (1962) have since shown, is its guarantee that any change will be efficiency-enhancing: If all voters support the change, it cannot be the case that someone is made worse off by it. Wicksell's advocacy of the unanimity rule, however, rested not on efficiency but on his belief that the rule would prevent a majority from exploiting a minority and as such would satisfy the dictates of justice.[33] The use of a unanimity rule forces officials to link

---

[31] Wicksell ([1896b] 1958: 108) did allow that justice in taxation under a unanimity rule assumes that the extant distribution of property rights and income is itself just. If not, he said, "society has both the right and duty" to modify the extant structure of property rights—which, he continued, should be done subject to a qualified majority assent rather than under the rule of approximate unanimity, since the latter would all but preclude any serious adjustments that might be necessary (109).

[32] This is subject to the hold-out qualifications mentioned in note 34.

[33] James Buchanan has placed the emphasis on the efficiency side, both in his interpretation of Wicksell and in his own contributions to the theory of public choice and constitutional economics. See, for example, Buchanan and Tullock (1962). Wicksell uses the term *efficiency*, however, only once in his discussion of the unanimity principle (at least as reprinted in Musgrave and Peacock 1958). Buchanan suggests that when using the term *rationality*, Wicksell is also alluding to efficiency concerns; but even this term is used very rarely by Wicksell, both absolutely (a couple of times) and relative to his use of *justice* (a term that he uses on numerous occasions throughout his discussion). When queried on this point by the author, Buchanan (letter to the author, 7 April 1999) acknowledged that justice was important for Wicksell, but he defended his view regarding the substantial import of efficiency (in Wicksell) in tandem with this. While Wicksell ([1896b] 1958: 90, emphasis added) does maintain that if the expenditure-and-tax package is not approved unanimously, we have "the sole possible ... proof that the state activity under consideration would not provide the community with utility corresponding to the necessary sacrifice and should hence be rejected on *rational* grounds," this would seem to be the only reference to efficiency amid Wicksell's myriad references to justice in this context. On this point, see also Sandelin (1988).

While it is common to link Wicksell's unanimity rule with the Pareto criterion (again, see Buchanan and Tullock 1962), it bears keeping in mind, as an interpretive matter, that Pareto

the tax and expenditure sides of the budgeting process, something that Wicksell (in contrast to Pantaleoni) felt was not usually the case in actual government budgeting. He also argued that the rule effectively precludes one group from financing its preferred projects off the backs of another part of the community ([1896b] 1958: 92, 94). In less representative governments, he said, the unanimity rule will keep the rich from exploiting the poor, and in more democratic systems it will keep the lower classes from exploiting the upper classes. Wicksell suggested that, as countries revise their constitutions in the process of moving to democracy, it will be important for them to institute the approximate unanimity principle, since "it is scarcely to be expected that the new ruling class will freely impose such self-restraint upon themselves if they do not already find it embodied in the constitution" ([1896b] 1958: 95–96).[34]

With a unanimity rule in place, the production and financing of public goods would take on the character of a voluntary exchange process, according to Wicksell. Taxes would no longer be regarded as a burden, but instead be viewed as the price necessary (and willingly paid) to secure the benefits associated with certain services that could not be secured through the market or by other means ([1896b] 1958: 97). Indeed, this system somewhat blurs the lines between market and government, as it envisages government operating largely according to the pricing system. In fact, said Wicksell, one may well witness the absorption of certain previously private activities into the state under such a system ([1896b] 1958: 91).

THE ITALIANS AND WICKSELL RECONCILED

It remains to develop the links between Wicksell's theory and the Italian literature and relate this to our larger narrative. Let us begin with the optimal-equilibrium theorists. Wicksell (1896b: 91, n. 13) assumed in his central case that "the legislative assembly is truly representative of all interest groups within the people"—akin to the assumption underlying Italian

---

did not set down his criterion until 1906, a decade after Wicksell wrote *Finanztheoretische Untersuchungen*. For an excellent treatment of the similarities and differences between the perspectives of Wicksell and Pareto, see the work of Pieter Hennipman (1980, 1982). See also p. 99 n. 39, infra.

[34] We see here a commonality with Mill, who was also a bit suspicious of the effects of the extension of the franchise—although Mill's concerns were more related to competence issues.

Wicksell ([1896b] 1958: 117) is not ignorant of the potential for holdouts and other obstructionist tactics under unanimity. He believed, however, that the desire of each group to have its interests served through the legislative process would likely minimize these tendencies. Somewhat ironically, modern game-theory insights would suggest that, in making this assertion, Wicksell was the victim of a nirvana-like perspective not entirely dissimilar to that for which he criticized the extant public finance depictions of government.

optimal-equilibrium theory. Even with this assumption, however, efficiency is by no means ensured; in fact, it is unlikely. Efficiency requires that the marginal balancing conditions be satisfied, but if one or more individuals vote against a proposal, it must be that there is some possible reallocation of expenditures and/or tax shares that will increase utility across society. If the legislative body is in fact representative of the people, the votes on tax-and-expenditure packages will be unanimous if the marginal balancing conditions are actually satisfied in the legislation.[35] Indeed, this result holds even if we do not assume that legislative behavior is representative. If the marginal balancing conditions are satisfied and the goal of legislators is to maximize social utility, as Pantaleoni and others assert, then the legislation will achieve unanimous consent.[36] Legislation that does not receive unanimous approval must therefore reflect an inefficient allocation of resources. In sum, the satisfaction of the principle of maximum net returns, with its marginal equivalences between private and public sectors, is only possible (except by accident) under a unanimity rule.

Now, let us introduce some complications. Wicksell recognized that only individual agents know their subjective utilities associated with particular levels of public good benefits and the taxes necessary to finance them. Even so, he said, it may be difficult for individuals to judge their expected benefits versus the cost of taxes, and this has significant implications for legislative behavior ([1896b] 1958: 79):

> This much is certain: If the individual is unable to form an even approximately definite judgement on this point, it is a fortiori impossible for anyone, even if he be a statesman of genius, to weigh the whole community's utility and sacrifice against each other.... So far as the economic side of the question is concerned, that is whether the benefits of the proposed activity to the individual citizens would be greater than its cost to them, no-one can judge this better than the individuals themselves or those who represent their interests in the legislature.

But the difficulties go beyond this. There is, said Wicksell, the additional problem that the motivations of government officials are less than lofty—in spite of what the Italian optimal-equilibrium theorists assumed ([1896b] 1958:86–87):

---

[35] We are assuming, with both Wicksell and the Italian optimal-equilibrium theorists, the absence of opportunistic behavior here.

[36] As we noted earlier, Mazzola ([1890] 1958: 44) contended that efficiency is ensured so long as the political sector does not "represent the predominating interests of one class or one people." This is too weak a condition, however, as it still allows for departures from optimality in the absence of unanimous consent.

Neither the executive nor the legislative body, and even less the deciding majority in the latter, are in reality—or from psychological necessity can be—what the ruling theory tells us they should be. They are not pure organs of the community with no thought other than to promote the common weal.

The executive more or less selfishly pursues its own dynastic ends and seeks its own private economic advantage....

In their turn, the members of the representative body are, in the overwhelming majority of cases, precisely as interested in the general welfare as are their constituents, neither more nor less.[37] Otherwise they simply would never have been elected or would not be elected again. At best and in the most fortunate cases they are representative of a majority within the population.

In fact, Wicksell argued, legislative bodies tend not to be representative of all interests within the population, and the greater the divergence, the more necessary the veto power that the minority holds under an approximate unanimity rule ([1896b] 1958: 91, n. 13). Wicksell thus concluded that the efficiency claims of the Italian optimal-equilibrium theorists could not be sustained. The Italians had argued for efficiency under majority rule, but Wicksell believed that efficiency could be guaranteed only under popular democracy accompanied by a unanimity voting rule. That is, in Wicksell's system it is only under a unanimity rule that the marginal benefits and marginal costs accruing to individuals would be adjusted so that the marginal equivalences suggested by Pantaleoni and others were satisfied.

Wicksell's theory also has implications for the validity of the Italian theories of government failure. Puviani's theory of fiscal illusion rests on the notion that, when the political process is dominated by a ruling class, legislators can successfully overstate the benefits and understate the costs of public goods and services, thereby allowing inefficient projects to secure legislative passage. Under a unanimity rule, however, it would not be possible for the legislature to practice such deception if that body were to any degree—even with only a one-person minority—representative of interests besides those of the dominant class. As Wicksell ([1896b] 1958: 97) noted in this context (although not making reference to Puviani), "There would no longer be occasion for the many devious devices by which the true magnitude of the tax load [has] in the past been concealed from the people. The fiscal principle would have to yield to the economic principle; the direct method of raising state revenues should become the rule and the indirect method the exception." Wicksell went on to argue that unanimity is especially important when considering debt financing, owing to the risk that the interests of future generations would not be taken into consideration

[37] That is, not at all. See the previous quote from Wicksell ([1896b] 1958: 79).

(1896b: 105–6). In sum, so long as there exist both majority and minority interests in the legislature, unanimous consent cannot be obtained for measures that will serve the interests of the majority at the expense of the minority. Puviani's results, then, hold only if the voting rule does not mandate unanimity.

The ability of Montemartini's political entrepreneurs to harness the coercive power of government to engage in cost spreading is similarly influenced by the voting rule in place. Under the rule of unanimity, it would not be possible to impose on nonbeneficiaries of particular public goods and services costs that they would not otherwise be willing to assume, because some legislators would be attuned to the interests of their constituency and possess the veto power to ensure that this cost spreading did not occur. As with Puviani's results, Montemartini's theory holds true only if the voting process is not governed by the unanimity rule.

GOVERNMENT FURTHER MARGINALIZED

The approach to public sector issues taken by Wicksell and the Italians offers a significant contrast to the classical and Cambridge approaches. The most obvious difference concerns the extent to which these Continental scholars incorporated the political process within their theoretical analysis of public sector activity. The appropriate functions of the state, and their extent, were not something to be taken as given or gleaned from history, philosophy, jurisprudence, or even casual empiricism, nor were they to be determined by working out instances of market failure, devising associated remedies, and asserting the ability of government to undertake corrective actions—perhaps subject to some qualification about potential problems with state action. Rather, the appropriate functions of the state were seen as something that is or ought to be worked out and continually determined over time through the political process.

The import of this analysis, however, goes beyond the mere incorporation of the political side of the equation. As with the developments in Cambridge, the influence of the marginal revolution on the theorizing process was paramount. It brought to the analysis of public sector issues both the marginal calculus and a relatively sophisticated (as compared with its classical predecessor) theory of individual demands. The demands for goods and services, both private and public, could be considered just that—demands, a function of the relationship between utility and price. The distinction between private and public goods provision lay in the institutional processes through which their provision was worked out—the market in the one case and the political process, through which demands are registered and tax prices are established, in the other.

These Continental scholars saw a parallel between private and public sector activities that led them to model the political process like a market, or exchange process. Prices, quantities, adjustment mechanisms, marginal balancing exercises and conditions, equilibrium, efficiency analysis—all these market analysis constructs were overlaid onto the public sector. Perhaps not surprisingly, then, what emerged were government-success and government-failure stories that correspond to the market-success and market-failure stories that we have already encountered: When the political process works like a smoothly functioning market, private interest promotes public interest, and efficiency results; when there are impediments to that smooth operation, the political process, like the market, fails (to a greater or lesser extent) to perform optimally. Put slightly differently, the Continental scholars showed that it is possible to construct models of the *public* sector decision process where the pursuit of self-interest promotes the larger social interest, and also to construct models in which it does not.

The success stories of the Italian optimal-equilibrium literature seem not to account for the difficulties that self-interested behavior can cause on the road from maximization to efficiency within the political process. Wicksell's analysis revealed that the efficiency claims made by the Italian optimal-equilibrium theorists require the adoption of a unanimity rule; in fact, their theory, if correct, would imply that the societal-utility-maximizing legislators whom they describe would approve all expenditure bills unanimously. The converse of this, of course, is that in the absence of a unanimity rule, the efficiency results do not in fact obtain, and instead we see the types of political behavior outlined by Puviani and Montemartini. Inefficiency is thus guaranteed in the absence of a unanimity rule.[38] In essence, these Continental scholars had shown that the qualms of the classical and Cambridge economists were theoretically warranted. Their analysis also implies, however, that the Cambridge optimism about the future was misplaced, in that the accomplishment of efficiency—in the sense of making at least one person better off and no one worse off[39]—requires unanimity.

The concept of efficiency here is also different from that which we have seen to this point. The classical and Cambridge economists worked with

---

[38] In other words, the inefficiency claims of the Italian government-failure theorists require that the voting rule be something other than unanimity.

[39] This notion of efficiency owes to Pareto. See Pareto ([1906] 1971: 261): "We will say that the members of a collectivity enjoy *maximium ophelimity* in a certain position when it is impossible to find a way of moving from that position very slightly in such a manner that the ophelimity enjoyed by each of the individuals of that collectivity increases or decreases. That is to say, any small displacement in departing from that position necessarily has the effect of increasing the ophelimity that certain individuals enjoy, and decreasing that which others enjoy, of being agreeable to some, and disagreeable to others."

the notion of wealth maximization; the Continental scholars, in contrast, offered a set of marginal equivalences that came to be known as Pareto efficiency. The former allows for winners and losers, while the latter requires or commands unanimous consent. The implications of the use of one or the other of these efficiency concepts is just one of the issues that came to the fore in the work of Ronald Coase.[40]

---

[40] See also Medema and Samuels (2000).

CHAPTER FIVE

Coase's Challenge

All is for the best in the best of all possible worlds.
—*Dr. Pangloss in Voltaire,* Candide *(1759)*

These stories of what Heaven is like are not without
interest, but they are bound to have most interest for
people who are sure of getting there.
—*Ronald Coase (1970a: 61)*

WE HAVE SEEN that Smith and the nineteenth-century classical economists posited a much greater degree of harmony between individual self-interest and the larger social interest than did commentators of previous eras, and how, under the influence of John Stuart Mill and Henry Sidgwick, this view gradually began to erode. Both Mill and Sidgwick pointed to a number of factors, including what we now call externalities, that can cause individually optimal behavior to diverge from the social optimum, and argued that these divergences potentially call for the imposition of governmental corrective measures. It was through A. C. Pigou's analysis, though, that the theory of market failure, and the need for government correction of these failures, began to reach full flower. Pigou's ideas laid the foundation for the "modern" welfare economics of Samuelson, Graaff, Bator, Meade, and others, although it can also be argued with some justice that the modern, or "Pigovian," externality theory is in many ways a distorted reflection of Pigou's ideas.[1] Whatever the relationship between Pigou's own perspective and modern Pigovian analysis, however, there can be little question that Pigovian thinking had come to dominate this sphere by 1960.

The contrast between the classical and the neoclassical approaches was set out pointedly by James Buchanan, who, in 1962 (p. 17 n. 3), commented that

> If … "*laissez faire* welfare theory" was "largely concerned with demonstrating the optimal properties of free competition and the unfettered price system," it is surely equally accurate to suggest that modern welfare theory has been largely concerned with demonstrating that these conclusions are invalid; that is, that competitive markets do not satisfy the necessary conditions for optimality.[2]

[1] See chapter 3, and Aslanbeigui and Medema (1998).
[2] As Lionel Robbins points out, however, one must be careful in drawing implications for externality analysis from the laissez-faire classical thinking. He suggests that the classical

And in many instances—externality theory being primary among them—this conclusion led economists to recommend the use of governmental tax, subsidy, or regulatory instruments to remedy these market failures, and to do so on the grounds that these policy measures would generate the optimal outcomes associated with perfectly functioning markets.

The tide, however, began to turn in the 1960s. One gets a sense that a change was under way, or at least that cracks were beginning to appear in the foundation, from Stanislaw Wellisz's 1964 article on the analysis of externalities, where he said,

> Much of modern welfare economics is indeed concerned with the problem of market failure, and the analysis of market failure appears to imply the desirability of administrative intervention. *Until recently* everybody agreed that where there are externalities, market allocation is bound to be non-optimal; the only point of controversy concerned the frequency and the severity of the external effects and the urgency of administrative action. (1964: 345, emphasis added)

"Until recently" was not an abstract statement, for at the center of this turn was the publication of Ronald Coase's article on "The Problem of Social Cost" in 1960.[3]

Though most closely associated with the Chicago school of economics,[4] Coase did not arrive at the University of Chicago until relatively late in his career—1964—by which time he had already made the signal contributions to the discipline for which he was awarded the Nobel Prize in 1991.[5] Coase was trained at the London School of Economics, where he also spent most of the first two decades of his professional career before emigrating to the United States, to take up a position at the University of Buffalo in 1951. Much of Coase's research during the 1940s and 1950s dealt with public utilities, including the broadcasting industry, and it was this work—in particular, his analysis of the allocation of broadcast frequencies in the United States—that led him to the consideration of externality problems and, ultimately, to the writing of "The Problem of Social Cost."

---

economists did not realize the import of negative externalities (or nuisances) and that, had they realized their import, there is "no doubt that the Classical Economists would have admitted the desirability of their control," seeing the prevention of nuisance "as part of the necessary framework of law and order" (1976: 38, 39; see also 18–19).

[3] Coase was not the only person calling the received view into question. See also Buchanan (1962), Buchanan and Stubblebine (1962), and Davis and Whinston (1962). It is not coincidental that all of this work came directly or indirectly out of the University of Virginia. See chapter 6, infra, for more on the Virginia school during this period.

[4] On the Chicago school, see the essays in Emmett (2009).

[5] These were "The Nature of the Firm" (1937) and "The Problem of Social Cost (1960). He wrote the former article while working at the London School of Economics and the latter while on the faculty at the University of Virginia. Medema (1994b) surveys Coase's contributions to economic analysis.

In his article, "The Federal Communications Commission" (1959), Coase set out to show that government allocation of broadcast frequencies by administrative fiat was potentially misguided, and that it might be preferable to replace this system with some form of a market in broadcast frequencies. The extant regulatory structure in broadcasting had come about in response to a classic externality situation: the freedom of radio stations to broadcast on whatever frequency they desired led to chaos on the airwaves, as radio stations broadcasting on the same or adjoining frequencies interfered with each other's transmissions. In part to avoid these problems, the Federal Communications Commission was charged with the regulation of the broadcasting process. This included the allocation of broadcast frequencies, which the FCC did by administrative fiat.

Against the FCC's approach, Coase presented an argument familiar to every student of elementary microeconomic theory: all resources are in scarce supply, and the method usually used to resolve scarcity problems, in the United States, at least, is allocation by the market, not by government. Moreover, he said, the goal should be to obtain the optimal allocation of frequencies across users, which was nothing more than the allocation that would result "if the institution of private property and the pricing mechanism were working well" (1959: 29). Theoretically, at least, by employing some mechanism to specify property rights in broadcast frequencies[6] and establishing a market in these rights, broadcasting resources, including frequencies, would flow toward their highest valued uses. Thus, the tax-subsidy-regulation apparatus, suggested by Pigou and the Pigovian tradition as the only possible means of attaining an efficient solution in these situations, would not be necessary.

As Coase saw the situation, a big part of the problem was that the law ruled out the possibility of such "desirable" market transactions (1959: 27, n. 54). Alienable rights in broadcast frequencies did not exist. Coase suggested that if the law was structured so as to allow the pricing mechanism to work, there was no a priori reason to expect that it could not do a reasonable job of allocating frequencies where they were valued most highly. As a practical matter, Coase allowed that there might be problems with such a market-based approach, but he was troubled that no serious attempt had been made to examine the potential of the market option as against the fiat-based allocation method.

The points Coase raised in "The Federal Communications Commission," especially regarding the virtues of the market as compared with the Pigovian approach, were not immediately accepted. This is not surprising, of course, given the entrenched nature of the Pigovian approach to externalities. Looking back on this nearly four decades later, Coase (1988c: 11) said,

---

[6] Coase (1959: 30) seems to have preferred an auction.

I was led to restate my argument in ... more elaborate form because a number of economists, particularly at the University of Chicago, who had read the earlier article thought the analysis fallacious, and I hoped that I could overcome their doubts and objections by a fuller treatment.

What happened was that a group of about twenty economists from the University of Chicago, including Milton Friedman, George Stigler, and Aaron Director, met with Coase at Director's home for the purpose of discussing what Stigler (1988: 75, 76) later referred to as Coase's "obvious ... mistake" and even "heresy" in "The Federal Communications Commission."[7] While there was no transcript made of the evening's discussion, Stigler (quoted in Kitch 1983: 221) provided a vivid description a couple of decades later:

> At the beginning of the evening we took a vote and there were twenty votes for Pigou and one for Ronald, and if Ronald had not been allowed to vote it would have been even more one-sided.
>
> The discussion began.... My recollection is that Ronald didn't persuade us. But he refused to yield to all our erroneous arguments. Milton would hit him from one side, then from another, then from another. Then to our horror, Milton missed him and hit us. At the end of that evening the vote had changed. There were twenty-one votes for Ronald and no votes for Pigou.[8]

After this meeting, Director asked Coase to write up the ideas for the *Journal of Law and Economics*, and the article that resulted was "The Problem of Social Cost."

There is no small amount of irony in the fact that "The Problem of Social Cost" was written as the result of Coase having to defend himself against a group of Chicago school economists who thought his criticism of Pigou and the Pigovian tradition wrongheaded. That these Chicago luminaries—themselves no friends of government intervention—were ardent defenders of Pigou against Coase's challenge speaks to the grip that the Pigovian approach had on professional discourse. That Coase was able to convert them speaks to the effectiveness of his challenge.

THE RECIPROCAL NATURE OF HARM

That "The Problem of Social Cost" posed a fundamental challenge to the Pigovian approach was made clear by Coase right from the start. He led

---

[7] This meeting occurred in 1960. Director was the founding editor of the *Journal of Law and Economics*, in which "The Federal Communications Commission" had been published. For more on Director, see chapter 7, infra, and Medema (2008).

[8] Stigler referred to this evening as "one of the most exciting intellectual events of my life" (quoted in Kitch 1983: 221).

off the article by stating that the Pigovian recommendation that liability for damages, a tax related to damages, or some other form of restriction be placed on the party said to be the cause of the harm in an externality situation was "inappropriate." The reason, he said, is because these measures "lead to results which are not necessarily, or even usually, desirable" (1960: 2).[9] Coase's critique here went to the very framework within which economists, following Pigou, examined the problem of harmful effects—that of a divergence between the private and social costs associated with an activity, where the divergence is due to external costs generated by the harmful effect. As Coase (1960: 2) characterized it,

> The question is commonly thought of as one in which A inflicts harm on B and what has to be decided is: how should we restrain A?

While this seems straightforward enough, Coase suggested that it reflects a wrongheaded view of the problem, which is actually reciprocal in nature. Specifically, while A's actions do cause harm to B, avoiding harm to B inflicts harm on A. Thus, the factory that dumps toxic chemicals into a river causes harm to the downstream farmers who use the river water for irrigation, but laws put into place to protect the farmers from this damage will impose harm (costs) on the factory. When viewed from this perspective, the nature of the problem is altered, says Coase (1960: 2): "The real question that has to be decided is: should A be allowed to harm B or should B be allowed to harm A?"

So conceived, problems of externality are ultimately problems of legal rights and the dual nature thereof: the assignment of a right to one party simultaneously exposes others to the effects of the exercise of that right. Looking at this from an economic perspective, rights beget both benefits and costs, the costs being "the loss which is suffered elsewhere in consequence of the exercise of that right," whether that be "the inability to cross land, to park a car, to build a house, to enjoy a view, to have peace and quiet or to breathe clean air" (1960: 44). This has at least two significant implications. First, because rights are inevitably attended by exposures, externalities are ubiquitous. Second, decisions about how to deal with externalities

---

[9] Coase offered several subsequent commentaries on "The Problem of Social Cost" and the analysis of externalities. See Coase (1970a,b,c; 1981; 1988c; 1992; 1993b).

It should also be noted from the outset that while the issue of social cost analysis is a broad one, Coase's treatment in "The Problem of Social Cost" is quite narrow, focusing on what he calls "harmful effects"—more commonly known as negative externalities. (Coase prefers the term "harmful effects" to the term "externalities" because the latter "carries with it the connotation that when 'externalities' are found, steps should be taken by the government to eliminate them," in contrast to his own view that "it [is] sometimes desirable to eliminate them and sometimes not." [1988c: 26–27].) However, the framework that he proposed for the analysis of negative externalities applies to a wide range of market failure situations. See, for example, his analyses of marginal cost pricing policies for natural monopolies (1946) and of public goods provision (1974a).

are ultimately decisions about legal rights: Does A have the right to produce in a way that is to its greatest advantage, but which also imposes costs
on B, or does B have a right to be free from harm, which, as a consequence,
imposes harm on A?

Coase's point about the reciprocal nature of harm and the dual nature of
rights transformed the entire nature of the externality problem. He charged
that the Pigovian focus on the divergence between private and social costs
in the actions of one party, and its prescription of governmental remedies
to remove the divergence so as to obtain the socially optimal level of that
activity, obscures the fact that costs are running in both directions. It is
one thing, he said, to claim that it is best to restrain, say, pollution, but
it is quite another to say that restraining pollution will maximize the national dividend when one is not considering the costs associated with these
restraints. In deciding to whom rights should be granted, said Coase, the
"comparison of private and social products is neither here nor there." To
make efficiency judgments, "the proper procedure is to compare the total
social product yielded by these different arrangements" (1960: 34). To put
it in conventional terms, Coase was arguing that the efficient resolution of
externality problems is not simply a matter of internalizing costs, but also
of *how* costs are to be internalized.[10]

While the reciprocity argument represented a radical departure from the
received view of externality problems, the idea that economic analysis can
and should inform the analysis of legal rights may seem like an even more
significant leap. Coase, though, did not see it that way; he was merely asserting that rights pertaining to externalities are just like any other rights within
the economic system and should be analyzed as such. As he remarked in a
1970 commentary, the decision as to whether producers should be allowed
to emit externalities in the production process "is no different from deciding whether a field should be used for growing wheat or barley" (1970b:
9). This reasoning emphasized the dependency of economic activity upon
the structure of law—a theme that recurs throughout Coase's writings.[11]
What is traded, and how much, depends upon "what rights and duties
individuals and organizations are deemed to possess," and these rights and
duties are determined by the legal system (Coase 1988a: 656). Because of
this, he said, "the legal system will have a profound effect on the working
of the economic system and may in certain respects be said to control it"
(1992: 717–18). It thus becomes important to examine closely the effects of

[10] As we shall see later, it is also, for Coase, a question of *whether* costs should be
internalized.

[11] For example, already in "The Nature of the Firm" (1937) Coase had pointed out how
the law respecting the employer-employee relation played a fundamental role in differentiat-
ing internal (that is, firm) from market organization.

alternative legal rules (that is, the government legal-*cum*-tax-*cum*-regulatory structure generally) in determining the appropriate institutional structure for dealing with externalities.

DR. PANGLOSS MEETS EXTERNALITY THEORY

Having established the reciprocal nature of the problem, Coase next turned to an examination of the effects of alternative assignments of rights. In doing so, he followed the Pigovian literature in employing the basic assumptions of orthodox economic theory—including (and most importantly, for present purposes) the assumption that the pricing system works costlessly (1960: 2). In his earlier article dealing with the allocation of broadcast frequencies, Coase had argued that, with a smoothly operating pricing mechanism, rights in broadcast frequencies could be efficiently allocated through the market, and that this would constitute an improvement over the existing system of allocating frequencies by governmental fiat. It was this argument to which the Chicago economists had objected, and these objections led to the aforementioned meeting at Director's home. In "The Problem of Social Cost," Coase generalized this line of reasoning to the wider class of common law nuisance situations, an illustration of which was provided in his now-famous example of conflict between a farmer and a cattle rancher.

Suppose, said Coase, that a farm and a cattle ranch occupy adjoining parcels of property and that roaming cattle from this ranch damage crops on the farmer's land. The relation between the number of steer and the annual value of crops damaged is shown in table 5.1. It is assumed that the farmer's property can be fenced off at an annual cost of nine dollars.

Coase first considered the case where the rancher is liable for the damage caused by his cattle. Here, in deciding whether or not to increase the size of his herd, the rancher will weigh the marginal benefit against the marginal cost, where the latter includes the additional damage payment for the

TABLE 5.1
The Cost of Wandering Cattle

Number of cattle	Total crop damage	Marginal damage
1	1	1
2	3	2
3	6	3
4	10	4

additional crop loss caused. Of course, given that total damage when the herd includes four steer is ten dollars, the rancher who desired to have four steer would pay for installation of the fence, since the cost of doing so (nine dollars) would be lower than the compensation payment. The point, however, is that since the rancher is forced to take the reduced value of crop production into account in making his output choice, the value of production will be maximized, assuming perfect competition (Coase 1960: 5).

Coase went on to illustrate a situation where it may not be efficient to pay damage for crop loss per se, but where a mutually beneficial bargain may be struck that enhances efficiency. Suppose that the farmer's crop is valued at twelve dollars and that the cost of production is ten dollars, leaving the farmer with a profit of two dollars. Suppose further that the rancher, who had been raising one steer, suddenly finds it profitable to increase the size of his herd to two steer. This increases the damage payment required of the rancher to three dollars, but does not affect the profits of the farmer, since he is exactly compensated for the value of the crops destroyed. Thus, while herd size is a matter of indifference to the farmer, it is not for the rancher. Since the farmer's profits are two dollars, he can be induced to forgo cultivation for any payment in excess of that amount. Because the rancher would have to pay three dollars in compensation for damage caused, he would be willing to pay the farmer up to three dollars to forgo the cultivation of his land. This, of course, would result in the amount of damage, and hence the compensation payment, being zero, leaving the rancher better off than if the farmer were to cultivate. There is thus room for a mutually beneficial bargain to be struck where the rancher pays the farmer some amount between two and three dollars to take his land out of cultivation.[12] As Coase (1960:5) noted, the actual amount paid would be determined by the negotiation process:

> What payment would in fact be made would depend on the shrewdness of the farmer and the cattle-raiser as bargainers. But as the payment would not be so high as to cause the cattle-raiser to abandon this location and as it would not vary with the size of the herd, such an agreement would not affect the allocation of resources but would merely alter the distribution of income and wealth as between the cattle-raiser and the farmer.

This outcome, in which the farmer discontinues cultivation, "is desirable in all cases in which the damage that the cattle would cause, and for which the cattle-raiser would be willing to pay, exceeds the amount which the farmer would pay for the use of the land" (Coase 1960: 5–6).[13]

[12] This result generalizes to any subset of the farmer's land as well.

[13] The reason that the value of damage caused is qualified by the willingness of the cattle-raiser to pay is that there might be a cheaper method of preventing damage. For example, if the value of the damage is twelve dollars and the farmer's profits are ten dollars, then the

Coase next turned to an examination of the situation where the agent who causes the harm (here, the rancher) is *not* liable for damages. Referring to table 5.1, the value of crop loss can now be seen in a somewhat different light. In the previous case, where the rancher was liable for damage, the value of crop loss represented the compensation that the rancher had to pay the farmer to keep a given number of steer. When the rancher is not liable for damage, however, he will not take this cost into account in deciding on herd size. Given that the farmer now bears the cost of damage done to his crops by the wandering cattle, he would be willing to pay any amount up to the value of crops lost in order to avoid this damage. That is, if the rancher had three steer, the farmer would be willing to pay up to three dollars to induce the rancher to reduce his herd to two steer, up to five dollars if he would reduce his herd to one steer, and so on. Of course the farmer would never be willing to pay the rancher more than nine dollars to reduce the size of his herd, since the farmer could install fencing at a cost of nine dollars. The point for Coase, however, is that the costs of the crop damage *are* internalized to the rancher, even when he is not legally liable. The willingness of the farmer to pay to avoid damages internalizes the damage costs to the rancher in exactly the same way as if the rancher himself were liable. When the rancher is liable for damages, the cost of adding, say, a third steer includes the three-dollar compensation payment to the farmer; when the rancher is not liable, the cost of adding the third steer includes the foregone three-dollar bribe from the farmer. Thus, whether the rancher is liable or not, the size of the herd will be the same, as the cost conditions facing the rancher are invariant.

What Coase demonstrated with this example is that, if there are no impediments to bargaining, it does not matter which party is made liable for the harm caused by the straying cattle: The farmer and the rancher will negotiate a solution that generates the efficient outputs of both cattle and crops, with the negotiation process internalizing all relevant costs to both parties. As Coase pointed out, there does need to be some establishment of legal rights determining liability for damage, without which the sort of market transactions he described cannot take place. Nonetheless, once these rights are specified, he said, "[T]he ultimate result (which maximizes the value of production) is independent of the legal position if the pricing mechanism is assumed to work without cost (1960: 8).

To illustrate how this analysis would apply to actual instances of harmful effects, Coase next discussed four nineteenth-century British legal cases,

---

payment would be between ten and twelve dollars. If the cost of installing the fence is 9 dollars, however, the cattle-raiser would find it profitable to pay for the fence rather than to pay compensation for the damage or to bribe the farmer out of cultivation.

two of which will be sufficient to give us a sense for how Coase's ideas might work themselves out in practice. In *Sturges v. Bridgman*,[14] a problem arose when a doctor set up practice next door to a confectioner. The confectioner used two mortars and pestles in his manufacturing process. One had been in place for more than sixty years, and the other for more than twenty-six years. There were no problems until eight years after the doctor opened his practice, when he decided to build an examination room set right against the confectioner's kitchen. The noise and vibration emanating from the confectioner's kitchen made it difficult for the doctor to conduct examinations in this room, especially when he was using his stethoscope. The doctor sought an injunction against the confectioner's use of the machinery and the court granted his request, reasoning that to rule in favor of the confectioner " 'would ... produce a prejudicial effect upon the development of land for residential purposes' " (quoted in Coase 1960: 9).

Applying his economic analysis to the facts of this case, Coase noted that the court's decision determines the final allocation of rights only if the right is in its highest-valued use. That is, if the confectioner values the right to use his machinery at this location more than the doctor values peace and quiet, then he will be willing to bribe the doctor to allow him to remain in this location. Such a result would occur if the cost to the confectioner of moving or shutting down exceeded the cost to the doctor of remodeling his office in such a way that the noise did not interfere with his practice.[15] Thus, according to Coase, the court's attempt to promote residential and professional land use could only succeed if such uses were consistent with the relative valuations of the two parties. The ultimate resting place of the right is independent of the court's decision.

Another of the cases discussed by Coase was *Bass v. Gregory*,[16] which involved a pub owner who brewed beer in the cellar of his pub. A ventilation shaft ran from the cellar to the yard of the neighboring parcel of property. The owner of the neighboring parcel sealed the opening of the ventilation shaft, and the pub owner filed suit. The court found in favor of the pub owner based on the doctrine of lost grant, which states that " 'if a legal right is proved to have existed and been exercised for a number of years the law ought to presume that it had a legal origin' " (Coase 1960: 14). The shaft had been in existence for over forty years, and the court determined that the neighbor must have known about it when he purchased the property, since the air coming from the shaft made the entire parcel of property smell of beer.

---

[14] 11 Ch.D. 852 (1879).

[15] Similarly, if the court had given the right to the confectioner, the doctor would bribe the confectioner to move or shut down if the doctor placed a higher value on the right.

[16] 25 Q.B.D. 481 (1890).

Again, however, Coase points out that the right will find its final resting place in the pub owner only if the value of this shaft to the pub owner exceeds the value of clean air to the neighbor. If this is not the case, the neighbor would bribe the pub owner to dig a new ventilation shaft, to relocate his business, or to shut down altogether. If the parties can bargain costlessly, the right will gravitate to its highest-valued use, and, said Coase, "[T]he 'doctrine of lost grant' is about as relevant [to the final outcome] as the colour of the judge's eyes" (1960: 15).

What Coase had demonstrated, then, was that when transactions are costless, legal rules, attempts at social engineering and other such practices are all irrelevant. The economic problem is to maximize the value of production, and attempts by courts to assign rights on other bases will ultimately be defeated. In fact, it would not matter if courts determined rights based on a coin flip. As Coase (1960: 15) said,

> [I]t has to be remembered that the immediate question faced by the courts is *not* what shall be done by whom *but* who has the legal right to do what. It is always possible to modify by transactions on the market the initial legal delimitation of rights. And, of course, if such market transactions are costless, such a rearrangement of rights will always take place if it would lead to an increase in the value of production.

This was nothing more than an application of basic economic theory handed down at least since Smith—that resources gravitate toward their highest-valued uses if there are no impediments to such movement. Yet the implications here are stunning: If market transactions are costless, court decisions assigning liability for damages will have no effect on the allocation of resources (Coase 1960: 10).[17] Because the value of output will be maximized whatever the legal rule, the "only" difference between alternative liability assignments is in the distribution of income; there is no efficiency-based reason to prefer any particular legal rule.[18] This is the set of ideas that George Stigler (1966: 113) was soon to christen the "Coase theorem."[19]

---

[17] It was this result that Stigler referred to as "heresy" (1988: 76).

[18] "It is, of course, true that the distribution of wealth ... [is] affected by the decision, which is why questions of equity bulk so largely in such cases" (Coase 1959: 27, at note 54).

[19] While it is standard (and correct) to credit Coase with developing the insight that costless bargaining will lead to the efficient resolution of externality problems without the necessity of government intervention (apart from an initial specification of rights), we have already seen that the seeds of this idea are actually present in Sidgwick's *Principles of Political Economy* (1901: 409–10; see also pp. 44–45, infra). Coase, however, seems not to have known about Sidgwick's insight, and Sidgwick did nothing to develop it. See Medema (2007c).

While we shall have more to say about the Coase theorem in chapter 7, it is worth mentioning at this point that this result was by no means universally accepted. For surveys of the debate over the Coase theorem, see, for example, Zerbe (1980), Medema and Zerbe (2000), and the references cited therein.

Through this analysis, Coase had, virtually at the stroke of a pen, taken us back to classical welfare theory, where the pursuit of individual self-interest translates into the best interests of society.[20] For Coase, the market failure, such as it is, results not so much from the failure of the market itself to coordinate individual behavior satisfactorily as from the failure of *government* to establish well-defined property rights that will facilitate the transacting process. Once it does so, self-interested agents will efficiently resolve externality problems through a negotiation process. Pigovian remedies are thus rendered unnecessary in a Pigovian world—a world embodying the assumptions of orthodox economic theory circa 1960. It is important to note that Coase was not suggesting that there would be *no* externalities; what he said was that any external effects that did exist would be efficient because the parties to the situation would be bearing the full costs of their actions.[21] The application of Pigovian remedies in such a context would actually make the situation *worse* rather than better, reducing the externality level below that which is efficient.

THE MARKET IN THE REAL WORLD

The idea that the structure of law does not matter for the efficiency with which resources are allocated is so startling as to seem almost nonsensical, and would seem to fly in the face of a great deal of evidence to the contrary. In fact, it would seem to contradict Coase's emphasis on reciprocity, which calls attention to the need to look at both sides of the externality problem in determining the efficient assignment of rights. Coase recognized as much, having pointed out already in his article on "The Federal Communications Commission" that "if the efficiency with which the economic system operated was completely independent of the legal position, [distribution and equity] would be all that mattered. But this is not so." Coase then listed a number of factors that may preclude the attainment of the efficient result through the negotiation process:

> First of all, the law may be such as to make certain desirable market trans-actions impossible.... Second, it may impose costly and time-consuming procedures. Third, the legal delimitation of rights provides the starting point for the rearrangement of rights through market transactions. *Such transac-*

---

[20] Of course, the classical economists did not assume that market transactions are cost-less, nor did they even really contemplate the notion of transaction costs. They did seem to believe, however, that markets tend to operate with a minimum of friction if the state does not get in the way.

[21] Buchanan and Stubblebine (1962) have called these externality levels "Pareto irrelevant."

tions are not costless, with a result that the initial delimitation of rights may be maintained even though some other would be more efficient. Or, even if the original position is modified, the most efficient delimitation of rights may not be attained. Finally, a waste of resources may occur when the criteria used by the courts to delimit rights result in resources being employed solely to establish a claim. (1959: 27, at note 54, emphasis added)

The first three of these factors imply that the market itself may not function smoothly, with the result that efficiency may depend on the initial specification and/or the content of rights, while the fourth is a rent-seeking argument that raises the possibility of general inefficiencies in a market-based approach to externality problems.[22]

In "The Problem of Social Cost," Coase focused on the third of these "imperfections," the presence of transaction costs. After winding up his discussion of the effects of alternative rights assignments in a world without transaction costs, Coase allowed that this is "*a very unrealistic assumption*":

> In order to carry out a market transaction, it is necessary to discover who it is that one wishes to deal with, to inform people that one wishes to deal and on what terms, to conduct negotiations leading up to a bargain, to draw up the contract, to undertake the inspection needed to make sure that the terms of the contract are being observed, and so on. (1960: 15, emphasis added)

Coase recognized that he had just removed the linchpin of his earlier analysis. These processes "are often extremely costly," he said, and will "prevent many transactions that would be carried out in a world in which the pricing system worked without cost" (1960: 15).

Looking at the situation realistically, then, required accounting for the role played by transaction costs. This emphasis on transaction costs was nothing new for Coase, who had already made the existence and magnitude of these costs a centerpiece of his analysis of firm organization in "The Nature of the Firm" (1937). There, Coase suggested that if the operation of the market were costless, there would be no reason for the existence of the integrated firm; all productive activity would take place through a series of market transactions. If, however, there were costs associated with transacting through the market, internal organization would be employed when its cost was lower than the cost of organizing market transactions. A rationale for the existence of the firm and an explanation for its extent could thus be found in the relative cost of internal and market transactions.

Coase used a similar line of reasoning to explain the existence and persistence of social cost problems. He suggested that the persistence of

---

[22] On this point, see Medema (1997).

inefficient levels of externality could be attributed to the presence of transaction costs that are sufficiently large to preclude the functioning of the market-like mechanisms that, as he had shown, work to internalize all relevant costs.[23] Coase was not suggesting that market mechanisms cannot function, but, rather, that once these costs are taken into account, rearrangements of rights will occur only when and to the extent that the associated gains—which he measured in terms of "the value of production"—outweigh the costs (1960: 15–16). This, for Coase, calls into question not only the *optimality* of markets, but even the ability of markets to move resources in to higher-valued uses. The problem then becomes one of determining how these transaction costs actually affect the working of markets. In externality situations, at least, these costs are often a significant impediment; indeed, as Coase later pointed out, "[T]he main concern of public policy has always been with cases in which ... market transactions ... would be too costly to be carried out" (1970c: 36).

Transaction costs would thus seem to be partially responsible for the market failures pointed to by Pigou and others, and so reinforce the Pigovian position.[24] Yet, it is actually here that we find the second of Coase's criticisms of Pigou and the Pigovian tradition.[25] Pigovian analysis, from Pigou on down, did not contemplate the notion of transaction costs, and so implicitly assumed that transaction costs are zero. In fact, the implicit assumption that transaction costs are zero is pervasive in neoclassical economics. Yet, within such a framework inefficient externalities would not—could not—exist. Economists, Coase charged, were trying to explain divergences between private and social costs using a theoretical framework in which private and social costs were inevitably equal (1988c: 175). This, he said, led to nonsensical conclusions: "[T]he kind of government actions that economists thought to be required were completely unnecessary given the assumptions of their analytical system" (1993: 252). In fact, the point of Coase's zero transaction costs analysis was not to demonstrate that markets and private bargaining can efficiently resolve externality problems. Rather, as he said later, it was used to show "the emptiness of the Pigovian analytical system" and turn the discussion in a different and more realistic direction (1993: 252–53).

[23] Once again, there is good reason to question whether the general attribution of externalities to transaction costs is in fact proper. See Medema and Samuels (1997). This qualification should not, however, be taken to imply that transaction costs have no role to play in explaining the existence of externalities.

[24] I say "partially" because Coase also laid some of the responsibility on the lack of property rights assigned over the resources in question.

[25] Recall that the first was the neglect of reciprocity.

FOUR MECHANISMS FOR DEALING WITH EXTERNALITIES

Coase alleged that the Pigovian framework is erroneous, but yet he also acknowledged that transaction costs would likely prevent markets from generating optimal solutions to externality problems. Where, then, does this leave the analysis of externalities and, in particular, the means for dealing with them? Coase's basic answer was that there is no answer—or at least no singular one. Instead, he suggested that there are four alternatives for dealing with these problems of harmful effects.

One option—and the one most seized upon in the subsequent literature and in the policy realm—is to use the market, and it is in this context that much of the import of Coase's zero transaction costs analysis lies. This analysis showed that, under ideal conditions, the market can optimally resolve problems of harmful effects. As Coase pointed out, of course, actual markets are imperfect and are unlikely to provide an optimal resolution of externality problems in the sense of the traditional definition of optimality. Yet, he said, they may be able to offer some (perhaps substantial) improvement over the status quo. This was the point that Coase was arguing in "The Federal Communications Commission," although he allowed that the degree to which the pricing mechanism should be used to allocate broadcast frequencies could be determined only "on the basis of practical experience" (1959: 34). The difficulty that Coase had with the existing state of affairs was that policymakers seemed to give little consideration to the idea that some (perhaps limited, perhaps extensive) use of the pricing mechanism in the allocation of frequencies *may* offer an improvement on the existing system. Coase's feeling was clearly that some use of the pricing mechanism would improve the efficiency with which broadcasting resources are allocated.[26] The fact, however, that the process of negotiating agreements involves costs, that such agreements will in many instances not be reached, and that those agreements which are reached will leave potentially beneficial improvements unexploited (owing to transaction costs), suggested to Coase that other possible remedies should be explored.

The second alternative suggested by Coase drew on his analysis in "The Nature of the Firm." Coase pointed out that a single entity in possession of the rights of all affected parties will be forced to account for the costs associated with alternative employments of resources and will arrange the allocation of factors among competing uses in light of these costs. For example, if the cattle rancher also owned the agricultural land, he would

---

[26] "[T]here is good reason to believe that the present system, which relies exclusively on regulation and in which private property and the pricing system play no part, is not the best solution" (Coase 1959: 34).

balance the cost of the crop damage against the benefits from additional head of cattle. The internalization of all relevant costs, along with the firm's ability to substitute administrative fiat for bargaining, may allow it to resolve externality problems at a lower cost than the market. On the other hand, the administrative costs of firm organization could be very high, perhaps exceeding the costs of market organization, and the more so the greater the diversity of activities that are organized under this firm.[27]

The third alternative is what Coase (1960: 17) called "direct Government regulation." Once again drawing on the ideas presented in "The Nature of the Firm," Coase maintained that the government could act as a "super-firm" through its ability to allocate resources by administrative fiat. While government may be able to deal with externality problems more economically than could the market, Coase insisted that one cannot properly assess the merits of the regulatory option without considering the difficulties that may attend such schemes, including administrative costs, political pressures, the lack of any sort of competitive check, and incomplete information, including the lack of precise measures of benefit and cost as well as information about producer and consumer preferences.[28]

This brings us to another major flaw that Coase ascribed to the Pigovian approach to externality theory: the tendency to ignore the costs and other difficulties, such as computation of the optimal Pigovian tax or subsidy rate, associated with government intervention of this sort.[29] We have already noted in chapter 3 that the standard welfare analysis of externalities assumed a costless and smoothly operating governmental machine and derived policy implications based on this premise. Yet if the actual costs of government intervention are taken into account, said Coase, "[I]t follows that direct governmental regulation will not necessarily give better results than leaving the problem to be solved by the market or the firm" (1960: 18). On the other hand, though, Coase did not see government regulation as inevitably inferior to other options, either. He allowed that it could well increase efficiency, especially in cases, such as with air pollution, where the externality affects large numbers of agents and where the costs of market or firm organization are thus likely to be substantial (1960: 18).

Given the costs associated with the market, firm, and governmental options, Coase suggested a fourth possible option: in some cases the best

[27] See Coase (1960: 16–17; 1970c: 39). In addition, it goes virtually without saying that this type of remedy is not feasible for externalities to which consumers are party, although Coase's examples in "The Problem of Social Cost" all deal with externalities between producers.

[28] See Coase (1960: 17–18; 1959: 18; 1970c: 39–40). Of course, Pigou had mentioned many of these same factors, as we saw in chapter 3.

[29] Coase (1960: 41–42; 1988c: 181–85).

solution may be "to do nothing about the problem at all" because the costs of allowing the externality to persist may be less than the costs of implementing the market, firm, or regulatory remedies. In fact, given the ubiquity of externalities within the economic system and what he considered the "heavy" costs associated with government regulation, Coase asserted that "it will ... commonly be the case" that the costs of regulation will exceed the gains (1960: 18). In effect, Coase was suggesting that the governmental cure will often be worse than the market disease, at least from an efficiency perspective.

It is important to understand that Coase was not arguing against the use of Pigovian remedies. He *was* arguing that there are multiple options for dealing with harmful effects, that none of them is optimal, and that there is no single, obvious solution to problems of external effects. Each of the options has various imperfections associated with it, and the fact that the market performs less than optimally does not, for Coase, imply that government intervention is the answer. In adopting this cautionary attitude toward regulatory solutions to externality problems, Coase was *not*, in actuality, taking us back to what Buchanan labeled laissez-faire welfare economics, for he did not assert the efficacy of the market in channeling individual self-interest to society's best interest. He takes us back, rather, to Mill and Sidgwick, who, as we have seen, suggested that market imperfections are widespread, but also that their existence does not mean that government interference will improve matters.[30]

SLAYING THE PIGOVIAN DRAGON, OR PREACHING PRAGMATISM OVER PANGLOSS AND PIGOU

Having completed the presentation of his theory of harmful effects, Coase next turned to a critique of Pigou and the Pigovian tradition. Coase's analysis of Pigou can hardly be considered charitable, and he treated the Pigovian tradition with no more kindness than he treated Pigou himself, labeling the tradition "inadequate" and "incorrect," both in analysis and in policy conclusions. Coase found it "strange that a doctrine as faulty as that developed by Pigou should have been so influential," and attributes part of its success to a "lack of clarity" in Pigou's exposition. "Not being clear," said Coase, "it was never clearly wrong" (1960: 39).

---

[30] See chapter 2. The drawbacks cited by Mill and by Sidgwick are very similar to those pointed to by Coase in "The Federal Communications Commission" (1959: 18) and "The Problem of Social Cost" (1960: 18).

Coase was very critical of Pigou's failure to analyze externalities in a framework that recognized their reciprocal nature, as we have already seen. Pigou's analysis posited one party as the injurer and the other party as the victim. The externality was then modeled as a divergence between the marginal private net product and the marginal social net product of the injury-causing party, with the marginal social net product being smaller than the private one due to the damage caused by the harmful effect. Pigou suggested that the effects of this divergence could be rectified by requiring the injuring party to pay compensation, taxing that party, or regulating the harm-generating activity. But this, said Coase, puts no onus on the "victim" to mitigate the level of damages, even though the victim in many instances might be able to do so more cheaply than the injurer.

Coase placed some of the blame for this neglect of reciprocity issues on economists' propensity to focus on these marginal private and social products, a focus that he considered both misplaced and misleading because it resulted in the perception of a "deficiency" where the two diverge. Moreover, economists seemed to assume that this deficiency must be corrected in some way and at all costs. Coase, though, felt that the "comparison of private and social products is neither here nor there." Instead, he said, "When an economist is comparing alternative social arrangements, the proper procedure is to compare the total social product yielded by these different arrangements" (1960: 34). For Coase, that is, the concern of the economist should be wealth maximization. Removing divergences between the marginal private and social net products of ostensibly harm-causing activities does not guarantee the wealth-maximizing result, which means that the Pigovian focus is misplaced. Coase was also aware, however, that there is more to policy analysis than wealth maximization, as when he noted that "it is, of course, desirable that the choice between different social arrangements for the solution of economic problems should be carried out in broader terms than this [wealth maximization] and that that total effect of these arrangements in all spheres of life should be taken into account. As Frank H. Knight has so often emphasized, the problems of welfare economics must ultimately dissolve into a study of aesthetics and morals" (1960: 43).[31]

One way of encouraging the reciprocal view, according to Coase, would be to treat situations of harmful effects under the common law of nuisance rather than through the use of taxes or regulations. This encourages the reciprocal view by allowing the courts to weigh the benefits and costs of the harmful effects in determining whether, and to what extent, these effects should be restricted (1960: 38). Under the tax or regulatory methods,

---

[31] That having been said, Coase's position throughout "The Problem of Social Cost" and in subsequent writings argues against much weight being placed on this caveat.

in contrast, the "victim" is never made liable, which may preclude the attainment of the efficient result (1960: 37–38). While Coase granted that dealing with harmful effects involves more than the economic analysis of benefits and costs, he also said that if judges act sensibly, the flexibility of the law of nuisance seems likely to generate "more satisfactory results," in an economic sense, than the adoption of "a rigid rule" (1960: 38).

At the heart of Coase's criticism of Pigou's analysis, though, is his sense that Pigou considered government the solution to all problems of harmful effects. Coase certainly did not sense any sort of pragmatic element in Pigou's approach; in fact, his (1960: 29) portrayal of Pigou's thought process seems almost sarcastic:

> Pigou's underlying thought would appear to be: Some have argued that no State action is needed. But the system has performed as well as it has because of State action. Nonetheless, there are still imperfections. What additional State action is required?

Given the significant problems that Coase associated with governmental tax, subsidy, and regulatory schemes, it is not surprising that he would be so critical of what he perceived to be such a staunchly interventionist position.[32] That having been said, Coase's portrayal of Pigou does not necessarily resonate with the Pigou described in chapter 3—an issue to which we shall return.

The problems with Pigovian externality theory, as Coase conceived them, were not due simply to "a few slips in the analysis," but rather to "basic defects in the ... approach to problems of welfare economics" (1960: 42). He felt that the Pigovian approach committed what Demsetz (1969) later labeled the "nirvana fallacy," which, as Coase put it, in-

---

[32] Coase's also argues that, even abstracting from the costs associated with government action, the Pigovian tax will not lead to the socially optimal result (1960: 41–42). Making the tax equal to damages, said Coase, will result, for example, in too many people living near a polluting factory, since those people would not bear the full cost of their actions. If more people moved near the factory, the firm's taxes, and thus its costs, would increase, and this, in turn, would lead to a reduction in the firm's output (and the harmful effect) below the optimal level. Coase suggests that we are faced with a choice between too much smoke and too few neighbors on the one hand and too little smoke and too many neighbors on the other.

As William Baumol (1972) has pointed out, however, Coase's analysis represents a fundamental misunderstanding of the Pigovian tax. The tax should not vary with the level of damage, but instead should be set equal to marginal damage at the efficient level of output/pollution. In this case, as Baumol demonstrated, the Pigovian tax will lead to an efficient outcome. (Coase was correct, though, in his assertion that a tax which varied with damages would lead to inefficiencies.) A further limitation of Coase's critique is that he saw the Pigovian tax solely as a potential method of correcting harmful effects, and he failed to recognize that it is also serves as a potential revenue source for the government. In fact, Ballard and Medema (1993) have shown that Pigovian taxes may well be superior to taxes levied on things like labor income, output, and sales.

volves making "a comparison between a state of laissez faire and some kind of ideal world" (1960: 43). When a divergence is found, it usually is followed by prescriptions for how the ideal optimum may be attained, usually through some governmental remedy. Coase has referred to this as "blackboard economics," an economics in which "[f]actors of production are moved around, taxes are imposed, subsidies are granted, prices go up and down—a social optimum is achieved and the relationships which it implies are described—but it all happens on the blackboard" (1970c: 41–42). While Coase found this type of economic analysis rigorous and elegant, he considered it "largely irrelevant for questions of economic policy." Though the economist might be able to devise a theoretical construct of an ideal world and its attributes, said Coase, "it is clear that we have not yet discovered how to get to it from where we are" (1960: 43). Behaving as if we do, he said, often causes economists to reach erroneous conclusions about how to deal with fundamental problems of economic policy (1960: 2, 42).

Not surprisingly, then, Coase recommended a change of approach away from the methodology reflected in Pigovian analysis. The starting point, he said, should be the recognition that there are multiple institutional alternatives for coordinating the production and provision of goods and services, and these may generate very different outcomes. The basic problem is to determine the appropriate institutional structure of production in a given context. Second, Coase felt that economists must come to recognize that factors of production are, at their heart, legal rights rather than physical entities. Viewed from this perspective, rights to command labor, utilize capital, and to engage in actions that generate harmful effects are all factors of production (1960: 43–44). This means both that labor and externalities are analytically equivalent and that the question as to the appropriate institutional structure of production is really a question about what mechanism(s) will be used to allocate these rights/factors of production among competing uses. Third, Coase rejected both the optimal markets and optimal government approaches, arguing that economists will not make much progress until they realize that policy-making involves "choosing between social arrangements which are all more or less failures" (1964: 195).[33] This, for Coase, meant that deductively derived, generalized policy solutions must be combined with "studies of how various kinds of institutions (firms, markets, regulations) actually work in practice" (1970a: 61). Fourth, the assessment of institutional performance should involve the comparison of the value of output under alternative institutional arrangements (1960: 43).

For Coase, the distinction between the Pigovian approach and the approach that he was advocating can be summed quite simply: "Pigovian

[33] See also Coase (1970a: 61).

analysis shows us that it is possible to conceive of better worlds than the one in which we live," while, in reality, "the problem is to devise practical arrangements which will correct defects in one part of the system without causing more serious harm in other parts" (1960: 34).

PIGOU REDUX

Coase's withering criticism of Pigou and the Pigovian tradition was not without controversy. Indeed, it launched a debate that, in certain of its aspects, continues to this day. No one, however, was arguing that Coase had mischaracterized Pigou or the Pigovian tradition.[34] Instead, the debate was aimed at the correctness and adequacy of Coase's challenge.

Coase's critique reflected what amounted to a universally held view that the theory of market failure,[35] circa 1960, was built on the foundation laid by Pigou in *The Economics of Welfare*. This take was nicely summed up by Stanislaw Wellisz (1964: 347), who noted, "The Pigovian tradition, accepted by modern welfare economists, claims that whenever private and social costs diverge, steps should be taken to equalize the two."[36] There can be no doubt that Pigou's work inspired much of the literature that followed. Yet this evolution, and thus the history of the theory of market failure, rested on a particular view of Pigou's contribution set forth in *Economics of Welfare*, and a good case can be made that this literature represents a significant departure from Pigou's perspective. *The Economics of Welfare*, with its extensive array of market failures and prescribed government policies for correcting them, has been cited by supporters and critics alike as the basis for a neoclassical approach to market failures that dominated economic thinking from the 1940s onward. When read against the background of Pigou's larger body of writings, and particularly his essay on "State Action and Laisser-Faire" (1935d), however, one gets a very different picture of what Pigou intended in *Economics of Welfare*[37]—one rather at odds with both the subsequent Pigovian tradition and the characterization

[34] But see more recently DeSerpa (1993), Simpson (1996), and the reply by Coase (1996), as well as Aslanbeigui and Medema (1998).

[35] When we speak of "market failure" here, we are referring to what is traditionally called "allocation" failure, as reflected in the theories of externalities and public goods in particular. For a discussion of the larger welfare approach of Pigou and the Cambridge tradition, see Aslanbeigui (1990, 2001) and Backhouse (2006).

[36] In addition to Wellisz (1964), see also Meade (1952), Bator (1958), Mishan (1971), Coase (1960), Buchanan and Stubblebine (1962), and Baumol (1972).

[37] While one could argue that Pigou's position in 1935 may have been different than that elaborated in a book originally written in 1920 and revised in 1932, the revisions undertaken in editions published after 1935 do not contradict the basics of the earlier analysis. Moreover, his *Theory of Public Finance* (1928) evidences a perspective similar to that of his 1935 essay.

of Pigou's approach by critics such as Coase. Indeed, it seems that Coase, like James Meade and others working in the Pigovian tradition, treated Pigou's "prima facie case" as if it were the end point rather than a beginning and spent much of his time hammering away at Pigovian straw men erected from passages in Pigou's work that are taken out of context.

What, then, is the source of this nearly universal tendency to lump Pigou in with the neoclassical theory of market failure and the economists who promulgated it?[38] One need only scan the pages of *Economics of Welfare* to see the link. Here, Pigou applied the Marshallian framework to a host of economic problems and derived the attendant implications. The book is an "economics" of welfare that pushed the analytics to the limit in a manner not unlike what one would see some decades later in, for example, a Samuelson or a Becker. Issues of practice are given almost no place at all in *Economics of Welfare*—a few pages in a work of many hundred. If *Economics of Welfare* is taken to define Pigou's position in toto, then the received view, which is reflected in Coase's challenge, is correct.

As we saw in chapter 3, however, the contrast between *Economics of Welfare* and "State Action and Laisser-Faire" is both clear and significant. The former shows the prima facie case for intervention and whence it arises; the latter shows how one navigates the waters from the prima facie case to reality. "State Action and Laisser-Faire" is the practical application of the insights gained from the theorizing in *Economics of Welfare* and, one could argue, takes us places where economic theory cannot. The essay deals with issues of practice, to the complete exclusion of theory—to the extent, even, of taking a jab at those who wrap themselves in theory with no attention to practical matters. In this sense, the essay is almost the antithesis of *Economics of Welfare*. Writing in "State Action and Laisser-Faire," Pigou (1935d: 128) argued,

> High-sounding generalisations on these matters are irrelevant fireworks. They may have a place in political perorations, but they have none in real life. Accumulation of evidence, the balancing of probabilities, judgment of men, by these alone practical problems in this region can be successfully attacked.

This sounds remarkably similar to any number of statements made by Coase in "The Problem of Social Cost" and elsewhere.[39] In framing the analysis this way, Pigou was working with what Sidgwick (1901) called the "art" of political economy, not the science. The essay shows the import of the theory-practice distinction for Pigou himself, and this, in turn, calls

---

[38] As evidenced in the ubiquitous references to Pigovian externality theory in the literature, to say nothing of the conflation of Pigou and Pigovian within the Chicago tradition, most notably by Coase.

[39] See pp. 117–21, infra.

into question the accuracy of the "Pigovian" label that was placed on the neoclassical theory of market failures in the middle-third of the twentieth century.

It seems apparent that *The Economics of Welfare* was in later years made to do something that it was neither intended to do nor capable of doing. That it became the foundation for the purely theoretical, nonpractical, neoclassical theory of market failures, then, calls for some attempt at an explanation. To say that no one read "State Action and Laisser-Faire," and that everyone simply overlooked or glossed over the practical bits in *Economics of Welfare*, while perhaps accurate, does not suffice.[40] The analysis of market failure in *Economics of Welfare* meshed very nicely with the formalism—the mathematical tools and deductive approach to economic theorizing—that characterized the neoclassical ascendancy of the 1940s through 1960s. While Pigou's notion of the national dividend was pushed aside early on in the development of neoclassical welfare economics,[41] his treatment of market failure—in particular, via the distinction between private and social net products—lent itself to the formalization that was at the heart of the neoclassical push to firm up a "scientific" theory describing the role for the state in economic activity. The quest for determinate, optimal solutions to questions of economic theory and policy in postwar neoclassical theorizing left little room for the practical matters that Pigou dealt with in his essay. As such, the answer to our question may to some extent lie in the methodological narrowing that characterized economics during this period—a narrowing that moved economic analysis increasingly away from the pluralistic approach that Pigou found so useful.[42] *Economics of Welfare* would be fit into this framework by subsequent commentators, just as the Coase theorem was a few decades later. "State Action and Laisser-Faire," however, could not be, just as the last (and main) part of "The Problem of Social Cost" could not. That the demonstrated pervasiveness of market failure and the ability of government to move the market to or near to the social optimum, so central to the Pigovian approach, may have comported with Pigou's priors is neither here nor there.

It would appear, then, that Coase's call for a more practical approach to problems of harmful effects and the possibilities associated with government intervention is really not much different than what Pigou was arguing

---

[40] "State Action and Laisser-Faire" and the book in which it appeared, *Economics in Practice*, are all but unmentioned in the economics literature during the formative era of neoclassical economics, and not at all in any significant work of the period.

[41] See Aslanbeigui (1990) for a discussion of this point.

[42] "Divergent methods," such as the historical and mathematical approaches, "are partners not rivals" in building economic understanding (Pigou 1935a: 22). This is the same position that we see Pigou (1922) taking in the empty boxes debate.

in "State Action and Laisser-Faire."[43] In light of this, then, where does Coase's contribution lie? At the most general level, it may be his insistence that modern welfare economics went astray in positing Pigovian remedies as the necessary and correct solution to these problems. A further answer to this question, however, is that Coase's analysis pointed to the potential of the market for resolving problems of harmful effects. One aspect of this is the possibility of using markets to allocate externality-related rights. The increasing use of marketable pollution permits and the auctioning of licenses for the new portable telephone technologies are direct applications of Coase's insights and have offered evidence that the market can indeed be used to deal with externality-related situations. A second aspect of Coase's contribution is a new or at least heightened awareness that the initial outcome generated by the market (the so-called market failure) may be superior to the result that would obtain under Pigovian or other governmental corrective measures. Of course, all of this derives from the reciprocity insight, which opened the door to the benefit-cost approach in the first place.

As we noted earlier, Coase's analysis takes us back to Mill and Sidgwick, whose presumption was for self-interest channeled through the market unless some other mechanism could be demonstrated to provide coordination with greater efficiency. For Coase, as for Mill and Sidgwick, it seems ultimately to boil down to a lack of confidence in the ability of government to get things right, to match the efficiency of the market even when the market works imperfectly. Both Mill and Coase were pessimistic about the ability of institutional change to resolve the problems that they felt characterized the political system, while Sidgwick parted company with them in showing a measure of optimism about future possibilities. Meanwhile, Coase's lack of optimism on this score was finding reinforcement in the work of some of his colleagues at the University of Virginia, whose analysis of the political process was beginning to put the theory of government failure on the same theoretical footing as the theory of market failure.

---

[43] Allowing, of course, for the fact that Coase did not share Pigou's optimism about the future prospects for state action.

CHAPTER SIX

Marginalizing Government II

THE RISE OF PUBLIC CHOICE ANALYSIS

In scholarship it is not perhaps necessity, but prejudice,
that is the mother of invention.
—*Mancur Olson (1962: 1217)*

WHILE COASE was hinting at problems with the governmental machine in "The Problem of Social Cost," a small group of scholars was beginning to train the tools of economic analysis—in particular, the assumption of the rational, self-interested agent—on the political process. This economic analysis of political behavior, which eventually came to be known as "public choice analysis," was generating results that provided theoretical support for many of the qualms about the influence of the political process on economic policy-making that we have encountered in previous chapters. The development of public choice analysis, however, was not an isolated circumstance; it had parallels in the forays by economists into the various other social sciences during this period, a movement that Kenneth Boulding (1969: 8) labeled "economics imperialism" in his 1968 presidential address to the American Economic Association. Public choice and the economic analysis of law (which is the subject of chapter 7) have been the two most successful of these movements, but their paths to prominence have to do with much more than the development of the theories per se; the overt efforts to develop communities of scholars and the operation of various professionalization processes helped to solidify their status as distinct fields within economic analysis. This, in turn, helped to institutionalize the challenge that this analysis posed to the received view.

The role played by sociological forces at work within the economics profession has only recently begun to receive significant attention in the history of economics literature. Indeed, our discussion to this point has focused largely on the ideas themselves. Small communities of scholars, however, have often played a critically important role in the development of economic ideas and in how these ideas have come to occupy an established place in the profession. This has been particularly true during the twentieth century, as economics has become increasingly professionalized, and as "schools" and intellectual communities have become more commonplace. These intellectual communities played a defining role in the counterrevolution of self-interest that began to gather momentum in the 1960s and

1970s, with pubic choice and the economic analysis of law being perhaps the two most successful of these efforts.

While it is fairly common to think of public choice analysis solely in imperialistic terms—as an attempt to replace traditional political science approaches to politics with an economic one—it is essential to understand public choice against the background of the larger project that James Buchanan and others, including Warren Nutter, commenced in the 1950s: the development of what they believed to be a more appropriate theory of public economics. What specifically concerned Buchanan was that public economics—where the development of the economics of public goods and externalities, welfare economics, and so on, raised important issues relating to the process of collective decision-making—gave no place to the role of political forces within the economic policy-making process. This, of course, was also of great concern to Coase—then a colleague of Buchanan, Nutter, and Gordon Tullock at the University of Virginia— and was a major theme of his analysis in "The Problem of Social Cost."[1] Buchanan's goal was to reshape public economics in a way that took these forces into account. While his project was novel, it was not without precedent, as we have seen. Indeed, Buchanan was inspired to pursue this line of analysis after reading Wicksell's *Finanztheoretische Untersuchungen* shortly after completing his doctoral dissertation. Not too long thereafter, Buchanan discovered and immersed himself in the late-nineteenth- and early-twentieth-century Italian *la scienza delle finanze* literature. The Italian approach was of a piece with his own approach to things but had made no impact on public economics in Great Britain or the United States. Ultimately, Buchanan saw his modern political economy approach linking back to Adam Smith and the classical economists, and the study of the market process as it operated within and through "the framework of society, described by the 'laws and institutions' about which Adam Smith wrote" (Buchanan 1983: 6). What would emerge, however, was something far larger than what he had imagined.

SELF-INTEREST AND STATE ACTION

Public choice analysis emerged as a reaction against the Pigovian, Keynesian, and standard political science approaches that (implicitly or explicitly) assumed that the primary concern of government officials is to make policy choices in the best interests of society as a whole—a benevolent public servant approach, if you will. The technical economic formulation of this mindset was that the political process is an exercise in maximizing a particular social welfare function that translates the preferences of the members of society

[1] See chapter 5.

into the optimal outcome for the nation as a whole. Yet, we have also seen hints—some stronger than others—throughout our discussion to this point that the political process may well not generate the social-welfare-maximizing outcomes contemplated by economic theory, and, indeed, that political actors—voters, politicians, bureaucrats—may not have the larger social interest at heart at all. These notions of potential inadequacies in government behavior were never formally modeled or probed with any degree of sophistication, and certainly with nothing that resembled what was happening on the market failure side. In essence, there was a dichotomy—some would argue inconsistency—in the theory of market failure, which assumed that people pursue their self-interest in the market place but pursue the public interest in the political arena. This dichotomy was certainly evident in the Pigovian literature, as well as in the Italian optimal-equilibrium analysis. Coase's irritation with this approach to things was laid out forcefully in "The Problem of Social Cost" (1960) and was reflected in his concern that the theory of economic policy included a very nice analysis of market failure but no corresponding category or analysis of government failure. Public choice analysis began to change all of that.

In the simplest of terms, public choice is the economic analysis of politics—that is, the application of economic methods, and the model of the self-interested rational actor in particular, to the analysis of the political process, including voting, legislative and bureaucratic behavior, interest-group activity, and constitutional design.[2] Public choice pioneers James Buchanan and Gordon Tullock, writing in 1970 (and so in the very early years of the field's formalized existence), have described the field in the following terms:

> In barest summary, we may say that "the government" is analyzed not as an organization that pursues some "public interest" or other higher goals, but rather as a somewhat mundane machine for achieving the concrete desires of individual human beings. The central and pervasive research objective in Public Choice is that of understanding and explaining how the desires of citizens are transformed or translated into the observed outcomes of the political process.[3]

In undertaking this analysis,

> No assumption is made that the research scientist knows what the government should do any more than the economic theorist presumes to know what

---

[2] For extensive surveys of this literature, see Mueller (2003), Shughart and Razzolini (2001), Tullock, Brady, and Seldon (2002), Farber and Frickey (1991), and Johnson (1991).

[3] Center for Study of Public Choice National Science Foundation proposal, 1970, p. 4, Buchanan House Archives (hereafter, BHA).

goods the market should produce. In both cases, the ultimate results are observed as emerging from the processes of choice made by individuals within alternative sets of rules and decision-making institutions. It is this basically positive approach that perhaps distinguishes Public Choice research most clearly from traditional approaches to the study of political organization.[4]

The self-interested agent was at the center of this approach to the political process, but partnered with it was catallactics—the science of exchanges— which models collective action within the political process as a system of "complex exchange or agreement among all members of the relevant community" (Buchanan 1989: 15). It is through the combination of these two building blocks that public choice derives its insights into the operation of the political process and its normative suggestions for reform.

It would require a book much longer than this one just to survey the many facets of public choice analysis.[5] We do want to say a bit here, though, about how the application of the self-interest postulate to the political process led to a theory of government failure that parallels the theory of market failure.

At the individual voter level, public choice analysis posits that the choices people make at the polling place are those that they believe will best serve their own interests. As with markets, then, the pursuit of self-interest serves the interests of society only when self- and social interest are aligned. There are certainly instances when a voter's view of her self-interest coincides with the larger social interest. Nevertheless, there are a number of situations in which such coincidence will be lacking. For example, voters make their choices based upon their preferences and the stock of information that they have about issues and candidates. Because information is costly to acquire, voters, as rational individuals, will search for additional information—political or otherwise—only so long as the expected benefit is at least as great as the expected cost. The inevitable result is that voters carry a degree of ignorance, perhaps substantial, into the polling place with them. Voters will tend to be most informed about issues that coincide with their particular interests, both because the benefits of having such information are more substantial and because organized groups promoting that interest make it their business to provide information to like-minded voters and thereby lower the cost to those voters of acquiring pertinent information. We thus expect to see members of labor unions particularly well

---

[4] Center for Study of Public Choice National Science Foundation proposal, 1970, p. 4, BHA.

[5] In fact, Dennis Mueller (2003) has written that book, which, reflecting the burgeoning literature in the field, has grown from 297 to 788 pages over the course of three editions, the first of which was published in 1979.

informed about union-related issues and retired military officers especially knowledgeable about the candidates' positions on national defense.

The self-interest model suggests that the politician's interest lies in getting elected and then, as an office-holder, reelected. This, in turn, implies taking positions on issues and casting votes in the legislature based not on an assessment of the society's best interest,[6] but upon what the politician believes will appeal to the largest number of voters. As Tullock (1987: 104) has put it, politicians take positions "in terms of what they think the voters will reward, not what they think the voters *should* reward."[7] If politicians do indeed pursue their self-interest in the positions that they take on the issues, then we expect that the social interest will be served only if self-interest and social interest coincide.

It may seem at first glance that attempting to please the voters would be in the best interests of society. Because many citizens do not bother to vote,[8] however, there is already a disconnect between legislative positions that maximize votes and those that serve the larger social interest. Moreover, because voters are operating with limited information, the legislation that attracts their interest, and thus votes, may have little to do with what is best for society. For example, faced with a choice between a ten billion dollar project that provides substantial benefit to the nation but virtually none to the home district, and a ten billion dollar project that provides substantial benefit to the home district but is of nearly no import or even a net loss for the nation as a whole, we would expect the politician to vote for the latter, because it will generate more votes for him when he is up for reelection. Because every legislator faces this same incentive, we end up with a host of expensive projects that benefit particular constituencies but likely would not pass a social benefit–cost test. Legislative vote-trading ensures sufficient support to get these projects (often referred to as pork-barrel projects) approved, while the cost of these programs—in dollar and

---

[6] Here we use the word "society" to describe the relevant constituency, whether it be nation, state, city, or other jurisdiction.

[7] In Tullock's essay, there is a typo that causes "voters" to be italicized, rather than "should."

[8] This, too, is a utility-maximizing choice. The public interest or civic duty model suggests that everyone will vote, while the economic approach tells us that people will vote only if the expected benefit from doing so outweighs the expected cost. Because any given voter has only a small probability of influencing the election outcome, the expected benefit from voting actually seems to be quite small. In fact, while the civic duty approach has problems explaining why so few people vote, the economic approach is rather hard pressed to explain why *anyone* votes. There is a tendency to fall back on the idea that doing one's "civic duty" provides utility and thus is part of the marginal benefit from voting. That is, some vote and some do not because some people are more concerned than others about doing their civic duty. See Medema (2007b) for a discussion of the history of the rational voter hypothesis.

opportunity-cost terms—is spread across the community at large and thus remains largely hidden from the voters in any given district.

The vote-maximizing legislator will also be concerned to curry favor with special-interest groups that are particularly influential in his district. Should a candidate's background or voting record suggest an opposition to defense issues, for example, defense-related interest groups will be sure to get that information to pro-defense voters in his district. Given that special interests create voters who are informed and ready to act on issues that concern them, the theory predicts that they will have a disproportionate share of the influence on politicians and on election results. Of course, politicians receive much of their information about what voters will reward from the same special interests that provide information to the voters. This process involves the expenditure of vast sums of money to influence legislation, a phenomenon known as rent seeking.[9] This expenditure of resources, which is largely in the attempt to transfer resources from A to B (rather than to increase national welfare), is largely wasteful from an efficiency perspective.

Public choice analysis has also extended the self-interest assumption to the bureaucracy, which is charged with implementing legislation. Political theory has traditionally characterized bureaucrats as public servants who operate in the public interest, following the directions set out by the legislators or their superiors within the bureaucracy. If, instead, they are rational maximizers, the immediate question is what the pursuit of self-interest equates to within the bureaucratic realm. The answer given to this is that the self-interested bureaucrat seeks to expand his or her sphere of bureaucratic influence: the size of the budget, the number of people supervised, the range of activities overseen, perquisites of office, promotions—all of these being indicative of power, influence, and importance.[10] If every bureaucrat has an incentive to increase his or her domain, we would expect to see significant growth over time in the size of the government bureaucracy, particularly given that information problems limit the ability of legislators to oversee bureaucratic activity effectively. To the extent that the bureaucrat's self-interest and the social interest fail to coincide, then, we expect to see inefficiencies at the bureaucratic level.

In sum, the combination of voters voting their self-interest, politician-legislators taking positions on issues and legislation that they believe will maximize their likelihood of (re)election, and budget-maximizing bureaucrats calls into question the ability and even willingness of government to enact and implement the types of efficiency-enhancing policies that were contemplated by neoclassical welfare theory. Instead, by pointing to a wide

---

[9] On rent seeking, see Tullock (1967b, 1993) and Krueger (1974).

[10] See, for example, the treatments of bureaucracy in Tullock (1965), Downs (1967), and Niskanen (1971).

range of disparities between self-interest and social interest, the public choice models of political behavior point back to the types of concerns about state action that we have seen in the literature from Smith to Mill to Sidgwick and Pigou, but without supporting the optimistic prognostications of the Cambridge group.

GETTING THERE

If we define public choice analysis as the application of economic analysis to the political process, public choice is a relatively recent phenomenon. There are, however, a number of significant, albeit scattered, historical precursors to the contemporary work in the field.

One of these, as we have already seen, is found in parts of the Continental public finance tradition—in particular, in the literature of the Italian *la scienza delle finanze* and German *Staatswissenschaften* traditions and in the work of Knut Wicksell. Yet this analysis had virtually no impact on economic thinking outside of continental Europe prior to the middle of the twentieth century—at least in part owing to the almost complete absence of translations of these works into English. A second significant body of antecedent scholarship can be found in the mathematical analysis of voting processes, which originated in France in the work of mathematicians Jean-Charles de Borda, Marquis de Condorcet, and Pierre Simon LaPlace.[11] A major theme of this literature, which relied heavily on probability theory, was that standard majority voting methods could lead to the selection of a less-preferred outcome over a more-preferred one. This led to the development of alternative voting schemes, the outcomes of which, it was argued, would be more likely to comport with the will of the voters. This line of analysis was picked up in England a century later in the work of E. J. Nanson, Francis Galton, and Rev. C. L. Dodgson (Lewis Carroll).[12] Yet, these ideas were not developed in any significant way by those in the mathematical community, and the mathematical nature of these works made them inaccessible to students of political theory.[13]

The development of modern public choice theory dates to the late 1940s and early 1950s and to the work of Duncan Black and Kenneth Arrow.[14] Black, who was trained in economics and politics at the University of

---

[11] See Borda (1781), Condorcet (1785), and LaPlace (1812).

[12] See Nanson (1882), Galton (1907a,b), and Dodgson (1873, 1876, 1884).

[13] Both the Marxian and the American Institutional economics traditions have lengthy histories of attempting to link up political and economic processes. These traditions have been all but ignored within modern public choice analysis, owing at least in part to their very different methodological underpinnings and (real or perceived) ideological perspectives.

[14] See, for example, Black (1948), Black and Newing (1952), and Arrow (1951).

Glasgow, fleshed out significant aspects of the theory of majority rule and proportional representation—including, most famously, the median voter theorem—in a series of papers in the 1940s and 1950s. Black, however, was a loner; apart from his colleague and coauthor at the University of North Wales, Bangor, R. A. Newing (a mathematician), there was no one within the United Kingdom who seemed interested in the type of problems upon which Black was working, and it was not until the 1960s that his work began to receive any serious attention.[15] Arrow's place here was intimately connected with the work going on at RAND during the early Cold-War period.[16] RAND (the name comes from Research ANd Development) was a think tank, originally established immediately following World War II by the U.S. Air Force and McDonnell-Douglas, whose purpose was to engage in research dealing with military and national security issues. RAND supported a great deal of research in economics during the Cold War period, and the mathematical and game-theoretic advances made at RAND had a significant influence on the research of the economists working under its auspices and eventually had a profound influence on the course of economic analysis. Much of the theoretical inspiration for modern public choice theory came from the development of the theory of games and hard-nosed rational choice theory. The ability to model relationships among political actors as games of strategy opened up entirely new vistas for the analysis of agent responses to political decision rules and for the analysis of the formulation of the rules themselves. Two of the pioneers of public choice theory—Arrow and his student, Anthony Downs—were affiliated with RAND; and others at RAND—including Lloyd Shapley and Martin Shubik—though not prominent figures in the history of public choice theory, did devote some efforts to the game-theoretic analysis of the political process.[17] This line of research, however, was not taken up in any large way until a decade later, when Steven Brams, Peter Ordeshook, and others developed a highly technical game-theoretic approach to politics.

The work of Arrow and Black focused on the relationship between individual preferences, the voting process, and electoral outcomes. Arrow's

---

[15] Black and Coase were actually close friends, having worked together at the London School of Economics before serving together at Dundee School of Economics and Commerce in the early 1930s.

[16] See, for example, Amadae (2003).

[17] See Downs (1957) and Shapley and Shubik (1954). Buchanan, too, spent some time at RAND, but he says that this had no influence on his thinking regarding public choice analysis (interview with the author, November 5, 1998). When the scholars at RAND became aware of Black's work in the late 1940s, they sent a letter to him requesting offprints of his articles. Upon ascertaining, via the British Consul in San Francisco, the military-oriented mission of RAND, Black apparently decided not to comply with the request (McLean, McMillan, and Monroe 1998: xxiii).

Social Choice and Individual Values (1951) was the first of the influential works in modern public choice analysis and was stimulated by a RAND staff member's query as to whether countries could have utility functions—something required in order to use game theory to model strategic interactions between nations. *Social Choice and Individual Values*, the book that was originally Arrow's Ph.D. dissertation, was ultimately concerned with what he called "the public adoption of economic policy" and the mechanisms by which that takes place (1951: 108).[18] Arrow worked from the perspective that the democratic voting process, like the market process, serves as a mechanism for aggregating preferences—but, he asked, is the democratic process consistent or rational? Arrow adopted the assumption of individual rationality and set out five ethical axioms that he considered relatively noncontroversial, and which he argued that any social choice process or social welfare function should satisfy. Assuming a choice among three alternatives, *x*, *y*, and *z*, the axioms can be stated as follows:[19]

- *Unanimity*: If all individuals prefer *x* to *y*, the social choice process chooses *x* over *y*.
- *Transitivity*: If *x* is preferred to *y* and *y* is preferred to *z*, then *x* is preferred to *z*.
- *Independence of irrelevant alternatives*: A social choice between two alternatives must depend only on the ranking of those two alternatives, and not on the ranking of any other possible alternatives.
- *Unrestricted domain*: The social choice process allows for any possible ordering of preferences over alternatives *x*, *y*, and *z*.
- *Non-dictatorship*: No individual has a status such that when he prefers *x* to *y* and all other individuals prefer *y* to *x*, his preference is preferred in the social ordering.

Arrow showed in what became known as his "Possibility Theorem" that no social welfare function could satisfy all five of these axioms; the impossibility result can be avoided only if one or more of the postulates can be relaxed.[20]

---

[18] Most of the work on *Social Choice and Individual Values* was completed at the Cowles Commission, where Arrow was a research associate, though the project originated during the summer of 1948, when Arrow served as a RAND consultant while on leave from Cowles. A history of the early years of the Cowles Commission, written by economist Carl Christ, can be found in *Economic Theory and Measurement: A Twenty Year Research Report, 1932–1952*, available at http://cowles.econ.yale.edu/P/reports/1932-52b.htm.

[19] Arrow's analysis applies to social choices among three or more alternatives.

[20] For example, plurality voting violates independence of irrelevant alternatives, as fringe candidates can affect outcomes (for example, the third-party presidential candidate who garners 5 percent of the vote but in doing so hands the election to one of the major-party candidates). The unanimity rule violates the non-dictatorship principle, since one person's preferences can trump everyone else's. Standard majority rule gives rise to cycling problems

Arrow's analysis did not imply that there are no useful or reasonable voting methods, simply that none is ideal, or that there is no perfect way of moving from individual preferences to a societal choice among alternatives if we accept that these five axioms must be satisfied. The implication, from an economic perspective, is that we cannot rely on democratic voting processes to generate the optimal outcomes envisioned by Pigovian welfare theory, regardless of the motives of voters, politicians, and bureaucrats.

The works of Arrow and Black had no discernable impact on views of the political process found in the economics and political science literatures in the years immediately following their publication. Economists seemed unconcerned with endogenizing things political. William Mitchell (1999) has suggested that political scientists were largely ignorant of this literature (a hypothesis supported by a perusal of leading political science journals during this period), and that the problem which Arrow and Black addressed—the aggregation of individual preferences into collective decisions—was not of great interest to political scientists.[21] This is consistent with political scientist William Riker's complaint in 1961 that while "the work of Black and Arrow is of great importance both for political theory and the study of political behavior ... on the whole political scientists have tended to ignore this literature" (Riker 1961: 911). Some evidence for this indifference (apart from the paucity of citations) can be gleaned from the fact that a Northwestern University study called "Approaches to the Study of Politics" in the mid-1950s included not a single economist invitee to discuss what politics can borrow from economics (Riker 1959: 209).

Things began to change a bit in the late 1950s and early 1960s with the publication of several works that were to become seminal in the field: Downs' *Economic Theory of Democracy* (1957), Black's *Theory of Committees and Elections* (1958), Riker's *Theory of Political Coalitions* (1962a), Buchanan and Tullock's *The Calculus of Consent* (1962), and Mancur Olson's *Logic of Collective Action* (1965).[22] Taken together, these books and the publication over the next decade of the many articles and books that were stimulated by these early efforts were providing a body of ideas that challenged the orthodox view of the operation of government.

(i.e., x defeats y, y defeats z, but z defeats x, meaning that transitivity is violated); the outcome will then depend upon the order in which the votes are taken, which means that agenda control—a form of dictatorship—is an important determinant of outcomes. Vickery (1960) provides a somewhat simplified restatement of Arrow's proof and Mueller (2003, ch. 24) provides an excellent overview of the theorem and its implications.

[21] Of course, the problem of aggregating individual preferences also poses issues for the Italian literature, which evidences no recognition of the nature of the problem involved.

[22] Not long afterward came Tullock's *Toward a Mathematics of Politics* (1967c), Downs's *Inside Bureaucracy* (1967), and Niskanen's *Bureaucracy and Representative Government* (1971).

From its inception the axiom that has driven public choice analysis is the assumption that voters, politicians, and bureaucrats are self-interested rational actors. The extension of this axiom to the political realm assumed an underlying consistency in human behavior, so that the same forces motivating behavior in one context also do so in other contexts—what economists call "stable preferences."[23] If, as the economist assumes, it is self-interest that drives behavior in the marketplace for goods and services, this consistency demands that self-interest must also govern behavior in other decision-making contexts. This approach placed public choice scholars in the vanguard of a movement that was to see the application of the model of the self-interested rational actor to a wide range of traditionally noneconomic subjects.[24]

EARLY REACTIONS

Because of the relative lack of attention paid to the economics of politics in its formative years, the initial reception accorded to this literature must be traced primarily through the reviews of the major early works in the field.[25] It is interesting both to juxtapose the reactions of economists and political scientists to these works and to examine how these views evolved over a relatively short period of time. As one might expect, the debate centered on the usefulness of the economic/mathematical deductive method versus the more inductive approach of political science, and the extent to which the *homo economicus* assumption held promise for the analysis of the behavior of political agents.

Perhaps not surprisingly, most of the methodological opposition came from within the political science community. Foremost in the minds of these critics was the degree of attachment to the real world of politics evidenced in the economic models. Kenneth Vines (1963: 61) suggested that *The Calculus of Consent* demonstrates limited "political awareness" and that it "derives general propositions about politics according to

---

[23] On the issue of the stable preferences assumption, see Stigler and Becker (1977).

[24] This is further discussed in chapter 7.

[25] On Arrow, see reviews by Somers (1952), Baumol (1952a), and Houthakker (1952); on Black and Newing, see reviews by Richenberg (1953) and Simon (1952); on Black, see reviews by Downs (1959), Harsanyi (1965), and Kort (1959); on Downs, see reviews by Bergson (1958), Banfield (1958), Pennock (1958), Farris (1958), and Diamond (1959); on Riker, see reviews by Fagen (1963), Holz (1963), and Matthews (1963); on Buchanan and Tullock, see reviews by Olson (1962), Downs (1964), Meade (1963), and Ward (1963) within economics, and Gertzog (1964), C.M.P. (1963), Riker (1962b), Vines (1963), Milne (1962), Ulmer (1963), and May (1963) within political science, as well as reviews by sociologist McGinnis (1963) and lawyer Manne (1963).

economic theory but largely outside the political context."[26] This, in turn, led to a great deal of concern regarding the adequacy and usefulness of the results derived from this modeling process. L. J. Richenberg (1953: 131), for example, argued that Black and Newing's models "do not lead to any results that can be interpreted in words: no new propositions emerge about the general relations between private and social choice except at an inescapably mathematical level of abstraction. Mathematical niceties apart, the results are barren." This opinion was echoed by W. Hayward Rogers (1959: 483), who thought that the adoption of the methods and techniques of the natural sciences by political scientists was "producing some interesting and provocative suggestions," but also that an "eagerness to exploit the power of the methodology" had a tendency to lead to "misapplication or overextension" of the techniques employed. Downs's book was, for Rogers, a case in point, being in his opinion essentially devoid of real-world implications.

The gulf between economists and political scientists on the methodological front can be seen in Rogers's argument that a priori deductive theorizing is relevant only to the extent that the underlying assumptions are exactly correct. A useful political theory, he said, must be based upon empirical investigations, and it is only from empirically validated phenomena that further conclusions may be properly deduced (1959: 484–85). This perspective is diametrically opposed to that espoused by Milton Friedman in his "The Methodology of Positive Economics" (1953), where he argued that the ability of a theory to predict successfully is far more important than the realism of its assumptions. While Friedman's methodological position was finding increasing acceptance within economics, political scientists were operating from very different premises. Donald Matthews (1963: 579) summed up the position of many of the political scientist critics when he wrote the following:

> Even the most sympathetic reader ... is likely to put down [Riker's] book undecided as to the utility of such highly abstract and formal models. How much of our limited time, resources, and imagination should be invested in their construction and perfection? Game theory itself was developed in revolt against the constraints of the elegant but increasingly irrelevant model of classical economics. The realism and utility of models are a function, in part, of their inventors' prior understanding of how the real world operates. Do we know enough about politics to construct useful models now? Or do we need more and better empirical studies first?

[26] In fact, this concern was voiced on occasion even *within* this new paradigm—for example in Downs' (1959: 212) criticism of what he saw as the narrow internalism of Black's analysis, particularly his failure to relate his analysis of committee processes to the larger political context and a larger economic theory of politics.

If there was a common thread running through these critiques, it was a fear among political scientists that this work would promote "the *science* of political science at the expense of politics" (May1963: 113).

One aspect of the economic approach that political scientists found particularly vexing was the application of the self-interested rational actor assumption to the political realm. R. S. Milne (1962: 152), for example, compared *The Calculus of Consent* to "a colonizing expedition," and a number of commentators either rejected the rational actor model altogether or at least questioned whether *homo economicus* could move as seamlessly between the economic and political arenas as the theory assumed. Sidney Ulmer's enthusiastic reception of *The Calculus* was tempered by his feeling that the new scholarship had "assumed too hastily that the explicit and implicit assumptions of economic behavior can be carried over to political behavior," and that the extent of the transference could be determined only empirically (Ulmer 1963: 175). Some questioned whether an individualistic framework could be usefully applied to those aspects of the social process that embody a group dynamic and whether the notion of a fully informed rational utility maximizer makes any sense for groups or individuals who are not so well organized (Gertzog 1964: 974; Milne 1962: 152). This criticism was even present within the economics literature, where Abram Bergson—whose welfare economics was very much called into question by this literature—criticized the assumption of vote maximization. "Perhaps the economist himself," he wrote, "is often misguided about motives, if not of bakers then of corporate executives, but this is no reason to compound the error in politics" (Bergson 1958: 437–38, 440).

A number of political scientists, and most of the economist reviewers, however, had a decidedly more positive reaction, and even when disagreeing with the conclusions drawn were favorably disposed toward the possibilities offered by the new methodology. As several of those offering more positive assessments of this methodology were themselves tilling this or related soils, their reactions are perhaps not completely unexpected. Herbert Simon (1952: 638), for example, acknowledged that the assumptions underlying these models "will seem deplorably naïve" to those unfamiliar with them, but both he and John Harsanyi (1965) suggested that there are substantial benefits to treating political theory with the rigorous methods of economics, in no small part because they lend a degree of precision and determinateness to things that are otherwise rather fuzzy.

Downs and Meade were also of the mind that this work had much to offer the study of economics. Downs (1964: 88), in a bit of a slap at both economists and political scientists, noted that "[w]hile economists refine the theoretical conditions for perfect competition down to the last gnat's eyebrow, the gigantic problems of economic choice and allocation within our political institutions are left largely to political scientists and to a few economists working on defense-oriented problems." Yet, he said, the decision processes of government are the same as those analyzed by economists, and economists are "much better tooled" than political scientists to tackle such analysis. Curiously, even Meade (1963: 101) criticized economists for being "much too ready to call in the State as a *deus ex machina* to remove the imperfections of the laissez-faire market without examining the implications of this view for the political, as contrasted with the economic, behaviour of the individual citizen." He found *The Calculus*, with its "assumption that the individual citizen is wholly selfish in his behaviour in the voting booth and in the market-place," to be "a most laudable attempt to close [this] gap"—a somewhat surprising assessment since Buchanan and Tullock's analysis very much called into question the ability of government effectively to bring off the types of optimal policy solutions that Meade had championed in his writings.[27]

These sentiments go some distance toward explaining why this public choice literature received a favorable reception in parts of the economics community. It is fair to say that the theory of economic policy had long neglected to analyze the ability of government to carry out effectively the policies proffered by the theory. For those who were opposed to the interventionist possibilities suggested by the traditional theory, and for those who were simply intellectually curious about the ability of government to effect optimal interventions, the emerging economics of politics had much to offer—particularly given its formalist nature.

One is still left, however, with the question of why this work—when it was not ignored—was well received, or at least not rejected outright, within certain quarters of the political science community, where no strong opposing camp emerged for two decades. One possible answer is that there was no perceived threat here, since political scientists were not quick to pick up this stream of research en masse. Yet there is certainly more to it than this, given that the number of publications by economists in leading political science journals and citations to works in this area were rising steadily as the 1960s progressed.[28] One part of the explanation that emerges is that political science has historically been open to, and even relied upon, the insights of other disciplines in the furtherance of its own, and that this created a degree of receptivity for the economic approach that would not otherwise have been present. As Vines (1963: 160) pointed out,

> An endemic characteristic of political science has been its use of theories and data drawn from other disciplines. Traditional political science used methods and data from history, philosophy, and law. Present-day political science has

---

[27] See chapter 3.
[28] On publications, see section titled "Words Written Down" in this chapter.

supplemented these with data and theories drawn from modern social science, from psychology, sociology, economics and anthropology, and from mathematics. Definitions and methods may be initiated by political scientists, but these original efforts are apt to be either syntheses or else adaptations of data and methods used in the social sciences for the study of politics.

Irwin Gertzog (1964: 974), for one, found himself impressed by the perspective of the "sister discipline," economics, and lauded the "extension of economic terminology and orientations to the essential concepts of democratic political theory," particularly the application of the notion of economic or marketplace exchange to political organization and the interpretation of voting in terms of its economic value.

Additional evidence on this score can be found in a powerful new interdisciplinary movement—the behavioralist approach—that was emerging within political science at this same time.[29] The behavioral approach drew heavily upon insights from sociology and psychology to examine individual behavior, including power relationships, within the political realm. While both the behavioralist and economic approaches focused on individual behavior, their methods, the resulting analysis, and the ideological overtones were very different.[30]

A further piece of the explanation for the reception of this work can be found in what some political scientists perceived as limitations of the extant political science paradigm, and to a search for moorings within political science that would create an openness to a new body of theory that offered substantial promise. Gertzog (1964: 473–74), for one, said that the political scientists continued to search for theoretical frameworks that would "give perspective and direction to the study of politics," and, as Ulmer put it, "lift political theory out of the abyss of diffused speculation" (1963:171). It was thought that the economics of politics offered a potential solution. Indeed, both the behavioralist revolution, where empirical study and statistical analysis played an important role, and the economic approach were responses to the perceived unscientific shortcomings of the existing theory.

One particularly significant aspect of the dissatisfaction within political science was the felt need to give the discipline a more scientific, theoretical underpinning—which included, indeed required in the minds of some, working from restrictive and often unrealistic assumptions (Hotz 1963: 295; Banfield 1958: 324). The feeling was that "mathematical approaches

---

[29] See Mitchell (1999).

[30] This openness may help to explain why the invasion of economics into political science generated a less hostile reception than within law: the openness of political science contrasts sharply with the jurisprudential tradition of insularity and the view of law (from the inside) as an autonomous, self-contained discipline (Posner 1987). See chapter 7, infra.

to social phenomena ... are not merely fashionable endeavors, but ... serve the purpose of discovering or comprehending relationships that cannot be fully explored by exclusive reliance on qualitative interpretation" (Kort 1959: 327). In the process, these approaches would bring "formal elegance to the discussion of matters which are usually very muddy" (Banfield 1958: 325) and "do precisely what good theory ought to do: namely, give guidance to empirical research" (Pennock 1958: 541).

The opinions of political science held by those more closely associated with these new ideas were even more stridently critical. Henry Manne (1963: 1065), who figured prominently in the development of law and economics during this same period, commented that "it is a commonplace observation that political theory largely failed to develop systematic tools of analysis comparable to those of economics" and "allow(s) neither for quantification nor objective evaluations." Because of this, he argued, political science "has become more and more comparable to descriptive sociology than to a mathematical or logical science." Riker was even more abusive to his colleagues in political science, offering stinging commentaries on the state of the field:

> There is considerable intellectual ferment among political scientists today owing to the fact that the traditional methods of their discipline seem to have wound up in a cul-de-sac. These traditional methods—i.e., history writing, the description of institutions, and legal analysis—... can produce only wisdom and neither science nor knowledge. (1962a: viii)[31]

> As numerous writers have pointed out, political theory as a field of academic concentration has been in a confused and unproductive state for at least the last generation.... Refusing ... to theorize themselves, most academicians have been limited to a consideration of intellectual primitives or of, what amounts to the same thing, the rantings and ideological tergiversations of half-educated modern pamphleteers. In almost no other field do the professionals thus abase themselves before the ancients and the amateurs. (1962b: 408)

Meanwhile, economics had been able to broaden its scope as the result of developments within utility theory and the application of the theory of games—the result of which was that non-market interactions, such as those taking place within the political arena, could be brought under the economist's umbrella. Peter Ordeshook, who had been a student of Riker, said that political science had failed to develop theories that were as successful as those developed by economists and that this left political science

---

[31] Even some contemporary critics of the rational choice approach to politics acknowledge that "much of what passes for the scientific study of politics is anything but that" (Green and Shapiro 1994: 10).

at a "distinct disadvantage" in terms of "its ability to conjecture about, advise on, and devise policy" (1969: 1274). Rejecting other attempts then being made to revitalize the field, Riker (1962b: 409) argued that the economic approach to politics appeared to be the only thing on the horizon that offered "some hope of a really successful reorientation of political theory."[32]

All of this having been said, the positive-to-lukewarm reviews of the early works in public choice are almost certainly an upward-biased indication of the general reaction to public choice analysis within the political science community. One gets a hint of the more severely negative undercurrent within certain quarters from Buchanan: "*Successful* invasion of an established discipline by 'outsiders' generates strong emotions,"[33] he said, with the result that "some traditional political scientists of a narrow bent tend to become somewhat violently and irrationally prejudiced against all efforts in public choice theory. They see their own intellectual capital threatened with rapid depreciation, and they are led to resist."[34] Buchanan also suggested, however, that it was not resistance to "economic imperialism" per se that drove much of the political science community's hostility, but, rather, conflicts over ideology—individualist versus collectivist.[35]

It is indisputable that much of the public choice literature, both pro and con, has ideological overtones, even if little of the early reaction dealt explicitly with this issue. Interestingly, the one place where the ideological question does come out strongly is not in the political science literature, but in Mancur Olson's review of *The Calculus* in the *American Economic Review*. Olson (1962: 1217) called the book "a stimulating new addition" to the emerging economics of politics literature, but he was critical of what he considered the "implicit ideological emphasis" of the book. This perspective, he argued, distinguishes the book from most other work in the area, and at once raises cause for scholarly concern and is the source of scholarly possibilities: "The somewhat eccentric ideological quality that characterizes [the authors'] writing," he said, "unfortunately narrows the appeal and perhaps obscures the objective importance of some of their theories." Yet, he continued, "Their right-wing view is ... also a blessing in that it gives them an unusual perspective that must account for many of their fresh insights."

---

[32] As we will see in chapter 7, the same arguments were made about what economics could offer to law.

[33] Letter from James M. Buchanan to Frank L. Hereford, 25 August 1967; emphasis in original, BHA.

[34] Draft letter from Buchanan and Tullock to Dr. Leslie F. Malpass (not sent), May 1970, BHA.

[35] James M. Buchanan, interview with the author, November 5, 1998. Buchanan and Tullock have suggested on several occasions that these forces played a significant role in their departure from the University of Virginia. This matter is discussed later.

In a letter to Olson subsequent to the publication of this review, Buchanan took issue with the imputation of "right-wing prejudice." He argued that "the book was devoted to deriving a simple logic of political choice from a position of methodological individualism" and wondered whether Olson was actually suggesting that "anyone who tries to derive a logical basis for democratic government from a consideration of individual choice is guilty of right-wing prejudice."[36] Buchanan thought that Olson's interpretation was, "fundamentally, a reaction of a strong emotional nature to the ideas," rather than a "reasoned position that is based on careful examination of the arguments themselves."[37] He did allow that the book stimulated in others, especially political scientists, reactions similar to those expressed by Olson, but he believed that these reactions actually derived from the inability of the readers to distinguish between methodology and ideology.[38]

We have noted that the impact of the early published works in public choice on the larger professional communities of economics and political science was neither instantaneous nor widespread. One correspondent lamented to Buchanan in early 1970 that "so few economists are aware that this theory even exists, much less that it says some interesting things" and found "sadder yet ... the seeming unawareness of political scientists that exciting insights into collective behavior can be gleaned from simple models employing the behavioral assumption of rationality and the methodology of economics."[39] In fact, it is safe to say that the early scholarship in the field provided only a partial stimulus to the development of public choice; it was through other forces that the field really became established and solidified.

GETTING "CENTERED"

Science Meets Ideology: The Thomas Jefferson Center

One cannot properly understand the evolution of public choice analysis without an understanding of the integration of positive and normative elements surrounding its genesis—Buchanan's comments to Olson not-

---

[36] Letter from James M. Buchanan to Mancur Olson, not dated, BHA.

[37] Ibid.

[38] Ibid.

[39] Letter from Professor A. James Heins to Buchanan, March 1970, excerpted in Center for Study of Public Choice NSF Proposal, 1970, p. 9, BHA. On this point, see also Mitchell (1999).

withstanding. Public choice emerged out of the Virginia Political Economy tradition that began to crystallize in the late 1950s through the founding, by Buchanan and G. Warren Nutter, of the Thomas Jefferson Center for Studies in Political Economy at the University of Virginia. The center's first brochure describes its program as follows:

> The Center is organized to promote scholarly discussion of the basic ideals of Western civilization and of the solutions to modern social problems most in accord with those ideals.
>
> The Center is a community of scholars who wish to preserve a social order based on individual liberty. The Center will encourage students to see the philosophical as well as the technical issues entering into problems of social organization.[40]

This overtly normative purpose put Virginia political economy on a course that was consciously at odds with what Buchanan and Nutter saw as a left-wing, interventionist tide within academia at that time, and served to give it its highly distinctive flavor.[41] Interestingly, both Buchanan and Nutter were ardent socialists in their graduate student days; but under the spell of Frank Knight and others at the University of Chicago—what Buchanan has called their "enlightenment through an understanding of the market process" (1983: 7)—their socialist views melted away.[42]

But the center did not see itself simply as a countervailing force against academic radicalism. Fundamental to the center's orientation was a profound dissatisfaction with economic analysis as it was being practiced within the profession. As Buchanan (1983: 6) noted,

> We were concerned, first of all, by what seemed to us to be a developing neglect of the basics of economics. Both Warren Nutter and I were Chicago economists, and Chicago economists of the Frank Knight, Henry Simons, Lloyd Mints, Aaron Director vintage. The basics of economics were those of price theory, not formal mathematics, and price theory applied to real world issues. The economic organization, the market process, and the working of this organization operating through the pricing structure were the subject matter of the discipline. Political economy was nothing more than this subject matter embedded within the framework of society, described by the "laws and institutions" about which Adam Smith wrote. To us, quite simply, political economy meant nothing more than a return to the stance of the

[40] Brochure for the Thomas Jefferson Center for Studies in Political Economy, 1957–58, p. 1.

[41] Radicalism is a relative concept, of course. The radicalism with which Buchanan *et al.* were concerned was seen as anything but radical by the members of the Union for Radical Political Economics (URPE), which was founded in the late 1960s.

[42] Ronald Coase, who was at Virginia and affiliated with the Center during this period, reports a similar transformation of views, in his case under the influence of Arnold Plant at the London School of Economics. See Coase (1988b).

classical political economists. Aside from Chicago, we saw programs else-where in economics neglecting these very foundations of our discipline.[43]

This positive stance of analyzing the market process, however, had a larger normative goal, as Buchanan (1983: 6–7) himself has since said:

> Let me now also admit openly and without apology then or now, that we were motivated by our conviction that if these foundations are neglected, a society in which individuals retain their liberties is not sustainable. We had faith than an understanding of the price system offered the best possible av-enue for the generation of support for free institutions. We did not feel any need for explicitly ideological polemic.

Their purpose, Buchanan acknowledged, was intentionally *"subversive"* (1983: 7). Through research and the training of graduate students, the center hoped to alter the focus of economic analysis and the attitudes of the scholarly community regarding the efficacy of the market system.

The center's staff expanded steadily in the early years, and included Bu-chanan, Nutter, Leland Yeager, Rutledge Vining, Ronald Coase, Andrew Whinston, and Tullock (who was brought in as a postdoctoral fellow at its inception and returned on a "permanent" basis in 1962). Both the center and the individual scholars associated with it received significant financial support for their activities from a variety of sources.[44] Among other things, this financial support funded a range of scholarly research projects and allowed the center to establish an active program of visiting scholars, the roster of which included Frank Knight, Maurice Allais, Duncan Black, Bertil Ohlin, T. W. Hutchison, F. A. Hayek, and Michael Polanyi.

During these early years, it became increasingly clear to the center's scholars that their normative goals could not be accomplished simply through the study of the market process; securing "the intellectual-analytical foundations of a free society," said Buchanan, requires "a complementary understanding of the political process" (1983: 10). The result was a new focus on the study of political institutions and their interaction with the market system—a major component of which evolved into public choice analysis. In 1963, the center moved to solidify, in an institutional sense, its mission in the area of public choice analysis by forming the Commit-

---

[43] This statement assumes a degree of homogeneity between Smith and the nineteenth-century classical economists and between Smith and the Virginia and Chicago school ap-proaches that is by no means universally agreed upon. See Evensky (2005), Samuels and Medema (2005), Robbins (1952), Samuels (1962), and O'Brien (2004).

[44] In the center's early years, these sources included the Volker Fund, the Relm Founda-tion, the General Electric Foundation, and the Lilly Endowment, as well as the University of Virginia. Both the Volker Fund and the Relm Foundation were committed to supporting the ideals underlying the Thomas Jefferson Center's mission, as expressed in the previously quoted passages from the center's brochure.

tee for the Analysis of Nonmarket Decision-Making. The purpose of the committee, which consisted of Buchanan, Tullock, and Paul David, was to "coordinate the Center's continuing interest in the research of American scholars in this new and growing area of emphasis."[45] This interest, however, was not limited to America. By the mid-1960s there were signs of an emerging internationalization of the field, as scholars from Europe began to inquire about and hold visiting positions at the center to do research in the field, and graduate students from India, Europe, and Japan were in residence. Buchanan and Tullock also coordinated postdoctoral research programs for several scholars who went on to be significant players in the field, including Francisco Forte (Italy), David Chapman (England), and Thomas Borcherding (United States).

In spite of its successes in promoting new frameworks for economic analysis, in the end it was the Thomas Jefferson Center's normative aspect that, according to Buchanan, played the major role in its demise. An early hint of things to come appeared already in 1960, when the Ford Foundation refused to provide funding for the center. Buchanan has long insisted that Ford did so for ideological reasons.[46] In a chronology that he put together in the mid-1970s, Buchanan wrote of a meeting that included himself, Nutter, University of Virginia President Edgar Shannon, and Kermit Gordon of the Ford Foundation, during which Gordon cited "the statement that 'the Center is a community of scholars who want to preserve a social order based on individual liberty' as evidence that the Department of Economics at Virginia is opposed to academic freedom."[47] According to Buchanan, Gordon asserted that "the Ford Foundation cannot consider making any grants to support work in economics at Virginia until its Department becomes at least as well balanced as those at Yale and Harvard."[48] Of course, the feeling among the Virginia group was that a center such as this was needed precisely because these other departments were *not* balanced.

Whatever the merits of Buchanan's chronology of events, this experience with Ford was only the beginning. In 1962, according to Buchanan, the university administration began to investigate "ways of changing or offsetting the 'political orientation' of the Department of Economics."[49] In 1963, a faculty committee with no representative from the economics department wrote a secret self-study report on the department for an

---

[45] Thomas Jefferson Center Report, 1963, BHA.

[46] It should be noted, however, that Ford does not have a reputation for being a leftist-oriented foundation.

[47] Buchanan, "Chronology of Significant Events," April 1976, p. 1, BHA.

[48] Ibid.

[49] Ibid.

external accreditation committee.[50] This report contended that while the department enjoyed substantial repute within the profession, "the repute enjoyed is regarded by the vast majority of economists as of a distinctly unfavorable character."[51] The root of the problem, according to the report, was the wholesale commitment to a single point of view that "make[s] it difficult or impossible for other views to find expression, whether in instruction or research."[52] The result, it was maintained, was that hiring decisions, field offerings, fellowship awards, and dissertation topics were all pervaded by the department's ideological stance.[53] Regarding field offerings, for example, the report stated that "it appears that one of the major consequences of this ideological commitment has been to handicap students on both undergraduate and graduate levels by leaving them without access to those fields of economics which remain unrepresented in the department because rejected [sic] by the prevailing doctrinairism."[54]

Based upon these factors, the report concluded that the university "would seem to be failing in its responsibility to give its students in Economics the best possible comprehensive training, without seeking to commit them to any particular position."[55] The study recommended "additions to the staff of full professorial members of [a] different, 'modern,' outlook ... in order to inject pluralism into an otherwise closed society." In doing so, the report specifically stated, "Care should be taken in making or renewing non-tenure appointments, as well as those of higher rank, to avoid further recruitment from the Chicago School," and the attempt should be made "to insure that a more mixed body of graduate students is created by discriminating assignment of fellowship grants."[56] While the report focused on the economics department, the Thomas Jefferson Center did not escape criticism. The report charged that "the degree to which the Thomas Jefferson Center through its funds for research and study exercises undue influence upon what should be an independent University Department constitutes still another obvious center of needed administrative inquiry."[57]

Things moved steadily downhill following the completion of this report. In 1964, Ronald Coase received an offer from the University of Chicago, and the University of Virginia made no attempt to retain him. In 1966, the administration refused to match an offer that Andrew Whinston re-

---

[50] Buchanan notes that this report was not seen by members of the Department until 1974. Ibid., 5.

[51] Excerpt from Self Study Report, University of Virginia, 1963, p. 1, BHA.

[52] Ibid.

[53] Ibid., 2–3.

[54] Ibid., 3.

[55] Ibid., 3.

[56] Ibid., 3–4.

[57] Ibid., 4.

ceived from Purdue.[58] The department's recommendation that Tullock be promoted to full professor was denied in 1965, 1966, and 1967, after which he resigned to take up a full professorship at Rice University. The treatment of Whinston and Tullock led Buchanan to threaten resignation unless the university made a serious attempt to rehire these two individuals. This controversy spilled over into the local and campus newspapers when certain current and former graduate students charged that the university was "systematically destroying the Department because of its alleged conservatism."[59] This controversy continued for nearly three months, with attacks and defenses coming from all sides. When no effort to rehire Tullock and Whinston was forthcoming, Buchanan resigned and moved to UCLA.

In a letter to Leland Yeager informing him of his decision to resign from Virginia, Buchanan said that the decision was a difficult one given his strong loyalty to the department and the graduate program there. "By any reasonably fair evaluation," he said, "our whole efforts here must, I think, be judged a success, and I am personally very proud of the work we have accomplished as a team."[60] The question, at that point, was whether this success would continue.

Virginia Redux: The Center for Study of Public Choice

Shortly after the meltdown at Virginia, public choice was reestablished—indeed more defined and solidified—at Virginia Polytechnic Institute through the establishment of the Center for Study of Public Choice. Charles Goetz, a former student of Buchanan at Virginia, was on the faculty at VPI and spearheaded the push to bring in Buchanan and Tullock to establish public choice at VPI,[61] which made "strengthening the program in Public Choice" the centerpiece of its plan to develop a strong emphasis in the social sciences.[62] Tullock was appointed to the VPI economics faculty in 1968, and the Center for Study of Public Choice was established at that time with Tullock as interim director. Buchanan came over from UCLA in 1969, assuming the position of general director of the center, while Tullock moved over to the position of editorial director. Others affiliated with the

---

[58] Coase was offered $6000 more than he was making at Virginia; the University countered with an offer of a $500 raise. Whinston was offered a $4000 raise by Purdue, as well as a full professorship.

[59] Buchanan, "Chronology," 3. Much of the information reported in this paragraph is drawn from this source.

[60] Letter from James M. Buchanan to Leland Yeager, January 16, 1968, BHA.

[61] Interview with James Buchanan, November 5, 1998.

[62] Center for Study of Public Choice National Science Foundation proposal, 1970, p. ii, BHA.

center from its inception were Goetz, as well as Joseph Bernd and James Herndon, both of the VPI political science department. The decision to establish a "public choice" center rather than a "political economy" center, as at Virginia, was a logical consequence of the focus of the work being done by those affiliated with the center at VPI.[63]

The plans for the development of the center were substantial and included several new faculty lines, bringing in prominent visiting scholars for substantial periods, six postdoctoral fellowships annually, summer research fellowships, graduate student fellowships, the development of an experimental laboratory, efforts at instructional innovation—such as the use of experimental activities in the classroom—that would introduce the students to fundamental issues in public choice analysis, as well as the regular sponsorship of general and small thematic conferences. VPI committed to over a half-million dollars in funding for the center, and additional funds were secured from other sources.

An economics Ph.D. program was established at VPI in 1968 and, from the outset, it emphasized public choice analysis, including the option for students to take a double field in the area, the effect of which was that virtually all of a student's education beyond the core would be in the field of public choice. This course of study involved a year-long sequence in public finance with a substantial public choice flavor and a year-long sequence in "Collective Decisions" that examined the economic theory of democracy, the theory of constitutions, voting models, and so on, as well as incorporating heavy doses of game theory and model building and an original research project. A similar course of study was offered at the undergraduate level. Plans were also developed for a Ph.D. program in political science that would allow a concentration in public choice, and students in both the economics and political science Ph.D. programs were encouraged to take courses across the two departments.[64]

The center grew quickly, with a dozen permanent research associates on board by the mid-1970s and an active and wide-ranging program of research. Even with its overtly public choice emphasis, the Center, like the Thomas Jefferson Center, carried out a broad-based program in political economy—including the study of subjects such as crime, charity and income redistribution, fiscal federalism, and education. It also carried on an active program of publication, including a book and monograph series and the housing of the editorial office of the journal *Public Choice*.

The internationalization of public choice continued during this time, as the center received numerous inquiries annually from professors and graduate students, in both economics and political science, from around

[63] Ibid.
[64] Ibid., 11–12 and Attachment 4.

the world who wished to come to VPI to study public choice analysis. The extent of the attention that this work was attracting is evidenced in an excerpt from the Yugoslavian journal *Ekonomska Politika* in April 1970: "The political sciences have now found an application for electronic computers and mathematical models: at the Virginia Polytechnic Institute, for example, a young team is performing pioneering work in the field of 'the economics of politics' ... —and that is a field which offers economists a wide area of investigation for the next twenty years."[65]

Molding the Next Generation

Perhaps most important for the long-term growth of the field was the heavy emphasis placed by these centers, from the beginning, on the support and training of graduate students—funded by, among others, the Earhart Foundation. The role of these centers in turning out strong graduates who went on to make significant impacts in public choice and related areas should not be minimized. The University of Virginia turned out numerous successful graduates during the Thomas Jefferson Center's heyday, including a number of individuals who went on to become significant figures in the development of public choice analysis: Otto Davis, Charles Goetz, Mark Pauly, Charles Plott, William Craig Stubblebine, Robert Tollison, Richard Wagner, and Thomas Willett (Tollison 1991). This continued at VPI, where the graduate students included Richard McKenzie, James Marchand, Marilyn Flowers, Gordon Brady, Randall Holcombe, Eugenia Toma, and Mark Toma (Tollison 1991). Riker was also training students at Rochester, and several of his students, including Peter Ordeshook, Peter Aranson, and Kenneth Shepsle, went on to make their mark in the field. Vincent Ostrom was doing likewise at Indiana.

The students who came through the programs at Virginia and VPI diffused themselves across the nation's colleges and universities, and, significantly, a number of them came to occupy professorships at leading universities. Many of these scholars have also held temporary appointments in important governmental posts.[66] Their influence extended to the far reaches of the profession, and it may safely be said that if Buchanan, Tullock, and their colleagues made the world safe for public choice, their students helped to solidify its place within the academic culture.

---

[65] Translated from *Ekonomska Politika*, April 6, 1970, pp. 45–46, in Center for Study of Public Choice NSF Proposal, 1970, p. 9, BHA.

[66] These posts included the Council of Economic Advisors (as senior staff economist), the Federal Trade Commission, the Department of the Treasury, the National Science Foundation, and the economist staff of the U.S. Congress.

On a more broad level, however, public choice's inroads into the formal curricula of economics and political science outside of places like VPI, Rochester, and Indiana proceeded "indirectly and with little uniformity."[67] Even so, some important early strides were made. The decade of the 1960s saw a broadening of the content of standard public finance courses to include public choice analysis and applications. Courses specifically focusing on public choice were introduced at both the undergraduate and graduate levels in a number of institutions, and graduate research concentrations in the field began to emerge, albeit slowly. The introduction of the public choice perspective into the political science education proceeded more slowly. The first political science textbook written from a public choice perspective, Joyce M. Mitchell and William C. Mitchell's *Political Analysis and Public Policy*, was published in 1969, but it did not attract imitators. There was both resistance to the teaching of these new methods and not insignificant barriers to entry on the students' side, owing to the investment costs involved in mastering the requisite economics and mathematics. The much simpler quantitative tools employed by the behavioralists required a smaller investment and offered the additional attraction of being much more welcome within the professional community.

CARVING OUT A FIELD

Meetings of the Minds

The beginning of the institutionalization of public choice within the larger academic community came through the organization of several scholarly conferences in the 1960s. The first of these conferences, which was organized by Buchanan and Tullock following the initial favorable reviews of *The Calculus of Consent*,[68] has been referred to variously as the "Conference on Converging Trends in Politics and Economics," the "Conference on the Pure Theory of Collective Decision-Making," and the "Conference on Nonmarket Decision-Making."[69] It was held at the William Faulkner House at the University of Virginia under the auspices of the Thomas Jefferson Center in October 1963 and sponsored by the National Science Foundation. The conference included as participants prominent economists and political scientists,[70] and its organization was relatively informal:

[67] Center for Study of Public Choice National Science Foundation Proposal, 1970, pp. 6–7. See also Dow and Munger (1990) and Mitchell (1999).

[68] Letter from James M. Buchanan to Sonja Amadae, February 26, 1997, BHA.

[69] See, for example, Mancur Olson, "The Proposed Interdisciplinary Committee on Nonmarket Decision Making," 1966, BHA, and TJ Report, 1964, p. 7.

[70] The economists included Buchanan, John G. Cross (Institute for Defense Analysis),

rather than having paper presentations, the participants talked about the research currently underway in the field and what could be done to further the development of this work.[71] In spite of Buchanan's concerns up to a few days before the conference as to whether the event would even come off, he found that "a certain community of interest did develop" and thought the conference "a great success." He also suggested that, because of the diversity of perspectives present, the conference "takes the right-wing onus off us to an extent, and it establishes our claim to scholarship, so to speak."[72] In fact, the conference was sufficiently successful that the center formed the "Committee for the Analysis of Nonmarket Decision-Making," made up of Buchanan, Tullock, and political scientist Paul David. It was determined both that continued meetings were in order and that the center should look into the publication of a series of research papers in the area.[73]

A second conference was held at the Big Meadows Lodge in Virginia in October 1964 and featured papers by Mancur Olson, John Rawls, and Henry Manne.[74] The general discussion held at the meeting's end suggested that there were several issues "relating to title, formal organization, conference focus, and breadth of participation" that needed to be worked out, and a committee was appointed to deal with these issues.[75] Thereafter, and reflective of its quick maturation, the group attempted to establish a national organization loosed of its direct ties to the Thomas Jefferson Center. One significant aspect of this was a drive to seek status as a subcommittee under the auspices of the Social Science Research Council—an effort that was

---

Otto Davis (Carnegie, and Virginia alumnus), Anthony Downs (RAND), John Harsanyi (Wayne State), James March (Carnegie), Ronald McKean (RAND), Henry Oliver (Indiana), Mancur Olson (Princeton), Jerome Rothenberg (Northwestern), Craig Stubblebine (Delaware, and Virginia alumnus), Gordon Tullock (Virginia), and Andrew Whinston (Cowles and Yale). The political scientists in attendance were Edward Banfield (Harvard), Paul David (Virginia), Gerald Garvey (U.S. Air Force Academy), Stanley Kelley (Princeton), Gerald Kramer (Rochester), Vincent Ostrom (Resources for the Future), and William Riker (Rochester) (Thomas Jefferson Center Report, 1964, pp. 21–22).

[71] Conversation with James M. Buchanan, November 5, 1998.

[72] James M. Buchanan, "journal" entries, September and October 1963, BHA.

[73] TJ Center Report, 1964, pp. 6–8. Banfield, Harsanyi, McKean, Ostrom, and Riker were appointed to serve the "committee" in an advisory capacity.

[74] New to the conference in 1964 were philosophers Robert Cunningham (University of San Francisco) and Rawls (Harvard), law professor Henry Manne (George Washington), economist Charles Stewart (George Washington), and political scientists Harold Guetzkow (Northwestern), Frederick Roberts (Delaware), and Glendon Schubert (Michigan State) (TJ Center Report, 1964, pp. 21–22).

[75] W. C. Stubblebine, "Proceedings of the Big Meadows Conference, October 12–13, 1964," p. 17, BHA. Graduate students were also involved in these conferences as observers. Goetz and Plott were in attendance at the Faulkner House conference, and Plott and Wagner at the Big Meadows conference.

ultimately unsuccessful. The SSRC's Committee on Governmental and Legal Processes agreed to sponsor the third conference, which would allow them to scout out this new enterprise, and that conference (organized by Riker) was held in New York City in April 1966.[76] Although the group was growing, and evidenced "considerable unity of interest," Buchanan felt that the continued existence of the group was "highly uncertain."[77] A fourth conference, again sponsored by the SSRC, was held in Chicago in December 1967; attendance here numbered thirty-seven—indicative of the group's continued expansion. It was at this meeting that the group adopted the name "Public Choice Society" and began the process of establishing a formal organization, including the drafting of a constitution and the designation of Vincent Ostrom as chairman.

Thereafter, the field continued to grow and achieved institutional solidity. By 1970, the Public Choice Society had more than five hundred members, and the conference had become an annual event.[78] More than eighty scholars attended the 1971 meeting held in Blacksburg, Va., and although the ranks of economists participating exceeded those of the political scientists, there was substantial political science representation on the program. This meeting of the society represented a substantial expansion over the previous conferences: nearly twenty papers were presented, and there was a session that dealt with "Teaching and Courses Related to Public Choice." While the society had been divided on the issue of whether to retain the small, seminar-type format or attempt to expand the conference in the manner of larger professional societies,[79] this dramatic early expansion makes it quite clear that growth was the order of the day.

The decade of the 1960s also saw increasing acceptance of the study of nonmarket phenomena within the economics profession at large. With some aggressive pushing by Buchanan and Tullock, sessions on nonmarket decision-making were held at American Economic Association meetings in 1963, 1964, 1967, and 1968 (the last jointly with the Public Choice Society),[80] with papers presented by a number of the individuals who

[76] Papers were offered by Davis and Wildavsky on the appropriations process, Downs on bureaucracy, and Harsanyi on games with incomplete information, and each participant was afforded ten minutes to discuss his own current research in the area. New attendees included economists Julius Margolis (Stanford), Charles Plott (Purdue), and Oliver Williamson (Pennsylvania); political scientists Hayward Alker (Yale), John Crecine (Michigan), and Peter Ordeshook (Rochester graduate student); and sociologists James S. Coleman (Johns Hopkins) and Robert McGinnis (Cornell).

[77] James M. Buchanan, journal, April 23, 1966.

[78] Center for Study of Public Choice National Science Foundation proposal, 1970, p. 6.

[79] Ostrom, Memorandum to Members and Prospective Members of the Public Choice Society, September 10, 1969, BHA.

[80] Buchanan recalls that they were never invited, but still managed to get on the program. Interview with James M. Buchanan, November 5, 1998.

were active in the society's evolution—for example, Buchanan, Tullock, Downs, Black, and Harsanyi—and discussants ranging from pioneers in the field to a group as diverse as Nathan Rosenberg, A. Allan Schmid, and Benjamin Ward, none of whom would be identified with the perspective that came to be so closely associated with public choice analysis.[81] The topics of the papers ranged from standard economics of politics fare to the analysis of traditional issues in public finance in light of insights from the economics of political behavior, and these sessions succeeded in bringing this emerging field to the attention of a wider audience.

The decision of the Committee for the Analysis of Nonmarket Decision-Making at the 1966 New York conference to ask the SSRC "to create an interdisciplinary committee that would organize and finance ... a series of conferences and publications" on nonmarket decision-making[82] is interesting for the perspective that the group's proposal, written by Mancur Olson, sheds on its thoughts regarding its own work and the state of economics and political science at that time. We have already mentioned that many political scientists were dissatisfied with the state of their discipline. Likewise, many economists found both economics and political science less than useful for evaluating the government's ability to carry out policy successfully, and they felt that public choice offered the potential to remedy this deficiency. The rationale offered by Olson for the establishment of an SSRC subcommittee reflects this—specifically, "the conviction that certain problems and methods had been neglected in economics and political science, and that the previous meetings of this conference had shown promise of overcoming this neglect."[83] Those attending these early conferences felt that "the problems and approaches that were discussed at the conferences were generally neglected in professional meetings of both economists and political scientists"—in particular, that economists neglected "certain types of substantive problems" (those involving economic processes occurring outside of the market context) and that political scientists neglected "certain methods of theory construction and research."[84] Economists, Olson contended,

> have been working with considerable success for more than a century and a half to explain how well or how badly markets function in various circumstances, [but] they have barely begun to consider how governments or other types of organization will perform these functions. Economists will

---

[81] Rosenberg's research dealt with the economics of technical change; Schmid worked on law and economics and public choice issues from an institutionalist perspective; Ward was very much his own man but would be classified by many as a Marxist.

[82] Mancur Olson, "The Proposed Interdisciplinary Committee on Nonmarket Decision Making," 1966, p. 1, BHA.

[83] Ibid.

[84] Ibid., 1–2.

presumably have to draw upon the insights and evidence gathered by political scientists and sociologists as they attempt to develop appropriate models of the economic behavior of governments and other organizations.[85]

Political scientists, meanwhile, had, in the view of conference participants, "neglected to master certain scholarly methods of extraordinary importance," and only rarely used modeling techniques and statistical testing. The definition of modeling employed here by Olson was very specific: "There has been very little (nontrivial) *deductive* theory in political science—almost no model building or theory in the sense in which these words are used in economics."[86] The result was that "those political problems that are logically too complex to be feasibly capable of solution unaided by common sense, and which demand properly theoretical or mathematical modes of thinking, have not usually been studied."[87] Olson's suggestion that the economic method would serve to broaden political theory is particularly interesting given that the modeling approaches that became so central to economics over the course of the twentieth century are today usually accused of *narrowing* the scope of economic analysis.

Olson's memo reflected a similarly dismissive attitude toward the quantitative side of political science:

> Though not unmindful of the widespread use of quantitative research in political science and sociology, [the political scientists at the conferences on nonmarket decision-making] have been concerned that the emphasis has been on the use of non-parametric techniques for testing what are essentially qualitative hypotheses. This has been due in part to the fact that the existing political theory has not lent itself into ready translation into a specific mathematical model or a specific set of interrelated quantitative hypotheses. Even when a specific theoretically derived hypothesis can be verified or falsified empirically, the overall importance of the empirical test is often unclear because of the non-deductive character of political theory. It is not, for example, clear

---

[85] Ibid., 3. It is worth noting that the borrowing here has been much more of political science from economics than of economics from political science.

[86] Ibid., 3, emphasis in original. This view is echoed in remarks that Tullock made to Buchanan in a letter written sometime in the late 1950s or early 1960s: "I think that you are too kind to the modern political scientist. His position is really based on no line of reasoning at all. Vague feelings and confused emotions, together with a lot of description of institutions and historical development make up the intellectual equipment of this discipline. Letter from Gordon Tullock to James M. Buchanan, n.d., BHA.

[87] Mancur Olson, "The Proposed Interdisciplinary Committee on Nonmarket Decision-Making," 1966, p. 3. This is consistent with the view that economics has brought added rigor to these traditionally noneconomic areas. See, for example, Lazear (2000).

whether, or how, or how much, the refutation of a specific hypothesis will affect the overall conception of, say, democracy or political stability.[88]

This statement is somewhat ironic, given the record of the discussion at the 1964 Big Meadows conference. There, Otto Davis had raised the question of how one might go about validating models of nonmarket decision-making, and the discussion that followed does not appear to have been particularly fruitful.[89] Indeed, by the standards of evidence reflected in the Olson memo, the evidence-to-theory ratio in public choice remained very low for a long time, and the lack of empirical validation has long been one of the major charges leveled against public choice by its critics (Green and Shapiro 1994).

Interestingly, Olson urged the SSRC's support not simply because of the benefits of interdisciplinary activity, but because of the novelty of such regarding economics:

> Economics has been, in Talcott Parsons' words, an "hermetically sealed" discipline, isolated from other social sciences. This lack of communication between economics and the other social sciences has presumably been due, not to any lack of need for such communication, but to the narrowness of the concerns of most modern economists and the unwillingness of many other social scientists to master the relatively rigorous and deductive methods of economic theory.[90]

Not that this "narrowness" was completely absent from the nascent public choice; the lists of invitees to these early conferences, while perhaps a bit more broad ideologically than the standard caricature, did not evidence extensive methodological pluralism. The rational choice approach was clearly dominant, and heterodox voices were hardly in evidence. In any event, Olson has proven quite prescient in his prediction that the new-found desire of some economists to examine the role and effects of the political process, along with the adoption by a small number of political scientists and sociologists of the tools of economics, promised "to undermine the thick wall that separate[s] economics from the other social sciences."[91] Public choice, the economic analysis of law, the economics of the family, and other traditionally noneconomic fields became significant growth areas

[88] Mancur Olson, "The Proposed Interdisciplinary Committee on Nonmarket Decision-Making," 1966, p. 4.

[89] Stubblebine, Proceedings of the Big Meadows Conference, pp. 17–18.

[90] Olson, "The Proposed Interdisciplinary Committee on Nonmarket Decision-Making," pp. 4–5. Of course, Parsons was very much responsible for the division between economics and sociology. See Parsons (1935a,b).

[91] Ibid., 5.

within economics, and the rational choice approach has gained a great deal of ground within the social sciences generally. While none of these so-called imperialistic movements was received with open arms outside of economics, their impacts—measured in terms of scholarly inroads and even the eventual rise of strong opposing camps within these other disciplines—cannot be minimized.

WORDS WRITTEN DOWN

While these various professionalization efforts were stimulating scholarship in the field, this continued growth presented a problem for its dissemination. As Tullock pointed out in 1967, "The field has suffered ... from the absence of a specialized journal. Articles are hard to place since most learned journals regard them as outside their scope and once published are hard to find. In a new and developing field, rapid interchange of ideas is extremely important. The existing journals are not organized to provide this exchange in an area which lies between (and overlaps) the traditional disciplines of economics and political science."[92] Moreover, he argued, the establishment of such an outlet, particularly as a multi-issue annual journal, would serve as an important stimulus for quality research in the field, owing to the greater publication potential offered by a specialized journal.[93]

Because of this perceived difficulty, the Committee for the Analysis of Nonmarket Decision-Making, in the person of Tullock, decided to take matters into its own hands. The first thrust at this was *Papers on Non-Market Decision Making*, the initial volume of which was published under the auspices of the Thomas Jefferson Center in the summer of 1966.[94] Within a year, it had sold 265 copies with almost no formal advertising. The process of putting together the first volume made it evident that a series of such volumes could easily be sustained by the submissions, and a second volume was issued in the first half of 1967. *Papers II* contained an expanded number of articles, a new book-review section, and, perhaps as important as any of this, the publication of a bibliography of books and articles in the field (compiled by Mark Pauly)—something that was to be repeated in later issues of the journal and that served the very useful function of keeping scholars abreast of the

[92] Tullock, National Science Foundation proposal for *Papers*, 1967, p. 1, BHA. These sentiments were echoed from the political science side by Vincent Ostrom, Chairman, in a memo to Public Choice Society members in 1969. Ostrom, Memorandum to Members and Prospective Members of the Public Choice Society, September 10, 1969, BHA.

[93] Tullock, National Science Foundation proposal for *Papers*, 1967, p. 11.

[94] It contained articles by Black, Coleman, Davis, Dempster and Wildavsky, E. A. Thompson, Tullock, and Wagner, and it appeared in book form (hard- and paperback).

far-flung publications in this newly emerging area of inquiry. The flavor of the articles in the second volume was also different: There was more of a "new public finance" (as opposed to "economics of politics") orientation than in the first volume. This was an artifact of the type of articles being submitted rather than a conscious editorial choice, and Tullock remarked on this in his foreword to the volume, saying, "We hope that this will not continue to be the case, and that we will have even more direct analysis of political phenomena in later issues" (Tullock 1967a: i).

By the time that the third volume of *Papers* appeared in the fall of 1967, the operation had evolved to the point that an editorial board had been put into place: Tullock served as editor and Mark Pauly as book review editor; Riker, Olson, Downs, Harsanyi, Black, Coleman, and Buchanan served on the editorial board. Even so, the status of the journal and its operations was by no means settled. While there was an intention to offer two issues in 1968, three in 1969, and four in 1970, they were not sufficiently confident of this to be willing to solicit subscriptions paid in advance, choosing instead to bill "subscribers" at year's end for whatever number of issues had been published (*Papers III*, Fall 1967, inside front cover). Some sense for the fledgling nature of this project is revealed in William Breit's insistence that his "comment" on a paper by Louis De Alessi, which appeared in *Papers III*, was actually written by Tullock based on a lunch-line conversation between the two of them, and that he did not know about the paper until he saw it in published form (Breit 1986: 8)!

In 1968, *Papers* was formally converted to a journal and given the new name, *Public Choice*. The journal was sponsored by the newly founded Public Choice Society[95] and funded from a three-year grant provided by the NSF, after which time it was expected that the journal would become self-supporting. In an "Editor's Note" to the maiden issue of *Public Choice*, Tullock opined that, in light of all of this, "We are still a struggling journal, but our struggle will be a bit less desperate in the future."

While we shall not trace in any depth the history of the journal beyond this point, suffice it to say that its growth was quite rapid. In 1973, the journal added a third annual issue, and circulation was approximately 900; in 1976, it was up to four issues per year with a circulation of 1300;[96] in 1980, the journal was publishing five annual issues. Tullock, who had served both as editor and as the principal referee since the journal's inception, stepped aside in 1990. By 1998, the journal was publishing nine

---

[95] Tullock (1997: 125) reports that the name of the journal was changed after a vote by the members of the society at the 1967 Chicago meeting. The journal's operations were moved to VPI and the newly established Center for Study of Public Choice in 1968.

[96] The center also inaugurated a new annual entitled *Frontiers of Economics* in 1976. The Center's annual report indicated that *Frontiers* "deals with applications of economics too far out even for *Public Choice*" (Center for Study of Public Choice Annual Report, 1976, p. 16).

issues annually under the editorship of Charles Rowley, Robert Tollison, and Friedrich Schneider (the journal's "European editor"), and the editorial board had expanded to include forty-five scholars. To accommodate the vast growth in and range of scholarly output, a sister journal, *Constitutional Political Economy* (*CPE*) was established in 1990 under the auspices of the Center for Study of Public Choice, with Viktor Vanberg and Richard Wagner serving as editors.[97] The internationalization of public choice has been much in evidence on the publications front, too, with the founding of the *European Journal of Political Economy, Economia delle Scelte Pubbliche* (*Journal of Public Finance and Public Choice*), and, in Japan, *Public Choice Studies* over the past three decades.

While the rise of specialized journals in a field is certainly one mark of its maturity as a scholarly endeavor, another is the publication of scholarship in the field across a broad spectrum of journals and, in particular, in the best general journals. The extensive bibliographical work done by Charles Plott and Mark Pauly in the early years of the public choice movement is instructive as to the range of literature and the broad spectrum of journals in which it was published—from elite journals such as the *American Economic Review, Journal of Political Economy, Economic Journal, Econometrica*, and the *American Political Science Review* to second- and third-tier journals— to say nothing of the numerous books and the research annual entitled *Mathematical Applications in Political Science*. Well over four hundred books and articles were published in the 1960s alone. In the *American Political Science Review*, for example, roughly 5 percent of the articles published in the mid-1960s embodied a rational choice perspective. By the early 1970s, this had increased to 20 percent, and by the early 1990s to around 35 percent (Green and Shapiro 1994: 2–3). All of this seems to call into question the assertions of Tullock and others regarding the lack of receptivity to this work within traditional professional outlets. Nonetheless, there was undoubtedly much to be gained from the establishment of an outlet such as *Papers/Public Choice*, which was overtly receptive to and encouraging of this work, and which served to bring together in one place work that would otherwise have been widely scattered and thus difficult to keep abreast of.

In an interesting commentary on the economics profession's view of this new scholarly enterprise, and in spite of Buchanan's decade-long effort to expand the scope of public finance to include the analysis of the relation-

[97] The term "constitutional economics" owes to Richard McKenzie, who used the term to define the subject matter of a Heritage Foundation conference that he organized in 1982 (Buchanan 1990: 1). Constitutional economics, as described by Buchanan, is "a research program that directs inquiry to the working properties of rules and institutions within which individuals interact, and the processes through which these rules and institutions are chosen or come into being" (1990: 1).

ship of the political process to public finance, the *American Economic Review* chose to locate its review of *The Calculus of Consent*—a piece written by Olson—not under "Public Finance" but under the "Related Disciplines" subject heading. By 1970, however, the scholarship in the field and its impact had grown to the point where it was given a separate *Journal of Economic Literature* classification, "025 Social Choice," falling under the heading "020 General Economic Theory" (*JEL*, September 1970).[98] The subject is now classified under "D Microeconomics" as "D7 Analysis of Collective Decision-Making," and it has no less than seven subcategories. The generalization and widespread acceptance of the public choice perspective is perhaps best illustrated by the perception that the best work in the field is no longer being published in *Public Choice*, but in the profession's top general journals.

While the effort to transform political science ultimately proved less than fully successful, the diffusion of public choice throughout the economics literature provides a clear indication of the manner in which this work forced economists to reexamine the theory of the economic role of government. The idea that self-interested behavior pervades the governmental process—from citizen and representative voting activities to the operation of the bureaucracy—led to the development of a theory of government failure that stood side-by-side with market failure, each "demonstrating" the limits of society's ability to attain the type of optimal results contemplated by welfare economics.

[98] This was changed to "Social Choice and Bureaucratic Performance" in the late 1970s and back to "Social Choice" in the late 1980s—a label that is more than a little ironic given the relative paucity of interaction between "social choicers" in the tradition of Arrow and Sen and "public choicers" within the tradition that we have been discussing here.

CHAPTER SEVEN

Legal Fiction

THE COASE THEOREM AND THE EVOLUTION

OF LAW AND ECONOMICS

For the rational study of law the black-letter man may
be the man of the present, but the man of the future is
the man of statistics and the master of economics.
—*Oliver Wendell Holmes (1897: 469)*

PUBLIC CHOICE THEORY was by no means the only manifestation of the backlash against the Pigovian approach to the analysis of market failures. Coase's analysis in "The Problem of Social Cost" contributed to the development of another significant movement, the Chicago approach to law and economics. Like public choice, law and economics employed the model of self-interested behavior—in this case, to analyze behavior in the legal arena. In doing so, it purported to show how the legal system can, and often does, cause self-interested behavior to generate outcomes consistent with efficiency, suggesting that observed, ostensibly inefficient behavior may in fact be efficient, and that common law remedies imposed by the courts can offer an alternative to legislative action and its attendant inefficiencies.

It is fairly commonplace for law and economics to be described as a post-1960 phenomenon, originating at the University of Chicago and dating roughly from the founding of the *Journal of Law and Economics* in 1958 and the publication of Coase's "The Problem of Social Cost" in 1960.[1] In fact, though, law and economics, conceived of as the study of the interrelations between legal and economic processes, is as old as economics itself. While not a prominent topic in economic or legal discourse prior to the twentieth century, it is on display in the ancient Greek discussions of the regulatory environment for the ideal state and the Scholastic discussions of usury and pricing (undertaken in light of Roman civil law), and atten-

---

[1] See, for example, Kitch (1983) and Parisi and Rowley (2005). This literature also tends to convey the impression that law and economics is a rather homogeneous mainstream enterprise, which is also misleading—although only somewhat so. See the discussion in Mercuro and Medema (2006).

tion to legal-economic relationships can be found in the writings Smith, McCulloch, Marx, Sidgwick, the German Historical School, and Pigou.[2]

The first four decades of the twentieth century saw a surge of interest in law and economics within both the legal and economics communities. The vast majority of this scholarship, though, was of a form very different from contemporary law and economics—not just in the techniques brought to bear, but in the general approach to and conception of the subject itself. In fact, the existence of this early work in the field is noted barely, if at all, in contemporary legal-economic scholarship, and, when taken note of, it is largely waived aside as something very different from and irrelevant to contemporary practice.[3] The history of law and economics at the University of Chicago is a part of this larger story, having begun well before the 1960s birth of the "new" law and economics, or "economic analysis of law," that is now synonymous with the Chicago school. Indeed, this history is not only more extensive but also more intertwined with phenomena outside of Chicago than is commonly understood or than many would care to believe. While the Chicago school was the launch vehicle for the development of an economic analysis of law that eventually spread to law schools, economics departments, and courtrooms across the United States and, eventually, around the world, the broad-based past of law and economics is not only important historically but also has a great deal to do with what is happening in law and economics today.[4]

THE LEGAL-ECONOMIC BACKDROP

The social sciences have long suffered from an inferiority complex as compared to the natural sciences.[5] The second half of the nineteenth century was no exception, and it witnessed the attempt among practitioners in certain social science disciplines to apply formalistic principles that would give their fields the status accorded to the natural sciences. In economics, this gave us the "marginal revolution." The legal manifestation was "doctrinalism," which held that legal principles are embodied in legal cases and that law is a scientific enterprise in which these legal principles are revealed through a careful examination of case law—as opposed to being the product of a

---

[2] See, for example, McCulloch (1848, 1853, 1856). Heath Pearson (1997) provides an illuminating examination of the nineteenth-century Continental traditions. On Sidgwick, see Medema (2007c).

[3] For example, in Kitch (1983) and Parisi and Rowley (2005).

[4] For a survey of the contours of contemporary law and economics, see Mercuro and Medema (2006).

[5] This section draws on the discussion in Mercuro and Medema (2006, ch. 1).

search for those principles ordained by God or nature.[6] The doctrinal approach had the effect of making the judicial opinion preeminent in law, with opinions embodying "a handful of permanent, unchanging, and indispensable principles" that revealed themselves in different guises in different cases (Posner 1990: 15). Law was said to consist of a set of objectively inferable rules and procedures, logically applied. Jurisprudence thus became both formal and insular, consisting only in an established body of legal doctrine, a set of principles that minimized judicial discretion, and where ethics, social conditions, politics, ideologies, and the insights of disciplines outside of the law had no proper place.

The reaction against doctrinalism began to gain strength before the end of the nineteenth century. The first salvo, "sociological jurisprudence," challenged both the formalism of the doctrinal approach and the traditional concepts of natural or objectively determinable rights. Oliver Wendell Holmes, Jr., Benjamin Cardozo, and Roscoe Pound,[7] among others, claimed that law cannot be understood without reference to social conditions. They also rejected the idea that law should be autonomous, and they instead argued both that insights from other social science disciplines should be integrated into the law and that judges should be aware of the social and economic conditions that influence and are impacted by the legal decision-making process. Cardozo, for one, believed that when precedent conflicted with the greater interests of justice or social welfare, the latter should carry the day (Bodenheimer 1974: 120–21). Law, in Holmes's view, is "a tool for achieving social ends"; to understand it "requires an understanding of social conditions," and judges thus ought to be acquainted with law's historical, social, and economic aspects (Posner 1987: 762).[8]

These pragmatic and socially attuned conceptions of law set the stage for an even more pronounced move away from the doctrinal approach: legal realism. The legal realist movement, which peaked in the 1930s, was the most influential of the challenges to doctrinalism and was part of a more general intellectual move away from formalism and logical reasoning in the early twentieth century.[9] The realists rejected the idea that law was, could be, or should be a logical, self-contained discipline, arguing instead that law should become more overtly attuned to the social ends that it necessarily serves. The realists held a strong instrumentalist, consequentialist conception of law: for them, law was, and had to be seen as, a "working tool" (Friedman 1973: 592). Every legal decision was understood to have social,

[6] See, for example, Langdell (1871), as well as Friedman (1973: 530–36) and Grey (1983).

[7] See, for example, Holmes (1897, 1923), Cardozo (1921, 1924, 1928), and Pound (1911a, 1911b, 1912, 1954).

[8] See also Holmes (1923: 1; 1897: 469) and Bodenheimer (1974: 123).

[9] See, for example, Fischer, Horwitz, and Reed (1993) and Duxbury (1995, ch. 2).

ethical, political, and economic implications, and the realists maintained that these should be recognized and explicitly dealt with by judges rather than hidden behind a veil of logical reasoning. Understanding these implications, of course, entailed the exploration of the interrelations between law and the other social sciences, including sociology, psychology, political science, and economics.

Of particular import for present purposes is the realist interest in using economics to understand and guide the development of law, which they believed both influenced and was influenced by economic conditions and ideas.[10] Karl Llewellyn, a leading legal realist and later a law school faculty member at the University of Chicago, pointed to a number of ways in which law influences economic conditions, including—through its role in providing a foundation for the economic order—its influence on the operation and outcomes of the competitive market process (particularly through the structure of law pertaining to property, contract, and credit, and through restrictions placed by law on the competitive process), and the influence of taxation, social welfare legislation, and public enterprise on production and distribution.[11]

The legal community was not alone in pushing for greater interaction between law and economics; economists, too, increasingly saw a need for the integration of legal and economic analysis. Calls for the integration of law and economics and the undertaking of studies toward this end could be found in the presidential addresses of the American Economic Association, sessions at the annual meetings of the AEA, and numerous books and journal articles.[12] Many, but by no means all, of the economists tilling this soil were either tightly or loosely allied with institutional economics—including Walton Hamilton, Henry Carter Adams, Richard T. Ely, Robert Lee Hale, John R. Commons, and Gardiner C. Means[13]— and the relations between the institutionalists and the legal realist community were rather close. The affinity was a natural one, given the institutionalists' concern with the influence of legal and nonlegal institutions on the economic system and the revolt against formalism that characterized their methodological stance. What must be emphasized here is that while institutionalism is a heterodox movement today, the individuals urging this integration of law and economics in the early part of the twentieth century were not fringe players, but among the economics profession's most prominent members.[14]

[10] See, for example, Llewellyn (1925), Litchman (1927), and Holdsworth (1927–28).

[11] See Llewellyn (1925: 678–81) and the discussion in Samuels (1993: 247–48).

[12] See the discussion in Samuels (1993).

[13] See, for example, Hamilton (1930, 1932), Adams (1887/1897), Ely (1914), Hale (1924, 1927, 1952), Commons (1924, 1925, 1934), and Berle and Means (1932).

[14] For example, Adams, Ely, and Commons each served as president of the American Economic Association. While we have used the label "institutionalist" to describe these

From this realist-institutionalist project came numerous studies that attempted to probe the linkages between law and economy, and, in the process to inform legal and economic thinking and decision-making.[15] The perceived need for such analysis arose from the belief that economic performance, including the operation of markets, is influenced by the legal system, which, through rights creation, definition, and modification serves to channel power, opportunity, and so forth—and thus allocation and distribution—in particular directions. This could be seen in legal decisions as to the types of contracts that would be enforced, the valuation of property for pricing purposes (and the regulation thereof), rules governing combination of firms and workers, hours of work, allowable levels of concentration, and so on. Related to this was a belief that economic forces are significant factors in the promotion of legal change, which, in turn, feeds back into economic performance. This, then, made the institutionalists and the realists concerned to understand the influence of the economic system on law. In particular, economic forces were said to exert pressure for and against legal change, both to promote new economic interests and to protect old ones. Law, here, was seen as a means to achieve certain ends, and competing interests were said to bring pressure to bear on government in the attempt to use law to promote their own ends.

EARLY CHICAGO

This interest in analyzing the legal-economic nexus was not confined to the realists and the institutionalists. Another legal-economic interaction, with a somewhat different flavor, commenced in the 1930s at the University of Chicago.[16] The origins of Chicago law and economics can be traced back to the latter part of the 1930s, when the law school faculty, under the leadership of Dean Wilber Katz, instituted a four-year curriculum that included courses in economics, accounting, and other subjects outside of the traditional realm of legal training (Katz 1937). This curriculum was overtly linked to the realist tradition in its strong emphasis on the social sciences, including economics. In 1939, the law school appointed its first economist, Henry Simons, to staff the economics courses that were part of the new curriculum. Simons was not the first economist on a law school

---

economists, the lines between schools were actually very blurred during this pluralistic era. See Morgan and Rutherford (1998). On institutional economics and its history, see, for example, Samuels (1988) and Rutherford (1994).

[15] For a discussion of the links between realism and institutionalism, see Duxbury (1995: 97–111).

[16] See, for example, Reder (1982), Kitch (1983), Coase (1993b), Hovenkamp (1995), and Duxbury (1995, ch. 5).

faculty—Walton Hamilton (Yale) and Robert Lee Hale (Columbia) had both preceded him on that score. Nor was he the first nonlawyer on the Chicago Law School faculty—Mortimer Adler had this honor, having been appointed in 1930. He was, however, the first economist granted tenure by the University of Chicago Law School, this coming in 1945.[17]

Simons was a student of Frank Knight, who, along with Jacob Viner, was instrumental in establishing the price-theoretic tradition that has long been a hallmark of Chicago economics and that came to underpin the Chicago variant of law and economics.[18] Knight brought Simons with him when he migrated from the University of Iowa to the University of Chicago, but a political battle in the Department of Economics, combined with Simons's poor reputation as a teacher and very limited scholarly output, resulted in a departmental fight over his promotion and tenure. The matter was resolved with Simons's part-time appointment to the law faculty, where from 1939, he taught a course entitled "Economic Analysis of Public Policy."

Simons's scholarly connection with law and economics was relatively slim.[19] His 1934 pamphlet, *A Positive Program for Laissez Faire*, set down a blueprint for a legal/regulatory regime that would ensure the maintenance of competitive conditions in the face of increasing concentration in corporate America. Simons's proposals here ranged from nationalization, to legal limits on advertising, to redefining the courts' criterion regarding the maximum firm size consistent with competition. If Simons's position qualified as "market oriented," it was relative only to the New Deal liberalism of the day. As George Stigler (1988: 149) noted a half-century later, "Much of [Simons's] program was almost as harmonious with socialism as with private-enterprise capitalism."[20] Apart from giving far more credence to the possibilities of government than one would expect from a "founder" of the Chicago law and economics tradition, Simons provided no empirical underpinnings for his analysis,[21] offered no evidence for the ability of the government to bring off such competition policy or that such policies would ultimately enhance the efficiency with which the economy operated. That is, even in a methodological sense, Simons's approach was, as Coase put it, "the very antithesis of that which was to become dominant

---

[17] Stigler (1974) gives an excellent overview of Simons's career.

[18] On the relationship between Chicago price theory and Chicago law and economics, see Medema (2007a).

[19] He was ultimately best known for his work in monetary theory. See Simons (1936) and Friedman (1967).

[20] Given the long tradition, from Smith onward, of believing that institutions need to be designed in such a way that markets produce beneficial outcomes, this comment may say as much about Stigler as it does about Simons. In fact, one could argue that Simons's approach was deeply Smithian.

[21] Empirical testing of theories has been a hallmark of the Chicago price theory tradition.

as a result of the emergence of that new subject, law and economics" (1993b: 242).

While Simons had little to do with the development of the body of ideas that became modern law and economics,[22] his price-theoretic perspective had a significant influence on Aaron Director, Milton Friedman, George Stigler, Gordon Tullock, and Warren Nutter, and his belief that law should be structured so as to promote competition reflected the perspective that became a cornerstone of Chicago law and economics. He also played a major role in the establishment of the law and economics program at Chicago via his efforts (together with those of Friedrich A. Hayek and financial backing from the Volker Fund) to bring to the law school the individual most responsible for firmly establishing the Chicago law and economics tradition—Aaron Director.

Director received his graduate training at the University of Chicago, and although he came to Chicago in 1927 to work with Paul Douglas on labor economics, it was Frank Knight and Jacob Viner who, via their courses in price theory, had the greatest influence on him. Director remained at Chicago as a graduate student and part-time instructor until 1934. This was a heady period at Chicago, where the student body included George Stigler, Paul Samuelson (who credits Director's teaching with stimulating his interest in economics), and Milton Friedman—each of whom helped to reshape economic thinking in the middle third of the twentieth century.[23] Aaron Director was very much part of this milieu. He left the University of Chicago for the U.S. Treasury Department in 1934 and, save for an aborted attempt to complete a dissertation on the history of the Bank of England, remained in Washington, D.C., until 1946, when he returned to the University of Chicago to take up a position in the law school, where he remained until his retirement in 1966.

Director's appointment in the law school was a result of the efforts of Simons and of Hayek, whose *Road to Serfdom* (1944) was published in the United States largely because of Director's intervention with the University of Chicago Press. The plan, as laid out by Simons, was for Director to head up the "Free Market Study," a Volker Fund–financed project, housed in the University of Chicago Law School and dedicated to undertaking "a study of a suitable legal and institutional framework of an effective competitive system" (Coase 1993b: 246). Simons, however, committed suicide in the summer of 1946, and Director was asked to take on Simons's basic law-school price theory course, "Economic Analysis of Public Policy." This

[22] See Stigler (1974) and Coase (1993b: 242).

[23] Rose Director—Aaron's sister and, eventually, Rose Friedman—was also a graduate student at Chicago during this time. Medema (2008) provides an overview of Aaron Director's career.

provided Director an initial forum for bringing the perspective he had learned from Knight and Viner in the law school classroom.

The transition from having an economist on the University of Chicago Law School faculty to the establishment of a law and economics tradition at Chicago began not long after this, when Edward Levi invited Director to collaborate in the teaching of the antitrust course. Levi would teach a traditional antitrust course for four days each week; Director would then come in on the fifth day and, using the tools of price theory, show that the traditional legal approach could not stand up to the rigors of economic analysis. The basic pattern was very simple: Director would ask whether the business practice in question was, in general, consistent with monopolistic profit-maximization. The answer was often negative, which meant that there had to be some sort of legitimate rationale for the supposedly anticompetitive practice in question. What Director's price theory showed was that the "simple and obvious" answers were often wrong-headedly simplistic.

These pedagogical exercises had a profound impact on students and colleagues alike. Director's antitrust students—a group that included Robert H. Bork, Ward Bowman, Kenneth Dam, Edmund Kitch, Wesley J. Liebeler, John S. McGee, Henry Manne, and Bernard H. Siegan—have often spoken of the "conversion" they experienced in this class, and even Levi himself became a partial convert.[24] As Bork put it, "There is a quality about the teaching at that time that doesn't come through" to those who were not there during this period. He went on to say that many of those who took Director's courses "underwent what can only be called a religious conversion. It changed our view of the entire world" (Kitch 1983: 183).

Director's most significant contribution on the missionary front may well have come after his retirement, when he and Richard Posner spent time together at Stanford in 1968. This was Posner's first year on the Stanford Law School faculty. He was interested in antitrust and in how economic analysis could inform it, and this led him to seek out Director when he arrived at Stanford. It was Director who taught Posner to think like a Chicago economist, introduced him to Stigler and Ronald Coase, and in this and other ways was instrumental in Posner's move to the University of Chicago Law School after only one year on the Stanford faculty.[25]

Although Director's published output was slight, his influence extended well beyond the classroom and the oral tradition. His insights made their way into the antitrust literature—and, eventually, antitrust policy—through

[24] See Kitch (1983) and Director and Levi (1956).

[25] Posner graduated from Harvard Law School (1962), clerked for Supreme Court Justice William J. Brennan, Jr., was appointed an associate professor of law at Stanford in 1968, and moved on to the University of Chicago Law School in 1969. Since 1981, he has served as a judge of the U.S. Court of Appeals for the Seventh Circuit, including Chief Judge from 1993 until 2000.

the writings of students and colleagues.[26] Director's primary legacies are in the analysis of predatory pricing, resale price maintenance, and tie-in sales.[27] His influence was also prominent in Stigler's view of oligopoly and antitrust policy, Posner's perspective on oligopoly and cartels, and Bork's influential articles on antitrust.[28] These contributions coalesced in a distinctive Chicago approach to antitrust analysis, an approach that antitrust historian Herbert Hovenkamp (1986: 1020) argues "has done more for antitrust policy than any other coherent economic theory since the New Deal," and the influence of which is inescapable.

Director's impact at the law school, however, went far beyond antitrust: He was also the prime mover in the early professionalization of law and economics. Director formally established the nation's first law and economics program, which maintained visiting fellowships for law and economics scholars, and, in 1958, he founded the *Journal of Law and Economics*, the aim of which was "the examination of public policy issues of interest to lawyers and economists" (Coase 1993b: 251). Within a few decades, Director's efforts at Chicago had been replicated in a set of thriving and well-funded law and economics programs at major law schools around the country.[29]

In 1964, as Director was approaching retirement, Ronald Coase was brought to the University of Chicago Law School from the University of Virginia to succeed Director on the faculty and as editor of the *Journal of Law and Economics*. Prior to Coase's arrival, the law school never had more than one economist on the faculty, although there were enough economics department and law school faculty with sympathies for examining antitrust cases and regulatory issues through the lens of economic analysis to form a small reading group. Yet, the presence of scholars such as Karl Llewellyn on the law faculty managed to ensure that there was strong resistance to expansion of the influence of price theory in the 1950s. Law school graduate and law and economics pioneer Henry Manne has reported that the economic analysis that was in the air "infuriated" Llewellyn, particularly when students would use it in order to attempt to refute positions that Llewellyn would take in the classroom (Kitch 1983: 184). Llewellyn even went so far as to question whether, given the influence of this economic mode of reasoning, Chicago was doing a proper job of training lawyers

---

[26] See Peltzman (2005) for a survey.

[27] See, for example, McGee (1958), Telser (1960), Director and Levi (1956), Bowman (1957), and Burnstein (1960), as well as the survey in Peltzman (2005).

[28] See, for example, Posner (1969), Bork and Bowman (1965), and Bork (1967).

[29] The John M. Olin Foundation was a major source of funding for the law and economics programs at Chicago and elsewhere. Like the Volker Fund, the Olin Foundation has had a reputation for supporting individuals, organizations, and causes identified with the Right. This has undoubtedly contributed to the ideological debate surrounding law and economics over the past several decades.

(Kitch 1983: 191).[30] Edward Levi, as Dean, protected and encouraged law and economics, but, as Director has pointed out, on the whole there was neither "any great resistance" to nor "any great enthusiasm for" law and economics—at least until it was proposed that a second economist be hired (Kitch 1983: 186). Indeed, the status of economics in the law school at that stage was such that Coase's initial appointment was partially in the business school.

Coase's arrival offered the promise of a measure of continuity in the legal-economic approach at the law school. While Coase was not trained in the Chicago brand of price theory, his approach was thoroughly Marshallian and very consonant with the Chicago view. Coase was educated at the London School of Economics, where he had studied under Arnold Plant, who had done pioneering work analyzing the economic implications of rules governing patents, copyrights, and intellectual property generally.[31] Coase's approach to the analysis of legal-economic policy issues, informed by Plant, resonated with the Chicago viewpoint.[32] Coase believed that there were important lessons to be learned by examining the relationship between law and economy—by "examining cases, examining business practices, and showing that there was some sense to them, but it wasn't the sense that people had given to them before" (Kitch 1983: 193). This is the perspective that was being applied at Chicago by Director and others in the area of antitrust, and it is reflected in Coase's several contributions to the *Journal of Law and Economics* prior to his arrival at Chicago. This commonality of approach almost certainly accounts for much of Director's interest in bringing Coase to Chicago, and the scope of its application was subsequently expanded to a wide range of issues in legal and regulatory policy, largely through the influence of Director and Coase as editors of the *Journal of Law and Economics*.

FROM LAW AND ECONOMICS TO ECONOMIC ANALYSIS OF LAW

While "The Problem of Social Cost" was written squarely within the old Chicago law and economics tradition that sought to get at the influence of

---

[30] Llewellyn was not inherently opposed to legal-economic analysis, but his preference was for something approximating the old institutionalist variety. See, for example, Llewellyn (1925).

[31] See Plant (1974).

[32] Coase has said that "[t]here were typical 'Chicago' lessons that I didn't have to learn, and I got them through Plant" (Kitch 1983: 214). Plant's most significant influence on Coase involved getting him to see that "there were many problems concerning business practices to which we had no satisfactory answer" (1982: 34; see also Coase 1986). Much of Coase's career was spent looking for these answers, and this perspective, along with Plant's approach of looking at real-world problems, is reflected throughout Coase's scholarship.

law on economic activity and performance, it also (unintentionally) triggered the development of something far more substantial and far-reaching. In the process of analyzing problems of harmful effects, Coase had applied his analysis to the courts, pointing to the economic questions at issue in a number of rather typical legal cases. He argued first, from a normative standpoint, that judges should, at minimum, take allocational—that is, efficiency—considerations into account in making decisions over rights that impact economic performance. He further suggested that "it is clear from a cursory study [of the case record] that the courts *have* often recognized the economic implications of their decisions and are aware (as many economists are not) of the reciprocal nature of the [externality] problem" (1960: 19, emphasis added). Coase went on to say that while the judges were not always explicit about the economic issues at stake, the interpretation of terms such as "reasonable" or "common or ordinary use" appears to reflect "some recognition, perhaps largely unconscious and certainly not very explicit, of the economic aspects of the questions at issue" (1960: 22).[33] These suggestions regarding judges' applications of economic thinking later stimulated a number of scholars—Richard Posner in particular[34]—to examine whether there might be an efficiency logic underlying the development of legal rules across the common law. Doing so involved the application of individual decision-making calculus to the analysis of agents faced with constraints imposed by common law rules, and the assessment of the resulting outcomes according to the dictates of efficiency. Of course, where extant rules were found to be inefficient, the determination of rules that would induce optimal behavior was a natural extension.

Coase was not alone in the use of economics to analyze tort cases; Guido Calabresi (1961) of the Yale Law School was doing so at the same time, and their work became the springboard for a new economic analysis of common law rules.[35] Suddenly, the economic nature of many of the questions of legal analysis—that legal rules and decisions across many traditional fields of law beget both benefits and costs, and thus are amenable to analysis in efficiency terms—and the potential for the application of economic analysis to these questions became apparent and began to stimulate research in the common law areas of property, contract, and tort.

---

[33] One finds a similar line of argument already in Commons (1924).

[34] Posner has acknowledged that his "interest in using economics to try to explain legal rules stems in significant part" from this aspect of Coase's analysis in "The Problem of Social Cost." See Kitch (1983: 226).

[35] It is, however, fair to state that Coase had the larger impact on both the development of law and economics at Chicago and among economists (as opposed to legal scholars). The case can be made that this also applies to law, given that "The Problem of Social Cost" is the most cited article in the legal literature. On Calabresi's contributions, see the 2005 symposium in the *Maryland Law Review*, as well as Grembi (2003).

The 1960s saw the emergence of a second and equally important strand of the economic analysis of law. In 1957, Gary Becker had published *The Economics of Discrimination*, a book that had itself contributed to the early development of economics imperialism by showing how the model of *homo economicus* could be applied to areas beyond the norm. Becker's now-classic 1968 article, "Crime and Punishment: An Economic Approach," extended the approach to the legal arena. Jeremy Bentham and Henry Sidgwick had analyzed criminal behavior and punishment issues in a utilitarian context during the nineteenth century,[36] but Becker pushed the self-interest–based approach to criminal behavior a step further by probing the implications of the rational actor model for the analysis of crime and its prevention. He assumed that criminals are rational utility maximizers like everyone else, but the relevant constraints and opportunity sets that they encounter generate maximizing outcomes that involve engaging in criminal activity. One implication of this is that criminal activity, like any other labor-occupational-economic choice, is subject to alteration when price incentives are scaled—that is, when legal rules are changed—in one direction or the other.[37] On the normative front, Becker examined the issue of optimal enforcement and showed how this varies with the nature of the punishment, with the costs of policing and of running the judicial system, and how individuals respond to changes in these variables. What some would consider an "extreme" application of economic logic to the analysis of criminal behavior made the applications to property, torts, and contracts—issues that, to the lay mind, are more overtly "economic" and less subject to the "deviance" label—seem relatively tame and much less inappropriate than they might have seemed otherwise. Becker's discussion thus brought increased attention to the economic analysis of legal rules, as well as contributing to the spread of economics imperialism more generally.

By the early 1970s, the economic analysis of law had developed to the point that Richard Posner could write a substantial treatise on the subject. His *Economic Analysis of Law* (1973) used basic price theory—"the assumption that man is a rational maximizer of his ... self-interest" (1973: 1), the law of demand, opportunity costs, and the idea that voluntary exchange allows resources to gravitate toward their highest-valued uses—as the lens through which law is examined. The book's contents spanned virtually the entire range of law and, as Posner calls it, "the legal regulation of non-market behavior" (1973: xix)—property, contracts, torts, family, criminal, antitrust, employment, utility and common carrier regulation, regulation

[36] See Bentham (1823, 1830), Sidgwick (1897, 1901), and the discussions in Posner (2001, ch. 1) and Medema (2007c).

[37] For example, the alteration of expected cost in the form of the product of probability of detection, probability of conviction, and monetized value of cost if convicted.

of financial markets, tax, inheritance, procedure, due process, federalism, discrimination, speech, and search and seizure. What is perhaps most surprising is the enormous scope of applications across the legal spectrum present even in the first edition, showing already in the days of the field's infancy the tremendous possibilities of the application of economic theory to legal analysis and outlining a framework for a field of analysis that others were only too happy to begin to fill.

Posner's *Economic Analysis of Law* was not the only sign of growth in the early 1970s. The *Journal of Legal Studies* was established in 1972 to handle the burgeoning output in the field and encourage the field's further development. Scholarship was mushrooming across the various areas in which legal rules affect individual behavior through the adjustment of incentives, and the analysis revolved around three core elements. First, in contrast to the standard legal view of individuals as reasonable agents behaving according to the norms and customs of society as reflected in legal rules, the economic approach posits agents as rational maximizers of their satisfactions. Second, legal rules are viewed as prices that are taken as given by individuals and used by them in the process of calculating their utility- or profit-maximizing response to these legal rules. Changes in legal rules thus function as changes in the constraints subject to which individuals maximize, with corresponding consequences for individual behavior. One of the implications of these first two points is that, while the traditional approach to law considers law-breaking and law-breakers unreasonable, the economic approach sees both law-breakers and non-law-breakers as rational—their behavioral differences being accounted for by the different constraints under which they maximize utility. Finally, the assessment of legal rules proceeds on the basis of the efficiency of the outcomes generated by these rules, in contrast with the "justice" or "fairness" criterion underlying traditional legal reasoning.

This last point raises the issue of the normative argument for efficiency as justice, which, from the start, was an important and controversial aspect of the economic analysis of law. The case for the use of the efficiency criterion in legal decisions was made both historically and philosophically. The historical aspect was accomplished by arguing that common law rules tend to exhibit an underlying economic logic—that, consciously or not, the decisions reached by judges over time have had a tendency to promote wealth maximization. This idea was first hinted at by Coase in "The Problem of Social Cost," but it was more extensively developed by Posner and others in the 1970s and 1980s. Posner's position is that "[t]he logic of the common law is an economic logic" (Landes and Posner 1987: 312), and, in an extensive body of published analysis—particularly *The Economic Structure of Tort Law* (1987), a book coauthored with William Landes—he has helped to build the case; in fact, he has been its primary architect. Like most collections of facts, the general sweep of common law case and doctrinal history shows consistency with multiple possible stories; nevertheless, the case made for the efficiency theory is a compelling one, whether the result of a conscious judicial logic or not.[38]

The philosophical component involved making the case for the use of the efficiency or wealth maximization criterion in legal decision-making as against other principles that could inform judicial reasoning. Here, Posner has played a particularly interesting role over time. In *The Economics of Justice* (1981: 48–115), he both distances wealth maximization from utilitarianism (see also 2001: 96–98) and attempts to ground an ethical defense of wealth maximization, or efficiency, in the notion of consent, operating via the Pareto criterion. A wealth-enhancing legal change is likely to hurt some and benefit others, but the net effect maximizes the size of the pie. It thus differs from the Pareto criterion in that it does not preclude losers. A wealth-maximizing legal change would, however, make one or more parties better off and no one worse off, if accompanied by appropriate side payments to compensate those who would otherwise be losers under the change. In that case, given that there are no losers, the change would command unanimous consent among rational agents. Posner's argument for wealth maximization (sans the side payments) rests on the idea that compensation comes ex ante or, at the very least, the wealth-maximizing set of rules—the one that offers the largest pie—is one that would command unanimous consent among rational agents ex ante. In recent years, Posner has moved away from, even rejected, the ethical defense of wealth maximization, though he does continue to hold the view that a wealth-maximizing rule for common law decision-making might command something like unanimous consent ex ante if some method existed for voting on the issue. Moreover, he continues to insist against his numerous detractors that efficiency "is perhaps the most common" meaning of justice (1992: 27).[39]

---

[38] There is no dominant explanation for the common law's efficient character (if it has such). The interest group theory—that inefficient rules will be litigated at a greater rate because of the net losses engendered, and will inevitably be overturned—offers an explanation that many find plausible. Posner has offered what some argue are compelling grounds for the idea that judges take efficiency considerations into account. The argument is not that all common law rules are efficient or that the application of rules from common law precedents is always efficient; the point, for Posner, is that "the law creates incentives for parties to behave efficiently," not that people actually do so (Landes and Posner 1987: 312).

[39] This poses a profound challenge to traditional legal approaches to justice and, not surprisingly, has been the source of substantial controversy within the legal community. Legal theorist Ronald Dworkin (1980, 2000) is perhaps Posner's most regular and severe critic. On the larger debate over the use of the efficiency criterion in legal theory and practice, see, for example, the articles appearing in the "Symposium on Efficiency as a Legal Concern," (1980) and the "Response to the Efficiency Symposium" (1980), both of which were published in

The Chicago school remained at the center of the meteoric rise of the economic analysis of law over the next twenty years, even while law and economics programs began to mushroom at elite law schools around the country. Fresh blood in the form of, among others, William Landes (a student of Becker), Dennis Carlton, Alan Sykes, Douglas Baird, and Daniel Fischel, brought new ideas and specialties into the law and economics program at Chicago and facilitated both its development and entrenchment.[40] Richard Epstein evolved from vociferous natural-rights-based critic to fellow traveler. Baird and Fischel went on to become deans of the University of Chicago Law School. As with public choice analysis, students went out to spread the economic analysis of law around the world. Perhaps the most prominent missionary among the Chicago graduates was Henry Manne, who founded or helped to develop multiple law and economics programs as well as a series of summer institutes, colloquially known as "Pareto in the Pines," which taught economic analysis to judges. Chicago law and economics has also been influential on the bench, particularly in the persons of Posner, Frank Easterbrook, Robert Bork, and Antonin Scalia. The former and latter pairs are indicative of the nonhomogeneity in the Chicago tradition, with Posner and Easterbrook being more activist along the lines implied by economic principles, and Bork and Scalia falling more heavily on the side of judicial restraint.[41]

THE COASE THEOREM

Explaining the success of the economic analysis of law requires both an understanding of the transition from a law and economics that sought to examine legal-economic policy issues to an economic analysis of

---

the *Hofstra Law Review*. Needless to say, the ethical case for efficiency as justice has its controversial, and even problematic, aspects, as pointed out by numerous commentators.

Posner has moved away from the ethical defense, practically, because of the questions regarding the relationship between efficiency and the distribution of wealth, and, philosophically, because his pragmatism now causes him to reject the idea of an underlying ethical basis for law. He nevertheless finds pragmatic justification for the wealth-maximization criterion on multiple fronts. First, political stability and average income in society tend to be positively correlated; that is, wealth maximization as a legal decision rule will tend to promote political stability (2001: 102ff). Beyond this, Posner argues that wealth maximization and the benefit-cost analysis that underlies it are operationally valid, tend to be more immune from political prejudices and pressures than are other decision rules, and can enhance the quality of government decision-making (2001: 123).

[40] Landes, Carlton, and Sykes are all trained in economics, with Sykes holding a J.D. as well.

[41] Bork has also criticized economic analysis of law, Chicago style.

legal rules, and the conditions within economics and law that facilitated this transformation. One can see the evolution of the field, from its "law and the economy" bent to its focus on the economic analysis of law, in the pages of the *Journal of Law and Economics*. The problem of pin-pointing the causes of this transformation is compounded by the fact that early law and economics was not homogeneous or monolithic, and that the transformation occurred in stages over time. The branch of law and economics that was rooted in the institutionalist-realist tradition was all but dead as an influential academic phenomenon by the mid-1950s. Meanwhile, early Chicago law and economics was only really coming into its own in the late 1950s. This brand of law and economics held strong within the Chicago school into the 1970s, before beginning a decline that was matched by the ascendance of the new economic analysis of law.

We have noted already that the economic analysis of law received much of its impetus from Ronald Coase's analysis in "The Problem of Social Cost." A goodly amount of that comes from the Coase theorem, which states that, absent transaction costs, conflicts over rights will be efficiently resolved through bargaining. The fact that the analysis that came to be codified in the Coase theorem was (intentionally) an exercise in pure fiction on Coase's part did not deter the erection of a substantial edifice of positive and normative analysis on this foundation.[42] In spite of the often heavily ideological overtones of the Coase theorem debate, the theorem is simply a positive proposition, stating that under certain conditions a particular result will follow. Yet, the Coase theorem has been assailed from the Left (as conservative dogma) and from the Right (as liberal dogma); its moral, philosophical, and political underpinnings have been called into question; its logic, applicability, and empirical content have been both trashed and defended; it has been hailed as offering a new way to conceptualize law and legal culture and attacked as anathema to the traditional common law process.[43] In the pages that follow we will attempt to explain how and why the Coase theorem quickly evolved from a debunking fiction to the basis for one of the most successful branches of applied economics in the last part of the twentieth century.

---

[42] Nor, for that matter, has subsequent elaboration of Coase's intent done anything to abate the interest in the theorem and its implications. Indeed, the controversy over the Coase theorem continues to this day. See, for example, Coase (1988c, 1992) and Medema (1994b, ch. 4; 1996a). For surveys, see Cooter (1987), Zelder (1998), and Medema and Zerbe (2000).

[43] The list of citations here is far too numerous to mention. See, for example, the citations in Gjerdingen (1986) and Medema and Zerbe (2000), as well as the references given in notes 50 and 66 of this chapter.

What Is the Coase Theorem?

Coase himself never stated or proposed a "Coase theorem." The theorem was derived from an argument, early on in "The Problem of Social Cost," that, in the presence of harmful effects,

> it is necessary to know whether the damaging business is liable or not for damage caused since without the establishment of this initial delimitation of rights there can be no market transactions to transfer and recombine them. But the ultimate result (which maximizes the value of production) is independent of the legal position if the pricing system is assumed to work without cost. (Coase 1960: 8)

The Coase theorem has been stated in several different ways, often with slight, but not necessarily unimportant, variations. Two of the classics are George Stigler's (1966: 113) statement that "under perfect competition private and social costs will be equal"—the first naming of the Coase theorem in print—and A. Mitchell Polinsky's (1974: 1665) assertion that "[i]f transaction costs are zero, the structure of the law does not matter because efficiency will result in any case."[44] A statement that closely follows the spirit of Coase can be worded this way: If rights are fully specified and transaction costs are zero, parties to a dispute will bargain to an efficient and invariant outcome regardless of the initial specification of legal rights. This statement of the theorem contains two explicit assumptions and two assertions regarding the results.

Let us begin with the results, which can best be understood as two theses regarding outcomes. The first is the *efficiency thesis*, which states that the outcome of the bargaining process will be efficient, regardless of who is initially assigned the right. The concept of efficiency underlying the Coase theorem is Paretian—the exhaustion of all potential gains from trade[45]—and much of the recent analysis by economists attempting to assess the validity of the theorem employs the Paretian notion of efficiency. Coase himself used the concept of efficiency in multiple ways in his analysis (maximizing the value of production and minimizing costs, in particular), while, within contemporary economic analysis of law, wealth maximization and cost minimization are the most frequently employed variants of the efficiency concept. The second of the implied results is the *invariance thesis*: The outcome of the bargaining process—the allocation of rights and resources (although not necessarily the distribution of income)—will be *the same*, regardless of who is initially assigned the right. That is, while the efficiency thesis contends that the final allocation of resources consequent to any particular assignment of rights will lie on the contract curve, the

---

[44] See Medema and Zerbe (2000) for a litany of Coase theorems.

[45] On this see point see Buchanan and Stubblebine (1962) and Buchanan (1986).

invariance thesis says that the final allocation will lie *on the same point* on that curve irrespective of who initially holds the rights over the resources in question. There are versions of the Coase theorem that employ both of these theses and those that state only the efficiency thesis. Indeed, one of the many oddities surrounding the theorem is that there is no singular Coase theorem. Both the form and content given to the theorem and the notion of efficiency employed affect the conclusions regarding the theorem's correctness.

The theorem's results can be illustrated using two simple examples—one from the realm of property law and the other from the realm of contracts. Suppose first that the discharge from an upstream polluting factory causes one million dollars in damage to downstream landowners. The polluter can prevent the damage by installing a filtering device at the cost of $600,000, whereas downstream landowners could eliminate the damage at a cost of $300,000. Efficiency clearly dictates that the pollution be eliminated, since the damage is greater than the cost of abatement. The optimal means of abating the pollution is for the downstream landowners to undertake the abatement, since they can abate at lower cost.

Suppose that the downstream landowners file suit against the factory and that the court subsequently assigns these landowners the right to be free from pollution damage. The polluting factory can abate the pollution at a cost of $600,000; however, recognizing that the downstream landowners can abate the pollution at a cost of $300,000, the factory owner will be willing to offer the landowners any amount up to $600,000 to undertake the abatement. The landowners, in turn, will be willing to accept a payment in excess of $300,000 to do so. Thus, in the absence of transaction costs, a mutually beneficial bargain will be struck that results in the landowners undertaking the abatement.[46] If, on the other hand, the factory is given the right to pollute, the downstream landowners, faced with a choice between one million dollars in damages and abatement costs of $300,000, will choose to abate the pollution. Thus, regardless of whether rights are initially assigned to the factory or to the landowners, the efficient result—abatement undertaken by the downstream landowners—will obtain.

Or, suppose that Ronald contracts to sell his house to Richard at a price of $100,000. Shortly before the transaction is consummated, Guido offers Ronald $110,000 for the house, and Ronald breaches his contract with Richard to sell to Guido. If the law allows for such contractual breaches, Guido, rather than Richard, ends up purchasing the house from Ronald. If the law states that such a breach is not allowable, Ronald must sell to Richard at the contracted price. Guido will then, however, offer Richard $110,000

---

[46] Note that the distribution of gains from this exchange will depend upon the relative bargaining power of the two sides.

for the house, an offer that Richard would certainly accept, assuming that he paid something approximating the house's value to him when he purchased it from Ronald. Thus, regardless of the law that governs breach, Guido ends up owning the house. The outcome is both efficient—the house ends up in its highest-valued use (owned by Guido)—and invariant under alternative assignments of rights. In each of these examples, the only thing that varies across alternative rights assignments is the distribution of income.

What about the assumptions that take us to these results? An implicit (and necessary) assumption in all formulations of the theorem is that rights are alienable. If they are not, the rights transfers contemplated by the theorem cannot take place. The further (explicit) assumption that these rights must be fully specified is rather noncontroversial. In its simplest form, this assumption says that some party must have legal control over the resource in question. If there are no rights established over said resources, or if rights are incompletely defined, bargaining solutions are all but precluded. For example, neither Richard nor Guido would enter into an agreement to pay Ronald $100,000 or more for the house if there were no preexisting rights of ownership.

The assumption of zero transaction costs is much more intricate, and it is the (often unrealized) source of most of the contention over the Coase theorem. Many a scholar has claimed to have demonstrated that the theorem is false by invoking what, in the end, is really just a class of transaction costs. The simple notion of transaction costs is that they consist of those costs associated with the negotiation process. While these costs are certainly significant in many cases, a more expansive definition is given by Douglas Allen (1998: 108): "Transaction costs are the costs of establishing and maintaining property rights"—perhaps the most important of which (from an application perspective) are information costs.[47] The necessity of the strict zero transaction costs assumption becomes clear after only a moment's thought. Sufficiently large transaction costs will preclude bargaining altogether. Yet even when transaction costs are very low, the marginal cost of additional negotiation will at some point exceed the marginal benefit, with the result that the final allocation of resources will indeed depend on to whom the rights are initially assigned.[48]

---

[47] On the definition and implications of transaction costs, see Dahlman (1979), Barzel (1985), and Allen (1991, 1998).

[48] For example, supposed that transaction costs are positive but low enough to make bargaining cost-effective, at least initially. If the factory is assigned the right to pollute, then the starting point for negotiation is the current level of pollution, and the marginal cost of additional negotiation will exceed the marginal benefit at some level of pollution greater than the optimum. Likewise, if the landowners are assigned the right to be free from pollution, then the starting point for negotiation will be zero pollution, and the marginal cost of additional negotiation will exceed the benefit at some level of pollution less than the optimum. Thus,

As Coase was not elaborating or proving a theorem, it is no surprise that he was not more specific and detailed about his assumptions or more probing about the details of his results.[49] Scores of scholars have undertaken this challenge, however, and the literature purporting to prove, disprove, confirm, or refute the theorem is voluminous. This much can be said with certainty: There exists no generalized proof of the Coase theorem. In contrast, there are an enormous number of "disproofs," many of them highly technical in nature—in stark contrast to Coase's intuitive formulation of these ideas.[50] Interestingly, most of the challenges to the theorem's correctness can be dismissed under appropriate (some would argue "correct") conceptualizations of the meaning of fully specified rights and zero transaction costs.[51] The validity of certain of the challenges also depends upon whether one considers the theorem to include both the efficiency and the invariance theses or the efficiency thesis alone. While Coase's original elaboration of these ideas included both efficiency and invariance, a number of subsequent commentators have dropped the invariance thesis on the grounds that it is invalidated by income effects and their implication that there is no unique efficient solution.[52] Without meaning to trivialize the

---

if transaction costs are positive, we will see less pollution when the landowners are assigned rights than when the factory is assigned the rights. Medema and Samuels (2000) and Mercuro and Medema (2006: ch. 2) have useful discussions of this, accompanied by diagrams.

[49] Some of this is also the result of Coase's methodological stance, which differs greatly from the methodology of contemporary mainstream economics. See Mäki (1998), Medema (1994a, 1995), and Zerbe and Medema (1998).

[50] This literature is far too vast to survey in any detail here, but is dealt with at great length in Medema and Zerbe (2000). Some of the more significant objections to the theorem include the emptiness of the core (Aivazian and Callen 1981), imperfect/incomplete/asymmetric information coupled with the effects of the resulting potential for strategic behavior (Cooter 1982; Samuelson 1985; Farrell 1987), nonseparabilities (Marchand and Russell 1973), nonconvexities (Starrett 1972), the necessity of rents (Wellisz 1964), entry and exit effects (Calabresi 1965; Tybout 1972; Frech 1979), and income and wealth effects (Mishan 1967). A further implicit assumption of the theorem is that agents are utility maximizers. There is, however, a growing empirical and experimental literature that calls into question the validity of this assumption in the context of the Coase theorem. Coase never made this assumption and in fact has criticized the rational utility maximization model (Coase 1984). He does, however, seem to work from the assumption that individuals will attempt to exploit opportunities for gains from trade. Apart from this, the adoption of the Paretian notion of efficiency brings into play the shape of the utility functions, which itself can affect the outcome (Hovenkamp 1990).

[51] For example, the challenges based on entry and even wealth effects can be shown to violate the assumption of fully specified property rights, while those based on nonseparabilities, nonconvexities, strategic behavior, risk, and so forth violate the assumption of zero transaction costs (Medema and Zerbe 2000).

[52] See Polinsky's (1974) statement of the Coase theorem, quoted on page 176, and that of Cooter and Ulen (1988: 105). It is worth noting that Coase (1960) used only examples of externalities between *producing* agents, rendering income effects irrelevant. In the case of

many objections that have been raised against the Coase theorem, for the sake of argument we will assume the position that the theorem is correct, full stop.

The Theorem's Implications

The power of the Coase theorem, as well as the fascination and infuriation with it, stems from its several implications. The first, and most obvious, is that if transaction costs are zero, as assumed by orthodox neoclassical economic theory, Pigovian remedies are unnecessary for externality correction.[53] A simple assignment of rights to one party or the other is sufficient to ensure the attainment of efficiency through market-like processes. To those predisposed to accept the idea that the pursuit of self-interest generally redounds to the larger social interest and who prefer so-called market-generated outcomes to so-called government intervention, the theorem offers an emphatic counter to what some perceive as the market-failure–driven interventionism of neoclassical economics. Presumed instances of market failure are revealed to be nothing more than the failure of law fully to specify rights—a failure that, once rectified, allows markets to generate optimal solutions. The fact that this "government versus the market" issue is nonsensical has not diluted the attractiveness of this implication for those who insist upon the primacy of the market. That the government is "intervening" both through the assignment of rights at law and through the imposition of Pigovian remedies should be clear, as should the attendant idea that all of this is apart from the fact that the same costlessly available information that allows the Coase theorem to work its magic in a market context would also allow government to resolve externalities efficiently using Pigovian instruments.

A second implication of the Coase theorem is that externalities will be resolved efficiently not only through an assignment of rights but also *regardless of to whom* these rights are initially assigned. This is very discomforting to traditional legal scholars, to those who adhere to traditional Pigovian externality theory, and to natural rights theorists. The theorem brings to the fore the reciprocal nature of externalities: A may be imposing costs on B, but to reduce the harm to B imposes costs on A. The question is who is going to be allowed to visit harm on whom. Pigovian externality theory, and to some extent traditional legal theory, have

externalities to which consumers are party, Douglas Allen (1991, 1998) contends that the fully specified rights assumption invalidates the income effects challenge.

[53] See chapter 5, infra.

not conceptualized the problem in these terms, assuming instead that one party (for example, the polluter) is *the* cause of the externality and that the other party is the victim, and prescribing restraints on the activity of the harm-generating agent.[54] By illustrating how both parties would be willing to pay to avoid having harm visited on them, the Coase theorem very nicely brings out the inherent reciprocity here.[55] But the controversial implication is that traditional notions of causation and harm go out the window.[56]

The idea that to whom rights are assigned does not matter for efficiency has an additional disquieting implication for law: The notion that courts determine rights, and thus outcomes, falls by the wayside, at least in part. The Coase theorem tells us that rights will inevitably end up in the hands of those who value them most highly, regardless of what the court decides or intends. Only the distribution of income will be affected by the initial assignment of rights, since it determines who makes payments to whom within the Coasean bargaining process. One of the many curiosities surrounding the Coase theorem is that the critics from the Left did not seize upon this insight with at least as much fervor as supporters on the Right. The Right can argue that the Coase theorem tells us that judicial attempts at social engineering are fruitless, since parties will bargain around that result when it is in their joint interest to do so. Those on the Left could well respond that, since the final allocation is not affected in any case, judges should feel free to assign rights in such a way as to satisfy their views about the principles of justice or their distributional preferences—for example, by assigning right to "victims" so that bribes flow to "victims" from the "harm-causing agent" rather than the other way around. Perversely, the Coase theorem is a friend to both proponents and opponents of the efficiency criterion.

[54] Traditional legal theory is much less guilty here, as Coase pointed out in "The Problem of Social Cost." Looking back on this several decades later, Coase (1993b: 251) noted that one of his goals in discussing court cases in that article was to show that the legal system did a much better job than the economics profession in recognizing this reciprocity.

[55] If efficiency is truly independent of the assignment of rights, as the Coase theorem implies, then the reciprocity issue is unimportant, from an efficiency perspective.

[56] In applying this notion of causation on the normative front, Landes and Posner (1983: 110) illustrate the causation-reciprocity-efficiency link very nicely in the context of tort law, noting that "[i]f the basic purpose of tort law is to promote economic efficiency, a defendant's conduct will be deemed the cause of an injury, when making him liable for the consequences of the injury would promote an efficient allocation of safety and care; and when it would not promote efficiency for the defendant to have behaved differently, then the cause of the accident will be ascribed to 'an act of God' or some other force on which liability cannot rest. In this view, the injurer 'causes' the injury when he is the cheaper cost avoider; not otherwise."

The Coase Theorem and the Economic Analysis of Law

UNLOCKING LAW

The analysis of externalities has been an important component of economic theory ever since Pigou made it a centerpiece of his *Wealth and Welfare*. Yet until the writing of "The Problem of Social Cost," the analysis proceeded largely absent any discussion of existing common law means of dealing with externalities and of common law solutions as potential instruments of externality policy. Coase's analysis essentially put forward an argument that the common law of property, contract, and tort is actually one large body of externality policy. This conception of the common law has two implications. First, the economists' focus on statutory remedies— Pigovian taxes, subsidies, and regulations—as the means for dealing with externalities is unnecessarily narrow. Second, and perhaps more important, economists became aware of a wealth of externality-related issues within the law to which economic analysis could be applied. Because a particular assignment of rights expands the opportunity sets of some agents and restricts those of others, legal decision-making can be conceived of as an exercise in allocation, to which one can readily apply the standard micro-theoretic tools in order to assess the incentive effects and relative efficiency properties of alternative structures of rights and to derive rules that will channel self-interested individual behavior toward the larger social interest—here, efficiency.

If there is a distinction to be made between the situations addressed by common law and the traditional economic theory of externalities, it lies in the context of the externality relationships: Common law problems have traditionally dealt with relations between small numbers of agents (as illustrated in the legal cases discussed by Coase), whereas the economic theory of externalities has tended to deal (at least implicitly) with situations involving large numbers, such as pollution. It is here that the Coase theorem found the foothold within the economic analysis of law that is less available within traditional externality theory. The simple (and somewhat simplistic) notion of transaction costs is that of bargaining or negotiation costs, and it is generally argued that these costs increase quickly as the number of parties to a bargain increases. This is illustrated in the extreme case by the public goods problem.[57] Given the magnitude of transaction costs, it is obvious that the bargaining solution will not work in the traditional externality situations, such as air pollution, contemplated by economic analysis[58]—except, perhaps, in the limit, where the number of parties on both sides is so large that the situation approximates that of perfect competition and, as such, brings us

[57] But see Coase (1974a).

[58] Coase accepted that the bargaining solution is not likely to apply to air pollution. See Coase (1960: 18).

within the bounds of the first optimality theorem, which says, in a nutshell, that perfectly competitive markets generate efficient outcomes.[59]

In the case of the "small-numbers" relations regularly contemplated by law, however, the bargaining solution takes on significant import. The simple notion of transaction costs suggests that impediments to bargaining here may well be minimal. If so, once legal rules are in place—ranchers are required to fence, surface rights owners also have beneath-the-surface rights, and so forth—attendant outcomes can be presumed to be efficient. Were the right in question more valuable to someone other than the party assigned it, that individual would have purchased the right through a voluntary transaction. This implies that legal or political pressures to alter the existing structure of rights are nothing more than rent-seeking by those unwilling to pay the price necessary to acquire them.

By implicitly favoring common law remedies, the Coase theorem logic enhances the probability of efficient resource allocation. Pigovian instruments have the effect of creating inalienable rights, whereas common law rights are usually alienable. A Pigovian remedy that deals with an externality problem in other than least-cost fashion is thus virtually guaranteed to generate an inefficient allocation, whereas common law rules simply set the stage for the bargaining that will lead to the efficient resolution of the problem.[60]

DOING WHAT COMES NATURALLY

A perusal of an issue of the *Journal of Law and Economics* or a textbook in the field does not reveal an inordinately large number of invocations of the Coase theorem. This might lead one to conclude that the whole Coase theorem issue is all smoke and no fire. What one does observe, however, is an enormous variety of legal-economic arguments couched in the language of the market, and this language, as well as the underlying logic, derives directly from the Coase theorem. Indeed, the most significant facet of the Coase theorem's legacy has been its role in placing issues of rights determination in a market context.

The idea of placing legal rights in a market context strikes many as wholly inappropriate. Yet, this is hardly an idea that originated with the Chicago school. One of the seminal insights of John R. Commons (1924), an American institutionalist and someone who would never be classed ideologically

---

[59] See Stigler (1966: 113) and Arrow (1969), as well as Blaug (2007).

[60] See Posner (1992: 251ff). The efficiency aspect of common law rules, combined with the legal-economic perspective on judicial behavior and the public choice perspective on legislative and bureaucratic behavior, underlies the preference, within the economic analysis of law, for common law rather than statutory remedies. See Posner (1992: ch. 19).

with the modern-day Chicago school, was that the fundamental unit of economic activity is the transaction—the transfer of legal rights of control—rather than the exchange of goods and services. At their core, input and output markets are vehicles for the transfer of legal rights between agents. To say that the market ought not to be the arbiter of rights is thus to say that markets ought not to exist. When the theory of markets or the theory of exchange tells us that, under particular conditions, resources will be allocated efficiently, what is really being said is that the rights over those resources will be allocated efficiently through the exchange process. This is noncontroversial. The Coase theorem extends this to the larger legal arena by asking the following: If these processes allocate rights over standard producer and consumer goods efficiently, why not also rights over, for example, pollution, unobstructed views, contractual promises, or, in the limit, the use of one's body for, say, prostitution? The argument here is that unless these classes of rights can be shown to have characteristics that cause them to differ with respect to their consonance with the underpinnings of exchange theory, there is no a priori reason to expect that the transactions contemplated by law (and thus the economic analysis of law) are any different than the standard transactions of the marketplace.

That the Coase theorem is a foundational element of the economic analysis of law should be obvious by this point. It is in its negation, however, that the theorem assumes its most significant import. The theorem says that the structure of legal rules does not matter, in an allocation sense. A moment's thought reveals that, if this were actually true in reality, the entire "economic analysis of law" enterprise would never have left the ground. The economic analysis of law takes as its mission the analysis of the efficiency properties of alternative legal rules—historical, actual, and potential. If any legal rule will generate an efficient and invariant allocation of resources, these studies would have all the import of one purporting to show, by reference to extensive empirical analysis, that the sun rises in the morning. Likewise, the advocacy of particular legal rules based upon their efficiency properties would be nonsensical.

Once it is allowed that transaction costs preclude the attainment of the optimum contemplated by the Coase theorem, we are immediately faced with the fact that the structure of rights does indeed affect the efficiency with which resources are allocated. We are also faced, however, with the recognition that these costs prevent agents from doing that which they would do in the absence of these costs. This has led some commentators to argue that two normative implications, both of which have become central to the economic analysis of law, can be drawn from the theorem.

The first claim is that the theorem implies that law should be structured so as to minimize the impediments to bargaining.[61] This would enhance

---

[61] Cooter and Ulen (1997: 89) call this the "normative Coase theorem."

the prospect that agents could consummate efficiency-enhancing (Pareto-improving) bargains, even if the bargaining process did not generate the wealth-maximizing result contemplated by the Coase theorem. The second implication is more important, as it goes to the heart of the normative economic analysis of law: Rights should be assigned so as to achieve the efficient (that is, wealth-maximizing) outcome. This idea—conventionally known as the "mimic the market" approach to rights determination[62]—is undoubtedly the most controversial aspect of the economic analysis of law within the greater legal community, and it has been both defended and assailed from a variety of directions.[63] Its claim to legitimacy is relatively powerful, however, and it rests on the Coase theorem.

The theorem says that parties will bargain to the efficient outcome, regardless of how rights are initially assigned, if they are not precluded from doing so. The "mimic the market" approach to legal decision-making simply allows parties to reach the allocative arrangement that they would have arrived at by mutual consent if transaction costs did not get in the way. The argument goes something like this: The Coase theorem shows us the allocation that parties would voluntarily agree to; since transaction costs preclude them from reaching this agreement, we should impose this result via judicial decree. Posner (1992: 93) illustrates this very nicely in his discussion of judicial gap-filling in contract law:

> The task for a court asked to interpret a contract to cover a contingency that the parties did not provide for is to imagine how the parties would have provided for the contingency if they had decided to do so. Often there will be clues in the language of the contract. But often there will not be, and then the court may have to engage in economic thinking—may have to decide what the most efficient way of dealing with the contingency is. For this is the best way of deciding how the parties would have provided for it. Each party, it is true, is interested just in his own profit, and not in the joint profit; but the larger the joint profit is, the bigger the "take" of each party is likely to be. So they have a mutual interest in minimizing the cost of performance, and the court can use this interest to fill out a contract along the lines that the parties would have approved at the time of making the contract.[64]

From this perspective, law simply becomes a vehicle that, via judicial decree, allows conflicts to be resolved in the manner that disputants would themselves mutually demonstrate that they prefer.

[62] See, for example, Posner (1992: 15). The efficiency focus is also an artifact of the idea that judges are best placed to concern themselves with issues of efficiency and that distributive issues should be left to legislative bodies (e.g., Posner 1990: 359; 1992: ch. 19).

[63] For a small taste of this debate, see Posner (1981: chs. 3, 4; 1990: 734ff), the *Symposium on Efficiency as a Legal Concern* (1980), and the *Response to the Efficiency Symposium* (1980).

[64] For illustrations and discussion of the application of economic reasoning in actual court cases, see Samuels and Mercuro (1984) and White (1987).

The fact that the economic analysis of law has concerned itself almost solely with issues of efficiency and virtually not at all with distribution is in part an artifact of this interpretation of the Coase theorem.[65]

In spite of the normative debate that, either implicitly or explicitly, seems to follow the Coase theorem wherever it goes, the theorem is a *positive* statement with no direct normative implications—it is an "is" statement, not an "ought" statement—going to the presence or absence of efficiency under particular assumed conditions. It does not tell us that efficiency is all that matters, or even that efficiency matters at all. The Coase theorem says nothing about the relative merits of market versus administrative (or Pigovian) remedies, nor does it establish the sanctity of property and contract. Yet, it is the normative baggage that has been appended to the Coase theorem that appears to have generated most of the hostility to it and, thereby, to the economic analysis of law.[66]

Indeed, the Chicago school has come under heavy criticism for the normative overtones that many believe go along with, or even drive, the economic analysis of law. There can be little question that the economic analysis of law has provided a sturdy intellectual foundation for a market-oriented approach to legal decision-making. The Coase theorem opened the door to the analysis of rights allocation within a traditional market framework and thus, potentially to a vast new scope for the operation of markets. In an era when so-called "activist judges" were making decisions that often seemed to conflict with the ideology of the market, the implications of the economic analysis of law were welcome ammunition for those who favored the market. As such, it is not surprising that the new law and economics movement was launched from within the Chicago school. The willingness of certain conservative-oriented organizations, such as the John M. Olin Foundation, to provide financial support for the law and economics movement helped to facilitate both the program of research and the classroom dissemination of these ideas.[67]

---

[65] An essential difference between the working of the theorem and the "mimic the market" approach to legal decision-making is that the former gives credence to distributional issues (mutual agreement on division of the gains from trade, so that each party is at least no worse off) while the latter generates a settled assignment of rights that creates winners and losers. The theorem and the "mimic the market" approach lead to the same allocation, but potentially to vastly varying distributive outcomes.

[66] See, for example, Samuels (1973) and Kelman (1979) for attempts to link the Coase theorem with right-wing ideology. Samuels has since recanted (Medema and Samuels 1997).

[67] As an aside, it should be noted that none of these normative conclusions is inherent in the analysis of legal rules using the tools of neoclassical economic analysis, and it is both incorrect and irresponsible to equate the new law and economics with conservative ideology. Indeed, the scholars working in the field come from a wide variety of perspectives and draw many conclusions at odds with conservative ideology. It would be difficult, however, to deny that law and economics has been used by some to promote normative agendas—not unlike,

USEFUL FICTION

It should have been evident from the beginning that the Coase theorem is not an accurate description of legal-economic reality. Yet, its implications were so fascinating, so challenging to the traditional economic and legal views of these issues, that the debate focused on ostensible proofs and disproofs or refutations rather than on the domain of the theorem's applicability. The reason for the intensity of the debate goes beyond the normative issues that we mentioned earlier. It also derives from some of the same professional forces that helped to drive the development of the Pigovian theory of externalities, including the interesting theoretical puzzle that the theorem poses and the fascination of economists with determinate, optimal solutions to questions of economic policy.

It has been argued that the Coase theorem is merely a tautology.[68] Perhaps it is, if by tautology we mean that the results follow directly from the assumptions.[69] The theorem is better understood, however, as a useful fiction. It shows what is implied by the standard assumptions of economic theory: If coordination is costless, both markets and government function optimally. Nevertheless, the theorem also shows us the converse: If coordination is costly, both markets and government can be expected to function suboptimally. The point, according to Coase, is that rhetorical and mathematical flourishes purporting to demonstrate that perfect markets trump imperfect governments or that omniscient governments dominate imperfect markets get us nowhere. The task for legal-economic policy here becomes the assessment of the magnitude and influence of the relative costs of coordination across alterative institutional structures and the resulting implications for alternative institutional-policy arrangements.[70]

The absurdity of the theorem's conclusions—or, rather, the absurd degree of emphasis that economists and legal scholars put on them—generated not only a great deal of heat in both the legal and economics communities, but also, many would argue, a significant amount of light. The theorem showed that legal rights are valuable entities that can be exchanged in broad or narrow markets, and it suggested that real markets do not operate nearly

---

at times, institutionalist-realist law and economics. When combined with the goal of facilitating competitive market outcomes, the Pandora's Box opened by "The Problem of Social Cost" gave ample opportunity for individuals so inclined to design legal rules that would comport with the dictates of competitive markets.

[68] See, for example, Regan (1972: 429–30), Veljanovski (1977), and Cooter (1987: 458).

[69] Then again, how many economic theories could escape such a charge?

[70] Given the tendency of certain supporters and detractors to act as if the theorem was intended as a depiction of reality, one could argue that the Coase theorem is as much a harmful myth as a useful fiction. The argument for the useful fiction view here is that it caused economists to pay increased attention to the role played by coordination costs in economic activity.

as smoothly as economic theory tends to contemplate. This insight led some economists—for example, Oliver Williamson, Scott Masten, Douglass North, Gary Libecap, Yoram Barzel, and Thrainn Eggertsson, to name just a few—to begin to explore the influence of coordination costs on economic activity and performance. This approach has come to be known as the "new institutional economics," and Coase has identified much more closely with it than with the economic analysis of law.[71] In some sense, this work took law and economics back to its pre-1970s roots by combining elements of the early Chicago law and economics with concerns that occupied the attention of (old) institutionalist law and economics scholars such as Hamilton, Commons, and Hale.

COASE AS ACCIDENTAL TOURIST

One of the great ironies surrounding the rise to prominence of the economic analysis of law is that the work on which it turns, "The Problem of Social Cost," was an unintended result of law and economics of the *old* variety, undertaken by someone with no interest in the economic analysis of legal rules. Viewed from the perspective of the present, "The Problem of Social Cost" immediately calls to mind contemporary work in the economic analysis of law. Yet, it was in fact a work in the older mode—the analysis of legal-economic policy issues.[72] Coase's work was not aimed at legal scholars and legal scholarship but, rather, at economists and the practice of economics. "What I wanted to do," said Coase (1993b: 251),

> was to improve our analysis of the working of the economic system. Law came into the article because, in a regime of positive transaction costs, the character of law becomes one of the main factors determining the performance of the economy.

Coase has consciously distanced himself from Posner, whose "main interest is in the legal system" (Coase 1993b: 251), noting that "I have no interest in lawyers or legal education" (Coase, quoted in Kitch 1983a: 192). He has also acknowledged that "[i]n the development of the economic analysis of the law ... Posner has clearly played the major role" (Coase 1993b: 251). Posner (1993a,b) has even taken Coase to task for this disavowal of his supposed progeny.

---

[71] See Eggertsson (1990) and Mercuro and Medema (2006: chs. 4, 5) for surveys of these literatures. Coase's attitude toward the New Institutional Economics, both absolutely and relative to the economic analysis of law, can be found in his 1984 and 1993a commentaries. Posner (1993a,b) is critical of Coase's position.

[72] Medema (1996b) discusses the commonalities between the law and economics of Coase and the institutionalists.

Coase's work in law and economics subsequent to the publication of "The Problem of Social Cost" consisted largely of further inquiries into the U.S. broadcasting industry and other regulatory institutions, attempting to come to grips with what he has called "the institutional structure of production." This work is decidedly *not* along the Coase theorem–related lines implied by what so many took to be the message of "The Problem of Social Cost" (Medema 1994b). Coase's rejection of the assumption of rational, utility-maximizing consumers is instructive here, particularly in contrast to subsequent developments in the field of law and economics.[73] Of course, Coase could not have anticipated the direction that law and economics would take subsequent to the publication of "The Problem of Social Cost." His analysis (and Calabresi's), however, raised many issues for both economists and lawyers, including revealing the choice-theoretic nature of the questions of legal analysis and the attendant potential for the application of economic theory to the analysis of legal rules and legal decision-making.

"The Problem of Social Cost" is an article which avowedly had nothing to do with legal scholarship, and was written by someone who has repeatedly emphasized his complete lack of interest in lawyers and legal education and who rejected the utility-maximizing approach so closely associated with the economic analysis of law and with economics imperialism generally. Yet, this article served as a springboard and foundation for the development, in the hands of others, of the economic analysis of law—the most significant movement within law during the last half of the twentieth century and one of the more significant developments within economics over this same time period. This raises a host of interpretive issues.[74] Indeed, perhaps no economic work written in the past century is as illustrative of the central tensions of hermeneutics as "The Problem of Social Cost."[75]

---

[73] See, for example, Coase (1984).

[74] While it has been argued that Coase's retrospectives on his own work are little more than revisionist history, the evidence—seen through the juxtaposition of "The Problem of Social Cost" with the entire corpus of Coase's writings—clearly suggests otherwise. See Canterbery and Marvasti (1992) and the response by Medema (1994a), as well as Medema (1994b). That much having been said, the emerging importance of the Coase theorem within public economics and law and economics, and the centrality of place given to Coase within the evolution of the economic analysis of law, proceeded apace with hardly a whimper of rebuttal from Coase. While there are a couple of relatively obscure publications circa 1970 in which Coase repeats what he considers to be the message of "The Problem of Social Cost," it was not until the publication of a collection of his seminal papers in the late 1980s that Coase (1988c) finally came out strongly in an attempt to set the record straight. The obvious question that arises is why Coase chose to keep silent for nearly three decades, in spite of what one might rightly call the abuse of his ideas—particularly at the hands of his colleagues at Chicago. Medema and Samuels (1997) offer a number of conjectures in this regard.

[75] Although John Maynard Keynes's *General Theory of Employment, Interest and Money*

UNDERSTANDING THE TRANSFORMATION

We have made the argument that the economic analysis of law was an accidental byproduct of Coase's analysis in "The Problem of Social Cost," and that the Coase theorem provided much of the fortification for this new approach to analyzing legal questions. We have yet to address, however, the issue of why the economic analysis of law proved so attractive relative to the older ways of doing law and economics. Much of the explanation can be found in the effect of larger professional forces at work in the post–World War II period—in particular, a simultaneous narrowing of the scope and perspective of economic theory to that of constrained maximization and rational choice and the expansion of its domain of application.

The postwar period saw a progressive narrowing of the bounds of what passed for theory within economics, with "theory" being equated with the presence of formal mathematical models and a deductive methodological approach. The questions addressed by economists, and the way of doing economics, became increasingly defined by the tools of theoretical analysis laid out in Paul Samuelson's *Foundations of Economic Analysis* (1947), Kenneth Arrow and Gerard Debreu's general equilibrium theory,[76] and, subsequently, game theory, while the more intuitive and empirical approach to theorizing characteristic of (among other things) the old law and economics was no longer considered solid economic analysis.[77] The standards for good empirical work came to be judged by the application of sophisticated econometric techniques, which rendered case studies unscientific. These tools of analysis were being used to open entirely new vistas in economic scholarship, but they were also singularly ill-suited to tackle the analysis of institutions. Such attitudes meant that work done in the old way had increasing difficulty gaining the attention of mainstream economists and publication outlets. Lacking the "aesthetic appeal" of postwar theory with its elegant systems of equations and sophisticated empirical techniques, the more intuitive and nonquantitative empirical nature of the old law and economics was not nearly so attractive to budding scholars, nor was such research the road to professional rewards.

(1936) would certainly give "The Problem of Social Cost" a run for its money on this score. See, for example, Backhouse and Bateman (2009).

[76] See, for example, Arrow and Debreu (1954) and the brief survey in McKenzie (2008).

[77] For example, the institutionalists were increasingly portrayed as little more than atheoretical or antitheoretical fact-gatherers within the profession at large and within the law and economics community in particular, as seen in George Stigler's comment—later echoed by Coase (1984)—that institutional economics "had nothing in it but a stance of hostility to the standard theoretical tradition. There was no positive agenda of research, there was no set of problems or new methods they wanted to invoke" (quoted in Kitch 1983: 170).

This formalist emphasis was closely linked to the increased professional emphasis on determinate, optimal solutions to the questions of economic theory and policy, and this, too, played a significant role in the reshaping of law and economics. Most of the standard problems of public economics—including externality theory, as we saw in chapter 3—had been quickly absorbed within the optimality framework. The old law and economics, in contrast, offered little in the way of a framework for determining the optimal legal structure for the economic system. It was entirely different, however, with the economic analysis of law. While Coase himself had little use for optimization techniques, the Coase theorem and the illustrations that Coase drew from his analysis of legal cases suggested that the analysis of legal rules, too, could be placed squarely within the optimizing framework. Because any given assignment of rights expands the opportunity sets of some agents while restricting those of others, legal decision-making could easily be converted into an exercise in optimal allocations, based upon which one could derive, in relatively straightforward fashion, the efficient legal rules to govern human behavior. Thus, by a curious reconstructive twist, Coase's analysis of how legal institutions influence economic performance was used to provide a basis for the analysis of all manner of legal rules within the optimization framework.

The application of economic theory to the analysis of legal rules was facilitated by the fact that many of the legal questions which the economists addressed had a substantial identifiable dollar-valued component. Rights are valuable: Alternative assignments of rights generate alternative patterns and levels of benefits and costs across affected parties. Moreover, legal rules, when established as precedents, provide incentives that channel individual decisions and actions in particular directions. It was just a short and (as some argued) natural leap from here to the conclusion that it is important to assess the degree to which legal rules promote the efficient allocation of resources, just as economists had for decades proposed efficiency-enhancing regulations through the political process. And it was just a further short leap to the analysis of *all* classes of legal rules (including those involving non-dollar-valued claims), given the assumption of stable preferences—that there exists a consistency of individual reasoning across the choice spectrum.

The second of the larger professional forces within economics that provided impetus for the development of the economic analysis of law was the expansion of the boundaries of economics, which began in the 1950s. This is actually tied to the emphasis on economics as the theory of constrained maximization or, more strongly, rational choice. Gary Becker is central to this part of the story, as he and his students set about analyzing all manner of social phenomena with a combination of price theory and econometric analysis. Such is the range of this work that almost no area of the social sciences and almost no aspect of human conduct remains untouched by economic analysis. This extension of economics beyond its traditional boundaries made the economic analysis of *law* a part of the rule rather than the exception to it.

The economic analysis of law and public choice were not only two of the earliest applications of the tools of economic theory to the analysis of "noneconomic" or "nonmarket" phenomena; they were also part of a larger professional dynamic within which economic analysis was coming to be viewed as an approach, method, or toolkit applicable to all areas of life in which choices are made, rather than simply as the study of the economic system per se. The old law and economics was concerned with analyzing the interaction between the law and the economy: it saw the study of the legal process as an important facet of *the study of the economic system*. The economic analysis of law, in contrast, is concerned with applying economic theory to analyze agent behavior within the legal arena and has little or nothing to do with understanding the legal bases of the economic system. This distinction is indicative of a larger professional move from a subject-matter definition of economics to a definition of economics as an approach or a toolkit for the analysis of individual behavior.

While the rational choice revolution across the social sciences is a many-faceted phenomenon,[78] the artistic license for economists to cross over into subjects traditionally noneconomic in nature came via Lionel Robbins' *Essay on the Nature and Significance of Economic Science* already in 1932. Rejecting the extant notion that the boundaries between "economics" and "not economics" are set by behavior that is or is not directed toward the enhancement of material welfare, Robbins argued that economics focuses on the form of behavior "imposed by the influence of scarcity." In particular, he defined economics as "the science which studies human behaviour as a relationship between ends and scarce means which have alternative uses" (1932,: 15). Robbins went on to note the implications of this definition for the subject matter of economics:

> It follows from this, therefore, that in so far as it offers this aspect, any kind of human behaviour falls within the scope of Economic Generalizations. We do not say that the production of potatoes is economic activity and the production of philosophy is not. We say rather that, in so far as either kind of activity involves the relinquishment of other desired alternatives, it has its economic aspect. There are *no limitations* on the subject-matter of Economic Science save this. (1932: 16, emphasis added)

When writing "no limitations," Robbins almost certainly did not anticipate how the boundaries of economics would be stretched in the decades to

---

[78] See, for example, Amadae (2003).

come. Nor, it would seem, did the rest of the profession, given that it took more than three decades for scholars to begin seriously extending the economic paradigm.[79] The practice of economics continued to reflect the traditional view that economics is the study of the economic system—the same view that characterized the early approaches to law and economics—even as it assimilated the idea that it is choice under scarcity within that context that defines what economists analyze.

There can be no question, however, that Robbins defined economics in a manner that naturally allowed for its extension beyond the analysis of standard market phenomena. The gradual institutionalization of an economics defined as the analysis of choice under scarcity[80] meant that it was only a matter of time before we began to see the "economic analysis of" a whole array of social phenomena,[81] with work in this area variously described as "the economics of nonmarket behavior," "the analysis of nonmarket decision-making," and "economic imperialism." Becker (1976: 4), whose work in this vein is without parallel, made this clear when he described the method that had motivated his own work: "The combined assumptions of maximizing behavior, market equilibrium, and stable preferences, used relentlessly and unflinchingly, form the heart of the economic approach as I see it." The logic of this extension is a simple one: Economics is the study of choice, and all of life involves making choices; should not economics, then, apply to all manner of human decisions and thus all areas of human life?

The common denominator of economics imperialism, according to Chicago economist Edward Lazear (2000: 100–102) is that economics has brought increasing scientific rigor to a host of academic areas and attendant analyses of social phenomena.[82] In Lazear's words, "The power of economics lies in its rigor. Economics is scientific; it follows the scientific method of stating a formal refutable theory, testing the theory, and revising the theory based on the evidence" (2000: 102). This rigor, in turn, "allows complicated concepts to be written in relatively simple, abstract terms" that "strip away complexity."

In economics, this abstraction comes via a trinity of attributes: (1) the assumption that individuals are rational maximizers, (2) the notion of equilibrium, and (3) the assessment of equilibria based upon their efficiency properties (Lazear 2000: 100–102). While of those working in these other fields have lamented what they see as excessive abstraction in the economic approach, Lazear argued that complexity, while perhaps adding descriptive

---

[79] On the reception and diffusion of the Robbins definition of economics, see Backhouse and Medema (2009). University of Chicago economist Frank Knight, for one, rejected the Robbins definition as over-broad.

[80] This process is described in Backhouse and Medema (2009).

[81] See Raditzky and Berholz (1987) and Lazear (2000) for surveys.

[82] This opinion is also held by Becker (1976) and Posner (2008), among others.

richness, "also prevents the analyst from seeing what is essential" (2000: 99–100). In fact, he said, it is this very abstraction that makes economics succeed "where other social sciences fail," because it allows for "analysis" in a way that the other social sciences do not (2000: 102, 103).[83]

Lazear (2000: 104) finds the case for the success of economics imperialism unambiguous, and observes that the widespread application of the economic paradigm has left the social sciences in a much stronger position:

> Economists generally believe in the market test. Economic imperialism can be judged to be successful only if it passes this test, which means that the analyses of the imperialists must influence others. The effort to extend the field measures its success by inducing others to adopt the economic approach to explore issues that are not part of classical economics. One possibility is that scholars outside of economics use economic analyses to understand social issues. Political scientists, lawyers, and sociologists come to use the methods of economics to answer the questions that are of interest in their fields. Another possibility is that economists expand the boundaries of economics and simply replace outsiders as analysts of "noneconomic" issues, forcing noneconomists out of business, as it were, or at least providing them with competition on an issue in which they formerly possessed a monopoly.

He maintains that both of these routes have been successful, and that the "fact" that economics has been successful in shedding new light in so many areas "attests to the power of economics" (2000: 142). Some may wish to contest Lazear's assertions,[84] but our purpose here is not to analyze or debate the explanatory power of the economic paradigm either in general or in its various specific applications. It would be difficult to conclude, however, that the economic analysis of law—and the same can be said of public choice—is anything other than a professional success, certainly within economics and most probably within law.

There is no question, though, that the growth of law and economics stirred up a great deal of controversy within the legal community—to the point of actually spawning the Critical Legal Studies movement as a reaction against the Chicago approach.[85] The situation in law during this

---

[83] Lazear's attitude here is virtually identical to that expressed by Olson regarding public choice and political science in the late 1960s. See pp. 153–55 in chapter 6.

[84] Ronald Coase (1977b), for one, predicted that economics imperialism was doomed to failure because of economists' lack of knowledge of these other fields. So far, though, that has not proved to be a deterrent to economists.

[85] For discussion as to why law and economics was so successful a movement in law, see Posner (1987). On Critical Legal Studies, see Unger (1983), Kelman (1987), and Boyle (1994). Mercuro and Medema (1997, 2006) discuss (without attempting to take sides) many of the criticisms that have been leveled at the Chicago approach.

period, however, also played a role in the process by which economic analysis of law became established as a scholarly endeavor, as Posner pointed out in his essay on "The Decline of Law as an Autonomous Discipline" (1987).[86] While the idea that economics could bring a much greater measure of rigor to the other social sciences helped to fuel the imperialist tendencies of economists, it took on particular import for the success of the law and economics movement because law was at this time engaged in a search for moorings following the decline of legal realism. There was a sense within the legal community that lawyers could not solve the problems of the legal system on their own, and that the traditional autonomous perspective had little new to say. As a result, legal scholars began to look elsewhere for interpretive principles. Beyond this, the increasing prestige and authority accorded scientific modes of inquiry, and the relative decline in prestige and authority accorded to the nonscientific method of legal analysis, pushed legal scholars to adopt more scientific methods. In the eyes of many legal scholars, economics, with its formalist approach, logical interpretive framework, and determinate solutions, offered exactly the sort of scientific basis for law that was needed to fill the void. In law, as in political science, economists were happy to do the void-filling.

This brings us to another irony: "[I]nterventionist" legal realism was a major reason why "market-oriented" law and economics could gain a foothold at Chicago in the first place and eventually sprout and spread in new form. The economic analysis of law, like legal realism, institutional law and economics, and the early Chicago law and economics, is *consequentialist*: Each takes the position that legal decisions should be made based on their impacts rather than based on a priori principles. The legal realism to which Chicago is so hostile opened a consequentialist door that could not be closed. Posner's (1995: 3) repeated attempts to dismiss such a link between realism and the economic analysis of law miss the point:

> The "crits" worry that the practitioners of law and economics will contest with them the mantle of legal realism. They needn't worry. We economic types have no desire to be pronounced the intellectual heirs of ... William Douglas, Jerome Frank, or Karl Llewellyn. The law and economics movement owes little to legal realism—perhaps nothing beyond the fact that Donald Turner and Guido Calabresi, pioneering figures in the application of economics to law, graduated from Yale Law School and may have been influenced by the school's legal-realist tradition to examine law from the perspective of another discipline. Although the legal realist Robert Hale anticipated some of the discoveries (inventions?) of law and economics, most modern law

[86] Here, Posner gives an in-depth analysis for how the state of legal study created an environment where the economic analysis of law could not only gain a foothold but also flourish in top-tier American law schools.

and economics scholars were unaware of his work until recently. It is difficult to measure and therefore treacherous to disclaim influence, but, speaking as one who received his legal education at the Harvard Law School between 1959 and 1962, I can attest that to a student the school seemed untouched by legal realism. And none of the legal and economic thinkers who since law school have most shaped my own academic and judicial thinking—Holmes, Coase, Stigler, Becker, Director, and others—was himself a product in whole or in part of legal realism.

That Coase, Stigler, Becker, and Director could shape and influence the perspective, scholarship, and judicial opinions of one of the most influential legal scholars of the late twentieth century—Richard Posner—and, by extension, stimulate the development of a new and now widely accepted approach to legal inquiry is not only a legacy of realism but also perhaps its foremost one.

Everywhere, Self-Interest?

THE ANALYSIS of the economic role of government has been bound up almost continuously in questions about the effects of the exercise of individual
self-interest on society as a whole. The preclassical commentators looked
for a means to coordinate or restrain the base effects of self-interested behavior and saw no means other than government regulation. Adam Smith
and the nineteenth-century classical economists saw the system of natural
liberty harmonizing, to a greater or lesser extent, self-interest and social
interest, allowing the market to function with less direct control by the state.
The marginal revolution and the subsequent development of neoclassical
economics illuminated divergences that the market seemingly could not
satisfactorily coordinate and showed how government could serve as an
efficient coordinating force. The backlash against this thinking, led by the
Chicago and Virginia schools, demonstrated that self-interested behavior
can also impact the operation of government, causing market failure and
government failure alike.

This is not to say that things had come full circle back to the classical view
by the end of the twentieth century. Indeed, far from it. What we have witnessed, though, is an acknowledgment (in certain quarters, at least) of the
inefficiencies of both markets and government, and a normative view of the
economic role of government that is quite heterogeneous, with individual
positions as to the efficacy of markets versus government resting largely on
one's opinion as to whether the limitations of the market are, in a given set
of circumstances, more or less severe than the limitations of government.

Given the centrality of self-interest in these two-plus millennia of literature, it is interesting that the assumption that individuals are motivated
by self-interest has been called increasingly into question in contemporary
economics. There have always been some economists who have argued
against the accuracy of utility theory and its more hard-nosed cousin, rational
choice theory, as descriptors of individual behavior, but with little impact on
professional practice, at east in its dominant, mainstream form. Yet recent
results in experimental economics—a number of which have involved tests
of the Coase theorem[1]—have led "mainstream" economists to reexamine

[1] See, for example, Elizabeth Hoffman and Matthew L. Spitzer (1982, 1985, 1986, 1993),
Harrison and McKee (1985), Coursey, Hoffman, and Spitzer (1987), Harrison, Hoffman,

the behavioral underpinnings of their theories, both without and within the realm traditionally considered economic. Bounded rationality, behavioral economics, and neuroeconomics, for example, are being used to offer alternative conceptions of how individuals make choices, and Nobel Prizes have already been awarded for some of this work.[2] While generally seen as a challenge to the traditional way of explaining, analyzing, and predicting individual behavior, these new approaches do not negate, or even attempt to refute, the motive force of self-interest in human behavior. Rather, they suggest that the choice process is richer and more complex than the rational actor model that dominated economic analysis over the last third of the twentieth century.

Then again, this is hardly an original idea, even within orthodox circles. When Alfred Marshall developed a formal demand-and-supply apparatus to analyze commercial society, he built it up from the actions of utility-seeking consumers and profit-seeking producers. He was no rational choicer, however. Marshall felt that economists should "deal with man as he is: not with an abstract or 'economic' man; but a man of flesh and blood" (1920: 22). He also drew a distinction between the economic and the noneconomic and said that "the side of life with which economics is specially concerned is that in which man's conduct is most deliberate, and in which he most often reckons up the advantages and disadvantages of any particular action before he enters on it" (1920: 17).[3] Marshall was convinced that there is much to be learned from using a conception of man that is grounded in utility maximization but took care to point out that this is not the sum total of the story. There are times, he said, when man's actions are guided by "habit and custom," and here man "proceeds for the moment without calculation"—though he allowed that in business-related affairs the habits and customs likely arise out of "a close and careful watching the advantages and disadvantages of different courses of conduct" (1920: 17).

If calculation does not govern all areas of life, or even particular areas in all circumstances, as Marshall and contemporary behavioral economists suggest, the economic approach becomes far less definitive in its theoretical conclusions and policy prescriptions. This consequence is clearly reflected in Marshall's demarcation of economics from natural sciences such as physics. Marshall argued that the results of economics are not like the laws of gravitation where, subject to a few ceteris paribus qualifications, we can state our expectations very concretely. Instead, economic theories are tendency statements, and of a somewhat weak sort. Moreover, as we move farther

---

Rutström, and Spitzer (1987), Kahneman, Knetsch, and Thaler (1990), and the discussion of this literature in Medema and Zerbe (2000).

[2] The prizes awarded to Herbert Simon in 1978 and to Daniel Kahneman and Vernon Smith in 2002 recognize this work.

[3] See more generally Marshall (1920: ch. 2).

and farther away from economic affairs proper within the social realm, those tendencies become progressively weaker (1920: 27).[4] There is, he says, "a continuous gradation from social laws concerned almost exclusively with motives that can be measured by price, to social laws in which such motives have little place." The latter, he went on to argue, are "generally much less precise and exact than economic laws," just as economic laws are much less exact and precise than those of physical sciences (1920: 27).[5]

A similar degree of indeterminacy may be said to characterize the relationship between self-interest, market, and state. The pendulum has swung back and forth over the past three centuries, and, if history is any indication, the recent ascendancy of the Chicago and Virginia approaches to these issues will be followed by a drift back to a more interventionist view. Indeed, the current economic crisis, with its attendant calls for new regulatory checks on the financial system, may well be a harbinger of exactly this. There remain "true believers" on both sides—those who argue that market failure is almost nonexistent and that government failure is ubiquitous, and others who see the market failure as ubiquitous and the government as something of a cure-all. But for the moment, at least, the debate seems to have settled at an intermediate point, with the majority of economists, like Coase, seeing neither the invisible hand nor the visible one as a panacea. The past two centuries of theoretical debate has suggested that the hand is hesitant—and increasingly, of late, so too is the economist.

---

[4] The terms "tendency" and "tendencies" are used roughly 150 times in Marshall's *Principles*. This was determined via a search conducted on the online version of the eighth edition of this work, which can be found at http://www.econlib.org/library/Marshall/marP.html.

[5] See Sutton (2000) for further discussion. The April 2002 issue of *Economics and Philosophy* contains a symposium that discusses the issues set forth in Sutton's book, particularly with regard to economic modeling and the relationship between theory and empirical evidence.

References

Adams, Henry C. ([1887/1897] 1954) *Relation of the State to Industrial Action and Economics and Jurisprudence*, edited by Joseph Dorfman. New York: Viking.

Aivazian, Varouj A., and Jeffrey L. Callen (1981) "The Coase Theorem and the Empty Core." *Journal of Law and Economics* 24 (April): 175–81.

Allen, Douglas W. (1991) "What Are Transaction Costs?" *Research in Law and Economics* 14: 1–18.

——— (1998) "Property Rights, Transaction Costs, and Coase: One More Time." Pp. 105–18 in *Coasean Economics: Law and Economics and the New Institutional Economics*, edited by Steven G. Medema. Boston: Kluwer.

Amadae, Sonja (2003) *Rationalizing Capitalist Democracy: The Cold War Origins of Rational Choice Liberalism.* Chicago: University of Chicago Press.

Aquinas, Thomas. ([1274] 1948) *Summa Theologica*, 5 vols. Notre Dame, IN: Ave Maria Press.

Aristotle (1946) *Politics.* Translated by Ernest Barker. Oxford: Clarendon.

Arrow, Kenneth J. (1951) *Social Choice and Individual Values.* New York: Wiley.

——— (1969) "The Organization of Market Activity: Issues Pertinent to the Choice of Market versus Nonmarket Allocation." In *The Analysis and Evaluation of Public Expenditures: The PPB System.* Joint Economic Committee, 91st Congress of the United States, 1st Session. Washington, DC: U.S. Government Printing Office.

Arrow, Kenneth J., and Gerard Debreu (1954) "Existence of an Equilibrium for a Competitive Economy." *Econometrica* 22 (July): 265–90.

Arrow, Kenneth J., and Tibor Scitovsky, eds. (1969) *Readings in Welfare Economics.* Homewood, IL: Richard D. Irwin for the American Economic Association.

Aslanbeigui, Nahid (1990) "On the Demise of Pigovian Economics." *Southern Economic Journal* 56 (January): 616–27.

——— (1995) "Pigou on Social Cost: Sophistry or Sophistication." Mimeo, Monmouth University.

——— (1996) "The Cost Controversy: Pigouvian Economics in Disequilibrium." *European Journal of History of Economic Thought* 3 (2): 275–95.

——— (2001) "Introduction." In A. C. Pigou, *The Economics of Welfare.* New Brunswick, NJ: Transaction.

——— (2008) "Pigou, Arthur Cecil (1877–1959)." In *The New Palgrave Dictionary of Economics*, edited by Steven N. Durlauf and Lawrence E. Bloom. 2nd ed. London: Palgrave.

Aslanbeigui, Nahid, and Steven G. Medema (1998) "Beyond the Dark Clouds: Pigou and Coase on Social Cost." *History of Political Economy* 30 (Winter): 601–25.

Backhaus, Jürgen, and Richard E. Wagner (2005) "From Continental Public Finance to Public Choice: Mapping Continuity." *History of Political Economy* 37 (Supplement): 314–22.

Backhouse, Roger E. (2006) "Sidgwick, Marshall and the Cambridge School of Economics." *History of Political Economy* 38: 15–44.

Backhouse, Roger E., and Bradley W. Bateman (2009) "Whose Keynes?" In *Keynes's General Theory: A Reconsideration after Seventy Years*, edited by R. W. Dimand, R. Mundell, and A. Vercelli. London: Palgrave for the International Economic Association.

Backhouse, Roger E., and Steven G. Medema (2008) "Market Failure, Government Failure, and the Cambridge School: A New View." Working paper, University of Colorado, Denver.

_____ (2009) "Defining Economics: The Long Road to Acceptance of the Robbins Definition." *Economica* (forthcoming).

Ballard, Charles L., and Steven G. Medema (1993) "The Marginal Efficiency of Taxes and Subsidies in the Presence of Externalities: A Computational General Equilibrium Approach." *Journal of Public Economics* 52 (August): 199–216.

Banfield, Edward C. (1958) "Review of *An Economic Theory of Democracy*, by Anthony Downs." *Midwest Journal of Political Science* 2 (August): 324–25.

Barzel, Yoram (1985) "Transaction Costs: Are They Just Costs?" *Journal of Institutional and Theoretical Economics* 141: 4–16.

Bastiat, Frédéric ([1850] 1996) *Economic Harmonies*, translated by W. Hayden Boyers, edited by George B. de Huszar. Irvington-on-Hudson, NY: Foundation for Economic Education.

Bator, Francis M. (1958) "The Anatomy of Market Failure." *Quarterly Journal of Economics* 72 (August): 351–79.

Baumol, William J. (1952a) "Review of *Social Choice and Individual Values*, by Kenneth J. Arrow." *Econometrica* 20 (January): 110–11.

_____ (1952b) *Welfare Economics and the Theory of the State*. London: London School of Economics and Political Science and Longmans, Green.

_____ (1972) "On Taxation and the Control of Externalities." *American Economic Review* 62: 307–22.

Becker, Gary S. (1957) *The Economics of Discrimination*. Chicago: University of Chicago Press.

_____ (1968) "Crime and Punishment: An Economic Approach." *Journal of Political Economy* 76 (March–April): 169–217.

_____ (1976) *The Economic Approach to Human Behavior*. Chicago: University of Chicago Press.

_____ (1981) *A Treatise on the Family*. Cambridge: Harvard University Press.

Bentham, Jeremy ([1793–95] 1839) *Manual of Political Economy*. In *The Works of Jeremy Bentham, Part IX*, edited by John Bowring. Edinburgh: William Tait.

_____ ([1823] 1970) *An Introduction to the Principles of Morals and Legislation*, edited by J. H. Burns and H.L.A. Hart. In *The Collected Works of Jeremy Bentham*. Oxford: Oxford University Press.

_____ (1830) The *Rationale of Punishment*. London: Robert Heward.

Bergson, Abram (1938) "A Reformulation of Certain Aspects of Welfare Economics." *Quarterly Journal of Economics* 52: 310–34.

_____ (1958) "Review of *An Economic Theory of Democracy*, by Anthony Downs." *American Economic Review* 48 (June): 437–40.

Berle, Adolf A., and Gardiner C. Means (1932) *The Modern Corporation and Private Property*. New York: Macmillan.

Bertrand, Elodie (2006) "The Coasean Analysis of Lighthouse Financing: Myths and Realities." *Cambridge Journal of Economics* 30 (May): 389–402.

Bharadwaj, K. (1972) "Marshall on Pigou's *Wealth and Welfare*." *Economica* n.s., 39: 32–46.

Black, Duncan (1948) "On the Rationale of Group Decision-Making." *Journal of Political Economy* 56: 23–34.

_____ (1955) "Wicksell's Principle in the Distribution of Taxation." In *Economic Essays in Commemoration of the Dundee School of Economics 1931–1955*, edited by J. K. Eastham. Coupar Angus, Scotland: William Culross.

_____ (1958) *The Theory of Committees and Elections*. Cambridge: Cambridge University Press.

Black, Duncan, and R. A. Newing (1952) *Committee Decisions with Complementary Valuation*. London: William Hodge.

Blaug, Mark (2007) "The Fundamental Theorems of Modern Welfare Economics, Historically Contemplated." *History of Political Economy* 39 (Summer): 185–207.

Bodenheimer, Edgar (1974) *Jurisprudence: The Philosophy and Method of the Law*, rev. ed. Cambridge: Harvard University Press.

Borda, Jean-Charles de (1781) "Mémoire sur les Élections au Scrutin." *Histoire de l'Académie Royale des Sciences*. Paris.

Bork, R. H. (1967) "Antitrust and Monopoly: The Goals of Antitrust Policy." *American Economic Review* 57: 242–53.

Bork, R. H., and W. S. Bowman, Jr. (1965) "The Crisis in Antitrust." *Columbia Law Review* 65: 363–76.

Boulding, Kenneth E. (1969) "Economics as a Moral Science." *American Economic Review* 59 (1): 1–12.

Bowman, W. S., Jr. (1957) "Tying Arrangements and the Leverage Problem." *Yale Law Journal* 67: 19–36.

Boyle, James (1994) *Critical Legal Studies*. New York: New York University Press.

Breit, William (1986) " 'Creating the Virginia School': Charlottesville as an Academic Environment in the 1960s." Second Annual Lecture in the Virginia Political Economy Lecture Series, April 16, 1986. Fairfax, VA: Center for Study of Public Choice.

Broadie, Alexander (2003) *The Cambridge Companion to the Scottish Enlightenment*. Cambridge: Cambridge University Press.

Buchanan, James M. (1960) "La Scienza delle finanze: The Italian Tradition in Fiscal Theory." In James M. Buchanan, *Fiscal Theory and Political Economy: Selected Essays*. Chapel Hill: University of North Carolina Press. Reprinted in James M. Buchanan, *Economics: Between Predictive Science and Moral Philosophy*, edited by Robert D. Tollison and Viktor J. VanBerg. College Station: Texas A&M University Press, 1987.

_____ (1962) "Politics, Policy, and Pigovian Margins." *Economica* 29: 17–28.

_____ (1983) "Political Economy: 1957–1982." *The G. Warren Nutter Lectures in Political Economy*. Washington, DC: American Enterprise Institute.

_____ (1986) "Rights, Efficiency, and Exchange: The Irrelevance of Transactions Cost." In J. M. Buchanan, *Liberty, Market and the State: Political Economy in the 1980s.* New York: New York University Press.

_____ (1989) "The Public Choice Perspective." Pp. 13–24 in J. M. Buchanan, *Essays on the Political Economy.* Honolulu: University of Hawaii Press.

_____ (1990) "The Domain of Constitutional Economics." *Constitutional Political Economy* 1 (Winter): 1–18.

Buchanan, James M., and W. Craig Stubblebine (1962) "Externality." *Economica* 29: 371–84.

Buchanan, James M., and Gordon Tullock (1962) *The Calculus of Consent.* Ann Arbor: University of Michigan Press.

Burnstein, M. L. (1960) "The Economics of Tie-in Sales." *Review of Economics and Statistics* 42: 68–73.

Cairnes, John Elliott (1873) "Political Economy and *Laissez Faire*." In *Essays in Political Economy*, London: Macmillan.

Calabresi, Guido (1961) "Some Thoughts on Risk Distribution and the Law of Torts." *Yale Law Journal* 70: 499–553.

_____ (1965) "The Decision for Accidents: An Approach to Nonfault Allocation of Costs." *Harvard Law Review* 78: 713–45.

Cannan, E. (1913) "Review of N. G. Pierson, *Principles of Economics*." *Economic Review* 23: 331–33.

Canterbery, E. Ray, and A. Marvasti (1992) "The Coase Theorem as a Negative Externality." *Journal of Economic Issues* 26: 1179–89.

Cardozo, Benjamin Nathan (1921) *The Nature of the Judicial Process.* New Haven: Yale University Press.

_____ (1924) *The Growth of the Law.* New Haven: Yale University Press.

_____ (1928) *The Paradoxes of Legal Science.* New York: Columbia University Press.

Chadwick, Edwin (1842) *Report on the Sanitary Conditions of the Labouring Population of Great Britain.* London: W. Clowes and Sons.

Cheung, Steven N. S. (1969) *The Theory of Share Tenancy.* Chicago: University of Chicago Press.

_____ (1973) "The Fable of the Bees: An Economic Investigation." *Journal of Law and Economics* 16 (April): 11–33.

_____ (1992) "On the New Institutional Economics." In *Contract Economics*, edited by Lars Werin and Hans Wijkander. Oxford: Blackwell.

Clapham, J. H. (1922) "Of Empty Economic Boxes." *Economic Journal* 32: 305–314.

Coase, Ronald H. (1937) "The Nature of the Firm." *Economica* n.s. 4 (November): 386–405.

_____ (1946) "The Marginal Cost Controversy." *Economica* n.s. 13 (August): 169–82.

_____ (1959) "The Federal Communications Commission." *Journal of Law and Economics* 2 (October): 1–40.

_____ (1960) "The Problem of Social Cost." *Journal of Law and Economics* 3 (October): 1–44.

_____ (1964) "Discussion." *American Economic Review* 54 (May): 194–97.

_____ (1970a) "Discussion." Pp. 60–61 in *Economics of Fisheries Management: A Symposium*, edited by A. D. Scott. Vancouver: Institute of Animal Resource Ecology, University of British Columbia.

_____ (1970b) "Discussion." *In Legal and Economic Aspects of Pollution*. Chicago: University of Chicago Center for Policy Study.

_____ (1970c) "Social Cost and Public Policy." Pp. 33–44 in *Exploring the Frontiers of Administration: Six Essays for Managers*, edited by George A. Edwards. Toronto: York University Faculty of Administration Studies, Bureau of Research.

_____ (1974a) "The Lighthouse in Economics." *Journal of Law and Economics* 17 (October): 357–76

_____ (1974b) "The Market for Goods and the Market for Ideas." *American Economic Review* 64 (May): 384–91.

_____ (1975) "Marshall on Method." *Journal of Law and Economics* 18 (April): 25–31.

_____ (1976) "Adam Smith's View of Man." *Journal of Law and Economics* 19 (3): 529–46.

_____ (1977a) "Advertising and Free Speech." Pp. 1–33 in *Advertising and Free Speech*, edited by Allen Hyman and M. Bruce Johnson. Lexington, MA.: D. C. Heath.

_____ (1977b) "Economics and Contiguous Disciplines." In *The Organization and Retrieval of Economic Knowledge*, edited by Mark Perlman. Boulder, CO: Westview.

_____ (1981) "The Coase Theorem and the Empty Core: A Comment." *Journal of Law and Economics* 24 (April): 183–87.

_____ (1982) "Economics at LSE in the 1930s: A Personal View." *Atlantic Economic Journal* 10 (March): 313–314.

_____ (1984) "The New Institutional Economics." *Journal of Institutional and Theoretical Economics* 140: 229–31.

_____ (1986) "Professor Sir Arnold Plant: His Ideas and Influence." In *The Unfinished Agenda: Essays on the Political Economy of Government Policy in Honour of Arthur Seldon*, edited by M. J. Anderson. London: Institute of Economic Affairs.

_____ (1988a) "Blackmail." *Virginia Law Review* 74 (May): 655–76.

_____ (1988b) "The Nature of the Firm: Origins." *Journal of Law, Economics, and Organization* 4 (Spring): 3–17.

_____ (1988c) *The Firm, the Market, and the Law*. Chicago: University of Chicago Press.

_____ (1992) "The Institutional Structure of Production." *American Economic Review* 82 (September): 713–19.

_____ (1993a) "Coase on Posner on Coase." *Journal of Institutional and Theoretical Economics* 149: 360–61.

_____ (1993b) "Law and Economics at Chicago." *Journal of Law and Economics* 36, Part 2 (April): 239–54.

_____ (1996) "Law and Economics and A. W. Brian Simpson." *Journal of Legal Studies* 25 (January): 103–119.

Colander, David (2009) "What Was 'It' That Robbins Was Defining?" *Journal of the History of Economic Thought* (forthcoming).

Collard, David (1999) "Introduction." In *A. C. Pigou: Collected Economic Writings, Volume 1*. London: Macmillan.

Commons, John R. (1924) *Legal Foundations of Capitalism*. New York: Macmillan.

———— (1925) "Law and Economics." *Yale Law Journal* 34 (February): 371–82.

———— (1934) *Institutional Economics*. New York: Macmillan.

Condorcet, M. J. A. N. de Carotat, Marquis de (1785) *Essai sur l'Application de l'Analyse à la Probabilitié des Décisions Rendues à la Pluralité des Voix*. Paris: Imprimerie Royale.

Cook, Simon (2009) *A Rounded Globe of Knowledge: The Intellectual Foundations of Alfred Marshall's Economic Science*. Cambridge: Cambridge University Press.

Cooter, Robert D. (1982) "The Cost of Coase." *Journal of Legal Studies* 11: 1–33.

———— (1987) "The Coase Theorem." In *The New Palgrave: A Dictionary of Economics*, edited by John Eatwell, Murray Milgate, and Peter Newman. New York: W. W. Norton.

Cooter, Robert, and Thomas Ulen (1988) *Law and Economics*. New York: HarperCollins.

———— (1997) Law and Economics, 2nd ed. Reading, MA: Addison-Wesley.

Coursey, Don L., Elizabeth Hoffman, and Matthew L. Spitzer (1987) "Fear and Loathing in the Coase Theorem: Experimental Tests Involving Physical Discomfort." *Journal of Legal Studies* 16: 217–48.

Da Empoli, Domenico (2002) "The Theory of Fiscal Illusion in a Constitutional Perspective." *Public Finance Review* 30 (September): 377–384.

Dahlman, Carl J. (1979) "The Problem of Externality." *Journal of Law and Economics* 22: 141–62.

Davis, Otto A., and Andrew Whinston (1962) "Externalities, Welfare and the Theory of Games." *Journal of Political Economy* 70: 241–262.

Debreu, Gerard (1954) "Valuation Equilibrium and Pareto Optimum." *Proceedings of the National Academy of Sciences* 40: 588–92.

Demsetz, Harold (1969) "Information and Efficiency: Another Viewpoint." *Journal of Law and Economics* 10 (April): 1–21.

DeSerpa, Allan C. (1993) "Coase and Pigou in Retrospect." *Cambridge Journal of Economics* 17 (1): 27–50.

De Viti de Marco, Antonio (1936) *First Principles of Public Finance*, translated from the Italian by Edith Pavlo Marget. London: Jonathan Cape.

Diamond, Martin (1959) "Review of *An Economic Theory of Democracy*, by Anthony Downs." *Journal of Political Economy* 67 (April): 208–11.

Director, Aaron, and Edward H. Levi (1956) "Law and the Future: Trade Regulation." *Northwestern Law Review* 51 (May–June): 281–96.

Dodgson, C. L. (1873) *A Discussion of Various Methods of Procedure in Conducting Elections*. Oxford: E. B. Gardner, E. Pickard and J. H. Stacy, Printers to the University, Oxford.

———— (1876) *A Method of Taking Votes on More than Two Issues*. Oxford: Clarendon.

———— (1884) *The Principles of Parliamentary Representation*. London: Harrison and Sons.

Dow, Jay, and Michael Munger (1990) "Public Choice in Political Science: We Don't Teach It, But We Publish It." *PS* 23 (December): 604–9.

Downs, Anthony (1957) *An Economic Theory of Democracy.* New York: Harper.

———— (1959) "Review of *The Theory of Committees and Elections*, by Duncan Black." *Journal of Political Economy* 67 (April): 211–212.

———— (1964) "Review of *The Calculus of Consent*, by James M. Buchanan and Gordon Tullock." *Journal of Political Economy* 72 (February): 87–88.

———— (1967) *Inside Bureaucracy.* Boston: Little Brown.

Dunbar, Charles F. (1886) "The Reaction in Political Economy." *Quarterly Journal of Economics* 1 (October): 1–27.

Duxbury, Neil (1995) *Patterns of American Jurisprudence.* Oxford: Oxford University Press.

Dworkin, Ronald M. (1980) "Is Wealth a Value?" *Journal of Legal Studies* 9 (March): 191–226.

———— (2000) "Philosophy and Monica Lewinsky." *The New York Review of Books* 47 (March 9).

Eggertsson, Thráinn (1990) *Economic Behavior and Institutions.* Cambridge: Cambridge University Press.

Einaudi, Luigi (1936) "Introduction." In Antonio De Viti de Marco, *First Principles of Public Finance*, translated from the Italian by Edith Pavlo Marget. London: Jonathan Cape.

Ellis, Howard R., and William Fellner (1943) "External Economies and Diseconomies." *American Economic Review* 33 (September): 493–511.

Ely, Richard T. (1914) *Property and Contract in Their Relation to the Distribution of Wealth*, 2 vols. New York: Macmillan.

Emmett, Ross, ed. (2008) *The Elgar Companion to the Chicago School.* Aldershot, England: Edward Elgar.

Evensky, Jerry (2005) " 'Chicago Smith' versus 'Kirkaldy Smith.' " *History of Political Economy* 37 (Summer): 197–203.

Faccarello, Gilbert (1999) *Foundations of "Laissez-Faire": The Economics of Pierre de Boisguilbert.* London: Routledge.

Faccarello, Gilbert, and Philippe Steiner (2006) "Interests, Sensationism and the Science of the Legislator: French 'Philosophie Économique,' 1695–1830." Working paper, Université de Paris II.

Fagen, Richard R. (1963) "Review of *The Theory of Political Coalitions*, by William H. Riker." *American Political Science Review* 57 (June): 446–47.

Farber, Daniel A., and Philip P. Frickey (1991) *Law and Public Choice: A Critical Introduction.* Chicago: University of Chicago Press.

Farrell, Joseph (1987) "Information and the Coase Theorem." *Journal of Economic Perspectives* 1: 113–29.

Farris, Charles D. (1958) "Review of *An Economic Theory of Democracy*, by Anthony Downs." *Journal of Politics* 20 (August): 571–73.

Fausto, Domenicantonio (2006) "The Italian Approach to the Theory of Public Goods." *European Journal of the History of Economic Thought* 13 (March): 69–98.

Fischer, Stanley (1977) "Long Term Contracting, Sticky Prices, and Monetary Policy." *Journal of Monetary Economics* 3: 317–23.

Fisher, William W., Morton J. Horwitz, and Thomas A. Reed (1993) *American Legal Realism.* New York: Oxford University Press.

Fossati, Amedeo (2006) "Needs, the Principle of Minimum Means, and Public Goods in De Viti de Marco." *Journal of the History of Economic Thought* 28 (December): 427–38.

Frech, H. E., III (1979) "The Extended Coase Theorem and Long Run Equilibrium: The Nonequivalence of Liability Rules and Property Rights." *Economic Inquiry* 17: 254–68.

Friedman, Lawrence M. (1973) *A History of American Law.* New York: Simon & Schuster.

Friedman, Milton (1953) "The Methodology of Positive Economics." In *Essays in Positive Economics.* Chicago: University of Chicago Press.

—— (1967) "The Monetary Theory and Policy of Henry Simons." *Journal of Law and Economics* 10 (October): 1–13.

Galton, Francis (1907a) "One Vote, One Value." *Nature* 75: 414.

—— (1907b) "*Vox Populi.*" *Nature* 75: 450–51.

Gertzog, Irwin N. (1964) "Review of *The Calculus of Consent,* by James M. Buchanan and Gordon Tullock." *American Political Science Review* 63 (December): 973–74.

Gjerdingen, Donald H. (1986) "The Politics of the Coase Theorem and Its Relationship to Modern Legal Thought." *Buffalo Law Review* 35: 871–935.

Gordon, Barry (1975) *Economic Analysis before Adam Smith: Hesiod to Lessius.* New York: Harper & Row.

Gordon, Scott (1955) "The London *Economist* and the High Tide of Laissez Faire." *Journal of Political Economy* 63 (December): 461–88.

Graaff, J. de V. (1957) *Theoretical Welfare Economics.* Cambridge: Cambridge University Press.

Grampp, William (1960) *The Manchester School of Economics.* Stanford: Stanford University Press.

Green, Donald P., and Ian Shapiro (1994) *Pathologies of Rational Choice Theory.* New Haven: Yale University Press.

Grembi, Veronica (2003) "The Actual Role of Ronald Coase's and Guido Calabresi's Contributions to the New Law and Economics." Working paper, University of Florence.

Grey, Thomas C. (1983) "Langdell's Orthodoxy." *University of Pittsburgh Law Review* 45 (Fall): 1–53.

Groenewegen, Peter (1995) *A Soaring Eagle: Alfred Marshall, 1942–1924.* Aldershot, England: Edward Elgar.

—— (2001) "From Prominent Physician to Major Economist: Some Reflections on Quesnay's Switch to Economics in the 1750s." In *Physicians and Political Economy: Six Studies of the Work of Doctor-Economists,* edited by Peter Groenewegen. London: Routledge.

—— (2002) "Laissez-faire: Reflections on the French Foundations." Pp. 211–21 in *Eighteenth-Century Economics: Turgot, Beccaria, and Smith and Their Contemporaries.* London: Routledge,

Haakonssen, Knud (2006) *The Cambridge Companion to Adam Smith.* Cambridge: Cambridge University Press.

Hale, Robert Lee (1924) "Economic Theory and the Statesman." In *The Trend of Economics,* edited by Rexford G. Tugwell. New York: Knopf.

_____ (1927) "Economics and the Law." In *The Social Sciences and Their Inter-relations*, edited by William F. Ogburn and Alexander A. Goldenweiser. Boston: Houghton Mifflin.

_____ (1952) *Freedom Through Law*. New York: Columbia University Press.

Hamburger, Joseph. (1965) *Intellectuals in Politics: John Stuart Mill and the Philosophic Radicals*. New Haven: Yale University Press.

Hamilton, Walton H. (1930) "Affectation with Public Interest." *Yale Law Journal* 39 (June): 1089–1112.

_____ (1932) "Property According to Locke." *Yale Law Journal* 41 (April): 864–80.

Harrison, Glenn W., Elizabeth Hoffman, E. E. Rutström, and Matthew L. Spitzer (1987) "Coasian Solutions to the Externality Problem in Experimental Markets." *Economic Journal* 97: 388–402.

Harrison, Glenn W., and Michael McKee (1985) "Experimental Evaluation of the Coase Theorem." *Journal of Law and Economics* 28 (October): 653–670.

Harsanyi, John C. (1965) "Review of The *Theory of Committees and Elections*, by Duncan Black." *Econometrica* 33 (July): 651–53.

Hayek, F. A. (1944) *The Road to Serfdom*. Chicago: University of Chicago Press.

Head, John G. (1974) *Public Goods and Public Welfare*. Durham, NC: Duke University Press.

Heckscher, Eli (1935) *Mercantilism*. London: Allen and Unwin.

Hennipman, Pieter (1980) "Some Notes on Pareto Optimality and Wicksellian Unanimity." Pp. 399–410 in *Wandlungen in Wirtschaft und Gesellschaft*, edited by Emil Küng. Tübingen: J.C.B. Mohr. Reprinted in Pieter Hennipman, *Welfare Economics and the Theory of Economic Policy*, edited by Donald Walker, Arnold Heertje, and Hans van den Doel. Aldershot, England: Edward Elgar, 1995, pp. 240–49.

_____ (1982) "Wicksell and Pareto: Their Relationship in the Theory of Public Finance." *History of Political Economy* 14 (Spring): 37–64. Reprinted in Pieter Hennipman, *Welfare Economics and the Theory of Economic Policy*, edited by Donald Walker, Arnold Heertje, and Hans van den Doel. Aldershot, England: Edward Elgar, 1995, pp. 214–39.

Higgs, Henry (1897) *The Physiocrats*. London: Macmillan.

Hill, Lisa (2006) "Adam Smith and the Theme of Corruption." *Review of Politics* 68: 636–662.

Hilton, Boyd (1979) "Peel: A Reappraisal." *The Historical Journal* 22 (3): 585–614.

Hodgson, Geoffrey (1988) *Economics and Institutions*. Philadelphia: University of Pennsylvania Press.

Hoffman, Elizabeth, and Matthew L. Spitzer (1982) "The Coase Theorem: Some Experimental Tests." *Journal of Law and Economics* 25 (April): 73–98.

_____ (1985) "Entitlements, Rights and Fairness: An Experimental Examination of Subjects' Concepts of Distributive Justice." *Journal of Legal Studies* 14 (June): 259–297.

_____ (1986) "Experimental Tests of the Coase Theorem with Large Bargaining Groups." *Journal of Legal Studies* 15 (January): 149–71.

_____ (1993) "Willingness to Pay vs. Willingness to Accept: Legal and Economic Implications." *Washington University Law Quarterly* 71 (Spring): 59–114.

Holdsworth, W. S. (1927–28) "A Neglected Aspect of the Relations Between Economic and Legal History." *Economic History Review* 1 (January): 114–23.

Hollander, Samuel (1973) *The Economics of Adam Smith.* Toronto: University of Toronto Press.

_____ (1985) *The Economics of John Stuart Mill,* 2 vols. Oxford: Blackwell.

Holmes, Oliver Wendell (1897) "The Path of Law." *Harvard Law Review* 10: 457–78.

_____ (1923) *The Common Law.* Boston: Little Brown.

Hotz, Alfred (1963) "Review of *The Theory of Political Coalitions,* by William H. Riker." *Midwest Journal of Political Science* 7 (August): 295–97.

Houthakker, H. S. (1952) "Review of *Social Choice and Individual Values,* by Kenneth J. Arrow." *Economic Journal* 62 (June): 355–58.

Hovenkamp, Herbert. (1986) "Chicago and Its Alternatives." *Duke Law Journal* 1986, 1014–29.

_____ (1990) "Marginal Utility and the Coase Theorem." *Cornell Law Review* 75 (May): 783–810.

_____ (1995) "Law and Economics in the United States: A Brief Historical Survey." *Cambridge Journal of Economics* 19 (April): 331–52.

Hutchison, T. W. (1953) *A Review of Economic Doctrines: 1870–1929.* Oxford: Oxford University Press. Reprinted Bristol, England.: Thoemmes, 1993.

Jevons, William Stanley (1871) *The Theory of Political Economy.* London: Macmillan.

Johnson, David B. (1991) *Public Choice: An Introduction to the New Political Economy.* Mountain View, CA: Mayfield.

Kahneman, Daniel, Jack L. Knetsch, and Richard H. Thaler (1990) "Experimental Tests of the Endowment Effect and the Coase Theorem." *Journal of Political Economy* 98 (December): 1325–48.

Kaldor, N. (1939) "Welfare Propositions of Economics and Inter-personal Comparisons of Utility." *Economic Journal* 49: 549–52.

Katz, Wilbur (1937) "A Four-Year Program for Legal Education." *University of Chicago Law Review* 4 (June): 527–36.

Kayaalp, Orhan (1985) "Public Choice Elements in the Italian Theory of Public Goods." *Public Finance/Finances Publiques* 3: 395–410.

_____ (1988) "Ugo Mazzola and the Italian Theory of Public Goods." *History of Political Economy* 20 (Spring): 15–25.

_____ (1989) "Early Italian Contributions to the Theory of Public Finance: Pantaleoni, De Viti de Marco, and Mazzola." Pp. 155–66 in *Perspectives on the History of Economic Thought, Volume 1: Classical and Neoclassical Economic Thought,* edited by Donald A. Walker. Aldershot, England: Edward Elgar.

Kelman, Mark (1979) "Consumption Theory, Production Theory, and Ideology in the Coase Theorem." *Southern California Law Review* 52: 669–98.

_____ (1987) *A Guide to Critical Legal Studies.* Cambridge: Harvard University Press.

Keynes, John Maynard (1936) *The General Theory of Employment, Interest and Money.* London: Macmillan.

Keyt, David, and Fred D. Miller, Jr., eds. (1991) *A Companion to Aristotle's Politics*. Oxford: Oxford University Press.

Kitch, Edmund W. (1983) "The Fire of Truth: A Remembrance of Law and Economics at Chicago, 1932–1970." *Journal of Law and Economics* 26 (April): 163–233.

Knight, F. H. (1924) "Some Fallacies in the Interpretation of Social Cost." *Quarterly Journal of Economics* 38: 582–606.

Kort, Fred (1959) "Review of *The Theory of Committees and Elections*, by Duncan Black." *Journal of Politics* 21 (May): 325–27.

Kraut, Richard (2002) *Aristotle: Political Philosophy*. Oxford: Oxford University Press.

Krueger, Ann O. (1974) "The Political Economy of Rent Seeking." *American Economic Review* 64: 291–303.

Landes, William M., and Richard A. Posner (1983) "Causation in Tort Law: An Economic Approach." *Journal of Legal Studies*, 12: 109–34.

——— (1987) *The Economic Structure of Tort Law*. Cambridge: Harvard University Press.

Langdell, Christopher C. (1871) *A Selection of Cases on the Law of Contracts*. Boston: Little, Brown.

Lange, Oscar (1942) "The Foundations of Welfare Economics." *Econometrica* 10: 215–28.

Langholm, Odd (1998) *The Legacy of Scholasticism in Economic Thought*. Cambridge: Cambridge University Press.

Laplace, Pierre-Simon, Marquis de (1812) "Leçons de Mathématiques, données à l'École Normale en 1795." *Journal de l'École Polytechnique*, tome II, septième et huitième cahiers: 1–173.

Lazear, Edward P. (2000) "Economic Imperialism." *Quarterly Journal of Economics* 115 (February): 99–146.

Litchman, Mark M. (1927) "Economics, the Basis of Law." *American Law Review* 61 (May–June): 357–87.

Llewellyn, Karl N. (1925) "The Effect of Legal Institutions upon Economics." *American Economic Review* 15 (December): 655–83.

Lowry, S. Todd (1987) *The Archaeology of Economic Ideas: The Classical Greek Tradition*. Durham, NC: Duke University Press.

Magnusson, Lars (1993) "Introduction." In *Mercantilist Economics*, edited by Lars Magnusson. Boston: Kluwer Academic Publishers.

——— (1994) *Mercantilism: The Shaping of an Economic Language*. London: Routledge.

Mäki, Uskali (1998) "Is Coase a Realist?" *Philosophy of the Social Sciences* 28: 5–31.

Maloney, John (1985) *Marshall, Orthodoxy, and the Professionalization of Economics*. Cambridge: Cambridge University Press.

——— (2005) *The Political Economy of Robert Lowe*. London: Palgrave Macmillan.

Malthus, Thomas Robert (1798) *An Essay on the Principle of Population*. London: J. Johnson.

Mandeville, Bernard. ([1714] 1988) *The Fable of the Bees*. Indianapolis, IN: Liberty Fund.

Manne, Henry G. (1963) "Review of *The Calculus of Consent*, by James M. Buchanan and Gordon Tullock." *George Washington Law Review* 31 (June): 1065–71.

Marchand, James R., and Keith P. Russell (1973) "Externalities, Liability, Separability, and Resource Allocation." *American Economic Review* 63: 611–20.

Marshall, A. ([1907] 1925) "Social Possibilities of Economic Chivalry." Reprinted in *Memorials of Alfred Marshall*, edited by A. C. Pigou, pp. 323–46. London: Macmillan.

_____ (1920) *Principles of Economics*, 8th ed. London: Macmillan.

_____ (1923) *Industry and Trade*, 4th ed. London: Macmillan.

_____ (1926) "Memorandum on Fiscal Policy of International Trade." In *Official Papers by Alfred Marshall*, edited by John Maynard Keynes. London: Macmillan.

Matthews, Donald R. (1963) "Review of *The Theory of Political Coalitions*, by William H. Riker." *Journal of Politics* 25 (August): 578–80.

May, R. J. (1963) "Review of *The Calculus of Consent*, by James M. Buchanan and Gordon Tullock." The *Australian Quarterly* (December): 111–13.

Mazzola, Ugo ([1890] 1958) "The Formation of the Prices of Public Goods," translated from the Italian by Elizabeth Henderson. Pp. 37–47 in *Classics in the Theory of Public Finance*, edited by Richard A. Musgrave and Alan T. Peacock. London: Macmillan. Originally published in Rome as *I dati scientifici della finanza pubblica*, chapter 9, pp. 159–83.

McCulloch, J. R. (1848) *Treatise on the Succession to Property Vacant by Death*, London: Longman, Brown, Green & Longmans.

_____ ([1853] 1968) "A Treatise on the Letting and Occupancy of Land." In J. R. McCulloch, *Treatises and Essays on Subjects Connected with Economical Policy: With Biographical Sketches of Quesnay, Adam Smith and Ricardo*. Clifton, NJ: Augustus M. Kelley, 1968.

_____ (1856) *Considerations on Partnership with Limited Liability*. London: Longman, Brown, Green & Longmans.

McGee, J. S. (1958) "Predatory Price Cutting: The Standard Oil (N.J.) Case." *Journal of Law and Economics* 1: 137–69.

McGinnis, Robert (1963) "Review of *The Calculus of Consent*, by James M. Buchanan and Gordon Tullock." *The Annals of the American Academy of Political and Social Science* 346 (March): 188.

McKenzie, Lionel W. (2008) "General Equilibrium." In *The New Palgrave Dictionary of Economics*, 2nd ed., edited by Steven N. Durlauf and Lawrence E. Bloom. London: Palgrave.

McLean, Iain, Alistair McMillan, and Burt L. Monroe (1998) "Editors' Introduction." Pp, xvii–1 in *The Theory of Committees and Elections, by Duncan Black and Committee Decisions with Complementary Valuation by Duncan Black and R. A. Newing*, revised 2nd eds., edited by Iain McLean, Alistair McMillan, and Burt L. Monroe. Boston: Kluwer.

Meade, James E. (1952) "External Economies and Diseconomies in a Competitive Situation." *Economic Journal* 62: 54–67.

_____ (1963) "Review of *The Calculus of Consent*, by James M. Buchanan and Gordon Tullock." *Economic Journal* 73 (March): 101–104.

Medema, Steven G. (1994a) "The Myth of Two Coases: What Coase Is Really Saying." *Journal of Economic Issues* 28 (March): 208–217.

_____ (1994b) *Ronald H. Coase*. London: Macmillan.

_____ (1995) "Ronald Coase on Economics and Economic Method." *History of Economics Review* 24: 1–22.

_____ (1996a) "Of Pangloss, Pigouvians and Pragmatism: Ronald Coase and Social Cost Analysis." *Journal of the History of Economic Thought* 18 (Spring): 96–114.

_____ (1996b) "Ronald Coase and American Institutionalism." *Research in the History of Economic Thought and Methodology* 14: 51–92.

_____ (1997) "The Coase Theorem, Rent Seeking, and the Forgotten Footnote." *International Review of Law and Economics* 17 (June): 177–178.

_____ ed. (1998) *Coasean Economics: Law and Economics and the New Institutional Economics*. Boston: Kluwer.

_____ (1999) "Legal Fiction: The Place of the Coase Theorem in Law and Economics." *Economics and Philosophy* 15 (October): 209–33.

_____ (2003) "The Economic Role of Government in the History of Economic Thought." In *The Blackwell Companion to the History of Economic Thought*, edited by Jeff Biddle, John B. Davis, and Warren J. Samuels. Oxford: Blackwell.

_____ (2007a) "Chicago Price Theory and Chicago Law and Economics: A Tale of Two Transitions." Working paper, University of Colorado, Denver.

_____ (2007b) "Creating a Paradox: Self-Interest, Civic Duty, and the Evolution of the Theory of the Rational Voter." Working paper, University of Colorado, Denver.

_____ (2007c) "Sidgwick's Utilitarian Analysis of Law: A Bridge from Bentham to Becker?" *American Law and Economics Review* 9 (Spring): 30–47.

_____ (2008) "Director, Aaron (1901–2004)." In *The New Palgrave Dictionary of Economics*, 2nd ed., edited by Steven N. Durlauf and Lawrence E. Bloom. London: Palgrave.

_____ (2009a) "Adam Smith and the Chicago School." In *The Elgar Companion to Adam Smith*, edited by Jeffrey Young. Aldershot, England: Edward Elgar.

_____ (2009b) "From Dismal to Dominance: Law and Economics and the Values of Imperial Science." In *Norms and Values in Law and Economics*, edited by Aristides Hatzis. London: Routledge.

Medema, Steven G., and Warren J. Samuels (1997) "Ronald Coase and Coasean Economics: Some Questions, Conjectures and Implications." Pp. 72–128 in *The Economy as a Process of Valuation*, edited by Warren J. Samuels, Steven G. Medema, and A. Allan Schmid. Aldershot, England: Edward Elgar.

_____ (2000) "The Economic Role of Government as, in Part, a Matter of Selective Perception, Sentiment, and Valuation: The Cases of Pigovian and Paretian Welfare Economics." *American Journal of Economics and Sociology* 59 (January): 87–108.

Medema, Steven G., and Richard O. Zerbe, Jr. (2000) "The Coase Theorem." Pp. 836–92 in *Encyclopedia of Law and Economics*, vol. 1, edited by Boudewijn Bouckaert and Gerrit De Geest. Cheltenham, England: Edward Elgar.

Meek, Ronald L. (1962) *The Economics of Physiocracy: Essays and Translations*. London: George Allen & Unwin. Reprinted Fairfield, NJ: Augustus M. Kelley, 1993.

Menger, Carl ([1871] 1981) *Principles of Economics*. Translated from the German by James Dingwall and Bert F. Hoselitz. New York: New York University Press.

_____ (1883) *Untersuchungen über die Methode der Socialwissenschaften*. Leipzig: Duncker & Humblot.

Mercuro, Nicholas, and Steven G. Medema (1997) *Economics and the Law: From Posner to Post-Modernism*. Princeton: Princeton University Press.

_____ (2006) *Economics and the Law: From Posner to Post-Modernism and Beyond*, 2nd ed. Princeton: Princeton University Press.

Mill, John Stuart ([1859] 1992) *On Liberty*. New York: Classics of Liberty Library.

_____ ([1861] 1977) *Considerations on Representative Government*. In *Collected Works of John Stuart Mill, Volume XIX: Essays on Politics and Society*, edited by J. M. Robson. Toronto: University of Toronto Press.

_____ ([1862] 1977) "Centralisation." In *Collected Works of John Stuart Mill, Volume XIX: Essays on Politics and Society*, edited by J. M. Robson. Toronto: University of Toronto Press, 1977.

_____ ([1865] 1969) "Auguste Comte and Positivism." In *Collected Works of John Stuart Mill, Volume X: Essays on Ethics, Religion and Society*, edited by J. M. Robson. Toronto: University of Toronto Press.

_____ ([1871] 1909) *Principles of Political Economy*, 7th ed. London: Longmans, Green.

_____ ([1873] 1977) *Autobiography*. In *Collected Works of John Stuart Mill, Volume I*, edited by J. M. Robson and Jack Stillinger. Toronto: University of Toronto Press.

_____ ([1879] 1967) "Chapters on Socialism." In *Collected Works of John Stuart Mill, Volume V: Essays on Economics and Society*, edited by J. M. Robson. Toronto: University of Toronto Press.

Milne, R. S. (1962) "Review of *The Calculus of Consent*, by James M. Buchanan and Gordon Tullock." *Political Quarterly* 33 (October).

Mirowski, Philip (1989) *More Heat Than Light*. Cambridge: Cambridge University Press.

Mishan, E. J. (1967) "Pareto Optimality and the Law." *Oxford Economic Papers* 19 (November): 255–87.

_____ (1971) "The Postwar Literature on Externalities: An Interpretive Essay." *Journal of Economic Literature* 9 (March): 1–28.

Mitchell, Joyce M., and William C. Mitchell (1969) *Political Analysis and Public Policy*. Chicago: Rand McNally.

Mitchell, William C. (1999) "Political Science and Public Choice: 1950–70." *Public Choice* 98 (March): 237–49.

Montemartini, Giovanni ([1900] 1958) "The Fundamental Principles of a Pure Theory of Public Finance," translated from the Italian by D. Bevan. Pp. 137–51 in *Classics in the Theory of Public Finance*, edited by Richard A. Musgrave and Alan T. Peacock. London: Macmillan. Originally published as "Le basi fondamentali di una scienza finanziaria pura." *Giornale degli Economisti*, II.

Morgan, Mary, and Malcolm Rutherford, eds. (1998) *The Transformation of American Economics: From Interwar Pluralism to Postwar Neoclassicism: History of Political Economy Annual Supplement* 30. Durham, NC: Duke University Press.

Mueller, Dennis C. (2003) *Public Choice.* 3rd ed. Cambridge: Cambridge University Press.

Musgrave, Richard A. (1959) *The Theory of Public Finance.* New York: McGraw-Hill.

———— (1985) "A Brief History of Fiscal Doctrine." In *Handbook of Public Economics,* vol. 1, edited by Alan J. Auerbach and Martin Feldstein. Amsterdam: North-Holland.

———— (1996) "Combining and Separating Fiscal Choices: Wicksell's Model at Its Centennial." *Public Economics Review* (June): 1–34. Reprinted in Richard A. Musgrave, *Public Finance in a Democratic Society,* vol. 3. Cheltenham, England: Edward Elgar, 2000.

Musgrave, Richard A., and Alan T. Peacock (1958) "Introduction." Pp. ix–xix in *Classics in the Theory of Public Finance.* London: Macmillan.

Nanson, E. J. (1882) "Methods of Election." *Proceedings of the Royal Society of Victoria* 19: 197–240.

Niskanen, William (1971) *Bureaucracy and Representative Government.* Chicago: Aldine-Atherton.

North, Douglass C. (1981) *Structure and Change in Economic History.* W. W. Norton.

O'Brien, D. P. (1970) *J. R. McCulloch: A Study in Classical Economics.* London: Routledge.

———— (1975) *The Classical Economists.* Oxford: Clarendon.

———— (1998) "Four Detours." *Journal of Economic Methodology* 5: 23–41.

———— (2004) *The Classical Economists Revisited.* Princeton: Princeton University Press.

O'Donnell, Margaret G. (1979) "Pigou: An Extension of Sidgwickian Thought." *History of Political Economy* 11 (4): 588–605.

Olson, Mancur, Jr. (1962) "Review of *The Calculus of Consent,* by James M. Buchanan and Gordon Tullock." *American Economic Review* 52 (December): 1217–18.

———— (1965) *The Logic of Collective Action.* Cambridge: Harvard University Press.

Ordeshook, Peter C. (1969) "Review of A Theory of Political Exchange: Economic Reasoning in Political Analysis." *American Political Science Review* 63 (December): 1294–96.

P., C. M. (1963) "Review of *The Calculus of Consent,* by James M. Buchanan and Gordon Tullock." *Ethics* 75 (October): 65–68.

Pålsson Syll, Lars, and Bo Sandelin (2001) "The Spread of Italian Economic Thought in Sweden, 1750–1950." In *From Economists to Economists: The International Spread of Italian Economic Thought, 1750–1850,* edited by Pier Francesco Asso. Florence: Edizioni Polistampa.

Pantaleoni, Maffeo ([1883] 1958) "Contribution to the Theory of the Distribution of Public Expenditure," translated from the Italian by D. Bevan. Pp. 16–27 in *Classics in the Theory of Public Finance*, edited by Richard A. Musgrave and Alan T. Peacock. London: Macmillan. Originally published as "Contributo alla teoria del riparto delle spese pubbliche." *Rassegna Italiana*, October 15, 1883; reprinted in Maffeo Pantaleoni, *Scritti varii di Economia*, vol. 1, Rome 1904.

―――― (1889) *Principii di economia pura*. Florence: G. Barbera.

Pareto, Vilfredo ([1906] 1971) *Manual of Political Economy*. Translated from the Italian by Ann S. Schwier; edited by Ann S. Schwier and Alfred N. Page. New York: Augustus M. Kelley.

Parisi, Francesco, and Charles K. Rowley (2005) *The Origins of Law and Economics: Essays by the Founding Fathers*. Cheltenham, England: Edward Elgar.

Parsons, Talcott. (1935a) "Sociological Elements in Economic Thought I. Historical." *Quarterly Journal of Economics* 49 (May): 414–453.

―――― (1935b) "Sociological Elements in Economic Thought II. The Analytical Factor View." *Quarterly Journal of Economics* 49 (August): 646–667.

Peacock, Alan (1987) "Wicksell and Public Choice." Pp. 69–95 in *The New Palgrave: A Dictionary of Economics*, edited by John Eatwell, Murray Milgate, and Peter Newman. London: Macmillan.

―――― (1992) *Public Choice Analysis in Historical Perspective*. Cambridge: Cambridge University Press.

Pearson, Heath (1997) *Origins of Law and Economics: The Economists' New Science of Law, 1830–1930*. Cambridge: Cambridge University Press.

Peltzman, S. (2005) "Aaron Director's Influence on Antitrust Policy." *Journal of Law and Economics* 48: 313–30.

Pennock, J. Roland (1958) "Review of *An Economic Theory of Democracy*, by Anthony Downs." *American Political Science Review* 52 (June): 539–41.

Petty, Sir William ([1662] 1986) *A Treatise of Taxes and Contributions*. In *The Economic Writings of Sir William Petty*, edited by Charles Henry Hull. Cambridge: Cambridge University Press, 1899. Reprinted Fairfield, NJ: Augustus M. Kelley.

Pigou, A. C. (1908) "Economic Science in Relation to Practice." In *A. C. Pigou: Collected Economic Writings, Volume 1*, edited by David Collard. London: Macmillan.

―――― (1912) *Wealth and Welfare*. London: Macmillan.

―――― (1922) "Empty Economic Boxes: A Reply." *Economic Journal* 32 (December): 458–65.

――――, ed. (1925) *Memorials of Alfred Marshall*. London: Macmillan.

―――― (1928) *A Study in Public Finance*. London: Macmillan.

―――― (1932) *The Economics of Welfare*, 4th ed. London: Macmillan.

―――― (1935) *Economics in Practice*. London: Macmillan.

―――― (1935a) "An Economist's *Apologia*." Pp. 1–25 in *Economics in Practice: Six Lectures on Current Issues*. London: Macmillan.

―――― (1935b) "The Economics of Restrictions." Pp. 129–54 in *Economics in Practice: Six Lectures on Current Issues*. London: Macmillan.

―――― (1935c) "Economy and Waste." Pp. 26–51 in *Economics in Practice: Six Lectures on Current Issues*. London: Macmillan, 26–51.

―――― (1935d) "State Action and Laisser-Faire." Pp. 107–28 in *Economics in Practice: Six Lectures on Current Issues*. London: Macmillan.

Pitavy-Simoni, Pascale (1997) "Vincent de Gournay, or 'Laissez-Faire without Laissez-Passer.' " Pp. 173–93 in *The State of the History of Economics*, edited by James P. Henderson. London: Routledge.

Plant, Sir Arnold (1974) *Selected Economic Essays and Addresses*. London: Routledge & Kegan Paul.

Polinsky, A. Mitchell (1974) "Economic Analysis as a Potentially Defective Product: A Buyer's Guide to Posner's *Economic Analysis of Law*." *Harvard Law Review* 87: 1655–81.

Posner, Richard A. (1969) "Oligopoly and the Antitrust Laws: A Suggested Approach." *Stanford Law Review* 21, 1562–1606.

_____ (1973) *Economic Analysis of Law*. Boston: Little Brown.

_____ (1976) *Antitrust Law: An Economic Perspective*. Chicago: University of Chicago Press.

_____ (1981) *The Economics of Justice*. Cambridge: Harvard University Press.

_____ (1987) "The Decline of Law as an Autonomous Discipline: 1962–1987." *Harvard Law Review* 100 (February): 761–80.

_____ (1990) *The Problems of Jurisprudence*. Cambridge: Harvard University Press.

_____ (1992) *Economic Analysis of Law*, 4th ed. Boston: Little, Brown.

_____ (1993a) "The New Institutional Economics Meets Law and Economics." *Journal of Institutional and Theoretical Economics* 149: 73–87.

_____ (1993b) "Ronald Coase and Methodology." *Journal of Economic Perspectives* 7 (Fall): 195–210.

_____ (1995) *Overcoming Law*. Cambridge: Harvard University Press.

_____ (2001) *Frontiers of Legal Theory*. Cambridge: Harvard University Press.

_____ (2008) "Norms and Values in the Economic Approach to Law." In *Norms and Values in Law and Economics*, edited by Aristides Hatzis. London: Routledge.

Pound, Roscoe (1911a) "The Scope and Purpose of Sociological Jurisprudence, Part I." *Harvard Law Review* 24 (June): 591–619.

_____ (1911b) "The Scope and Purpose of Sociological Jurisprudence, Part II." *Harvard Law Review* 25 (December): 140–68.

_____ (1912) "The Scope and Purpose of Sociological Jurisprudence, Part III." *Harvard Law Review* 25 (April): 489–516.

_____ (1954) *Introduction to the Philosophy of Law*, rev. ed. New Haven: Yale University Press.

Prest, Wilfrid (1991) "Judicial Corruption in Early Modern England." *Past and Present* 133 (November): 67–95.

Puviani, Amilcare (1897) *Teoria della illusione nelle entrate publiche*. Perugia, Italy.

_____ (1903) *Teoria della illusione finanziaria*. Palermo, Italy: Sandron.

Quesnay, François ([1757] 1993) "Corn." Pp. 72–87 in *The Economics of Physiocracy: Essays and Translations*, edited by Ronald L. Meek. London: George Allen & Unwin, 1962. Reprinted Fairfield, NJ: Augustus M. Kelley.

_____ ([1767] 1993) "The General Maxims for the Economic Government of an Agricultural Kingdom." Pp. 231–62 in *The Economics of Physiocracy: Essays and Translations*, edited by Ronald L. Meek. London: George Allen & Unwin, 1962. Reprinted Fairfield, NJ: Augustus M. Kelley.

────── (2005) *Œuvres Économiques Complètes et Autres Textes*, edited by Christine Théré, Loïc Charles, and Jean-Claude Perrot. Paris: L'Institut National d'Études Démographiques.

Raditzky, G., and P. Berholz (1987) *Economic Imperialism: The Economic Method Applied Outside the Field of Economics*. New York: Paragon.

Raffaelli, Tiziano, Giacomo Becattini, and Marco Dardi, eds. (2006) The *Elgar Companion to Alfred Marshall*. Aldershot, England: Edward Elgar.

Rawls, John (1981) "Foreword." In Henry Sidgwick, *The Methods of Ethics*, 7th ed. Indianapolis, IN: Hackett.

Reder, Melvin W. (1982) "Chicago Economics: Permanence and Change." *Journal of Economic Literature* 20 (March): 1–38.

Regan, Donald H. (1972) "The Problem of Social Cost Revisited." *Journal of Law and Economics* 14: 427–37.

Response to the Efficiency Symposium (1980) *Hofstra Law Review*, 8: 811–972.

Richenberg, L. J. (1953) "Review of *Committee Decisions with Complementary Valuation*, by Duncan Black and R.A. Newing." *Economic Journal* 63 (March): 129–31.

Riker, William H. (1959) "Review of *Approaches to the Study of Politics*, edited by Roland Young." *Midwest Journal of Political Science* 3 (May): 207–210.

────── (1961) "Voting and Summation of Preferences: An Interpretive Bibliographic Review of Selected Developments during the Last Decade." *American Political Science Review* 55 (December): 900–911.

────── (1962a) *The Theory of Political Coalitions*. New Haven: Yale University Press.

────── (1962b) "Review of *The Calculus of Consent*, by James M. Buchanan and Gordon Tullock." *Midwest Journal of Political Science* 6 (November): 408–11.

Robbins, Lionel (1932) *An Essay on the Nature and Significance of Economic Science*. London: Macmillan.

────── (1952) *The Theory of Economic Policy in English Classical Political Economy*. London: Macmillan.

────── (1976) *Political Economy Past and Present: A Review of Leading Theories of Economic Policy*. New York: Columbia University Press.

────── (1981) "Economics and Political Economy." *American Economic Review* 71 (May): 1–10.

Rogers, W. Hayward (1959) "Some Methodological Difficulties in Anthony Downs' *An Economic Theory of Democracy*." *American Political Science Review* 53 (June): 483–85.

Ross, Ian Simpson (1995) *The Life of Adam Smith*. Oxford: Oxford University Press.

Rothschild, Emma (2001) *Economic Sentiments: Adam Smith, Condorcet, and the Enlightenment*. Cambridge: Harvard University Press.

Rutherford, Malcolm (1994) *Institutions in Economics: The Old and the New Institutionalism*. Cambridge: Cambridge University Press.

Samuels, Warren J. (1962) "The Physiocratic Theory of Economic Policy." *Quarterly Journal of Economics* 76 (February): 145–62.

_____ (1966) *The Classical Theory of Economic Policy.* Cleveland, OH: World.

_____ (1973) "The Coase Theorem and the Study of Law and Economics." *Natural Resources Journal* 14: 1–33.

_____ ed. (1988) Institutional Economics, 3 vols. Aldershot, England: Edward Elgar.

_____ (1993) "Law and Economics: Some Early Journal Contributions." In Warren J. Samuels, Jeff Biddle, and Thomas W. Patchak-Schuster, *Economic Thought and Discourse in the Twentieth Century.* Aldershot, England: Edward Elgar.

_____ (2009a) *Essays on the Invisible Hand.* Cambridge: Cambridge University Press.

_____ (2009b) "The Invisible Hand." In *The Elgar Companion to Adam Smith*, edited by Jeffry Young. Aldershot: Edward Elgar.

Samuels, Warren J., and Steven G. Medema (1998) "Ronald Coase on Economic Policy Analysis: Framework and Implications." Pp. 65–94 in *Coasean Economics: Law and Economics and the New Institutional Economics*, edited by Steven G. Medema. Boston: Kluwer.

_____ (2005) "Freeing Smith from the 'Free Market': On the Misperception of Adam Smith on the Economic Role of Government." *History of Political Economy* 37 (2): 219–26.

Samuels, Warren J., and Nicholas Mercuro (1984) "Posnerian Law and Economics on the Bench." *International Review of Law and Economics* 4: 107–30.

Samuelson, Paul A. (1947) *Foundations of Economic Analysis.* Cambridge: Harvard University Press.

_____ (1954) "The Pure Theory of Public Expenditure." *Review of Economics and Statistics* 36: 386–89.

_____ (1964) *Economics: An Introductory Analysis*, 6th ed. McGraw-Hill.

Samuelson, William (1985) "A Comment on the Coase Theorem." Pp. 321–39 in *Game-Theoretic Models of Bargaining*, edited by Alvin E. Roth. Cambridge: Cambridge University Press.

Sandelin, Bo (1988) "Buchanan, Wicksell, and Finanztheoretische Untersuchungen." *History of Economics Society Bulletin* 10 (fall): 169–70.

Schabas, Margaret (2006) *The Natural Origins of Economics.* Chicago: University of Chicago Press.

Schlag, Pierre (1986) "An Appreciative Comment on Coase's 'The Problem of Social Cost': A View From the Left." *Wisconsin Law Review* 1986: 919–62.

Schultz, Bart (2004) *Henry Sidgwick: Eye of the Universe.* Cambridge: Cambridge University Press.

Senior, N. (1928) *Industrial Efficiency and Social Economy.* 2 vols., edited by S. Leon Levy. London: P. S. King.

Shapley, L. S., and Martin Shubik (1954) "A Method for Evaluating the Distribution of Power in a Committee System." *American Political Science Review* 48 (September): 787–92.

Shughart, William F., II, and Laura Razzolini, eds. (2001) *The Elgar Companion to Public Choice.* Northampton, MA: Edward Elgar.

Sidgwick, Henry ([1885] 1904) "The Scope and Method of Economic Science." In *Miscellaneous Essays and Addresses.* London: Macmillan.

_____ ([1886] 1904) "Economic Socialism." In *Miscellaneous Essays and Addresses*. London: Macmillan.

_____ (1897) *The Elements of Politics*, 2nd ed. London: Macmillan.

_____ (1901) *The Principles of Political Economy*, 3rd ed. London: Macmillan.

_____ ([1874] 1981) *The Methods of Ethics*, 7th ed. London: Macmillan, 1907. Reprint Indianapolis, IN: Hackett.

Simon, Herbert A. (1952) "Review of *Committee Decisions with Complementary Valuation*, by Duncan Black and R. A. Newing." *American Sociological Review* 17 (October): 638.

Simons, Henry C. (1934) *A Positive Program for Laissez Faire*. Public Policy Pamphlet No. 15, edited by H. D. Gideonse. Chicago: University of Chicago Press.

_____ (1936) "Rules versus Authorities in Monetary Policy." *Journal of Political Economy* 44 (February): 1–30.

_____ (1937) "Review of *First Principles of Public Finance* by Antonio De Viti de Marco." *American Economic Review* 45 (October): 712–17.

Simpson, A. W. Brian (1996) "*Coase v. Pigou* Reexamined." *Journal of Legal Studies* 25 (January): 53–97.

Skinner, Andrew S. (1996a) "The Role of the State." In *A System of Social Science: Papers Relating to Adam Smith*, 2nd ed. Oxford: Oxford University Press.

_____ (1996b) *A System of Social Science: Papers Relating to Adam Smith*, 2nd ed. Oxford: Oxford University Press.

Smith, Adam ([1759] 1977) *The Theory of Moral Sentiments*. Indianapolis, IN: Liberty Fund.

_____ ([1776] 1981) *An Inquiry into the Nature and Causes of the Wealth of Nations*. Indianapolis, IN: Liberty Fund.

_____ (1978) *Lectures on Jurisprudence*. Oxford: Oxford University Press.

Somers, Harold M. (1952) "Review of *Social Choice and Individual Values*, by Kenneth J. Arrow." *Journal of Political Economy* 60 (April): 170–71.

Sraffa, Piero (1926) "The Laws of Returns under Competitive Conditions." *Economic Journal* 36: 535–50.

Starrett, David A. (1972) "Fundamental Nonconvexities in the Theory of Externalities." *Journal of Economic Theory* 4: 180–99.

Steiner, Philippe (1994) "Demand, Price and the Net Product in the Early Writings of François Quesnay." *European Journal of the History of Economic Thought* 1 (Spring): 231–51.

_____ (1998) *La "science nouvelle" de l'économie politique*. Paris: Presses Universitaires de France.

Stigler, George J. (1965) "The Economist and the State." *American Economic Review* 55: 1–18.

_____ (1966) *The Theory of Price*, 3rd ed. New York: Macmillan.

_____ (1971) "Smith's Travels on the Ship of State." *History of Political Economy* 3 (Fall): 265–77. Reprinted in *The Economist as Preacher and Other Essays*, Chicago: University of Chicago Press, 1982, pp.136–45.

_____ (1974) "Henry Calvert Simons." *Journal of Law and Economics* 17 (April): 1–5.

_____ (1988) *Memoirs of an Unregulated Economist*. New York: Basic Books.

_____ (1989) "Two Notes on the Coase Theorem." *Yale Law Journal* 99 (December): 631–633.

_____ (1990) "The Place of Marshall's *Principles* in the Development of Economics" In *Centenary Essays on Alfred Marshall*, edited by J. K. Whitaker. Cambridge: Cambridge University Press.

Stigler, George J., and Gary S. Becker (1977) "De Gustibus Non Est Disputandum." *American Economic Review* 67 (March): 76–90.

Stigler, George J., and Kenneth E. Boulding (1952) *Readings in Price Theory*. Homewood, IL: Richard D. Irwin for the American Economic Association.

Sutton, John (2000) *Marshall's Tendencies: What Can Economists Know?* Cambridge: MIT Press.

Symposium on Efficiency as a Legal Concern (1980) *Hofstra Law Review* 8: 485–770.

Telser, L. G. (1960) "Why Should Manufacturers Want Fair Trade?" *Journal of Law and Economics* 3: 86–105.

Thomas, William (1979) *The Philosophic Radicals: Nine Studies in Theory and Practice, 1817–1841*. Oxford: Oxford University Press.

Tollison, Robert D. 1991. "Graduate Students in Virginia Political Economy: 1957–1991." Center for Study of Public Choice Occasional Paper on Virginia Political Economy. Fairfax, VA: George Mason University.

Toso, Stefano (1992) "The Italian School of Public Finance at the Turn of the Twentieth Century and the Ricardian Equivalence Theorem." *History of Political Economy* 24 (Winter): 819–41.

Tullock, Gordon (1965) *The Politics of Bureaucracy*. Washington, DC: Public Affairs Press.

_____ (1967a) "Foreword." *Papers on Non-Market Decision Making* (later renamed *Public Choice*) 2: i.

_____ (1967b) "The Welfare Costs of Tarrifs, Monopolies and Theft." *Western Economic Journal* 5: 224–32.

_____ (1967c) *Toward a Mathematics of Politics*. Ann Arbor: University of Michigan Press.

_____ (1987) "Public Choice." In *The New Palgrave: A Dictionary of Economics*, vol. 3, edited by John Eatwell, Murray Milgate, and Peter Newman. New York: W. W. Norton.

_____ (1993) *Rent Seeking*. Northampton, MA: Edward Elgar.

_____ (1997) "Origins of Public Choice." Pp. 122–40 in *The Makers of Modern Economics, Volume III*, edited by Arnold Heertje. Cheltenham, England: Edward Elgar.

Tullock, Gordon, Gordon Brady, and Arthur Seldon (2002) *Government Failure: A Primer in Public Choice*. Washington, DC: Cato Institute.

Tybout, Richard A. (1972) "Pricing Pollution and Other Negative Externalities." *Bell Journal of Economics* 3: 252–66.

Tynan, Nicola, and Tyler Cowen (1998) "The Private Provision of Water in 18th- and 19th-Century London." Mimeo, George Mason University, Department of Economics.

Ulmer, S. Sidney (1963) "The Role of 'Costs' in Political Choice: A Review of James M. Buchanan and Gordon Tullock, *The Calculus of Consent.*" *Conflict Resolution* 7 (2): 171–76.

Unger, Roberto (1983) "The Critical Legal Studies Movement." *Harvard Law Review* 96 (January): 561–675.

Van Zandt, David E. (1993) "The Lessons of the Lighthouse: 'Government' or 'Private' Provision of Goods." *Journal of Legal Studies* 22: 47–72.

Veljanovski, Cento G. (1977) "The Coase Theorem—The Say's Law of Welfare Economics?" *Economic Record* 53: 535–41.

_____ (1982) "The Coase Theorems and the Economic Theory of Markets and Law." *Kyklos* 35: 53–74.

Vickery, William (1960) "Utility, Strategy, and Social Decision Rules." *Quarterly Journal of Economics* 74 (November): 507–535.

Viner, Jacob (1927) "Adam Smith and Laissez Faire." *Journal of Political Economy* 35 (April): 198–232. Reprinted in Jacob Viner, *Essays on the Intellectual History of Economics*, edited by Douglas A. Irwin. Princeton: Princeton University Press, 1991, pp. 85–113.

_____ (1937) *Studies in the Theory of International Trade.* New York: Harper. Reprinted Clifton, NJ: Augustus M. Kelley, 1975.

Vines, Kenneth (1963) "Review of *The Calculus of Consent*, by James M. Buchanan and Gordon Tullock." *The Journal of Politics* 25 (February): 160–61.

Wagner, Richard E. (2003) "Public Choice and the Diffusion of Classic Italian Public Finance." *Il Pensiero Economico Italiano* 11 (1): 271–82.

Wakefield, Edward Gibbon (1829) *A Letter from Sydney, The Principal Town of Australasia*, edited by Robert Goucher, together with the *Outline for a System of Colonization.* London: Joseph Cross.

Walras, Léon ([1874] 1954) *Elements of Pure Economics*, translated from the French by William Jaffé. Homewood, IL: Richard D. Irwin.

Ward, Benjamin (1963) "Review of *The Calculus of Consent*, by James M. Buchanan and Gordon Tullock." *Southern Economic Journal* 29 (4): 351–53.

Weingast, Barry R., and William T. Marshall (1988) "The Industrial Organization of Congress; or, Why Legislatures, Like Firms, Are Not Organized as Markets." *Journal of Political Economy* 96 (February): 132–63.

Weiser, Friedrich von (1889) *Der natürliche Werth.* Vienna.

Wellisz, Stanislaw (1964) "On External Diseconomies and the Government-Assisted Invisible Hand." *Economica* 31: 345–62.

Whitaker, J. K., ed. (1975) *The Early Economic Writings of Alfred Marshall, 1867–1890*, 2 vols. Cambridge: Cambridge University Press.

White, Barbara (1987) "Coase and the Courts: Economics for the Common Man." *Iowa Law Review* 72: 577–635.

Wicksell, Knut (1896a) *Finanztheoretische Untersuchungen.* Jena, Germany: Gustav Fischer.

_____ ([1896b] 1958) "A New Principle of Just Taxation," translated from the German by J. M. Buchanan. Pp. 72–118 in *Classics in the Theory of Public Finance*, edited by Richard A. Musgrave and Alan T. Peacock. London: Macmillan.

Williamson, Oliver E. (1975) *Markets and Hierarchies: Analysis and Antitrust Implications.* New York: Free Press.

_____ (1985) *The Economic Institutions of Capitalism.* New York: Free Press.

Williamson, Oliver E., and Scott E. Masten, eds. (1995) *Transaction Cost Economics*, 2 vols. Aldershot, England: Edward Elgar.

Winch, Donald (1996) *Riches and Poverty: An Intellectual History of Political Economy in Great Britain.* Cambridge: Cambridge University Press.

Young, Allyn (1928) "Increasing Returns and Economic Progress." *Economic Journal* 38 (December): 527–42.

Zelder, Martin (1998) "The Cost of Accosting Coase: A Reconciliatory Survey of Proofs and Disproofs of the Coase Theorem." Pp. 65–95 in *Coasean Economics: Law and Economics and the New Institutional Economics*, edited by Steven G. Medema. Boston: Kluwer.

Zerbe, Richard O., Jr. (1980) "The Problem of Social Cost in Retrospect." *Research in Law and Economics* 2: 83–102.

Zerbe, Richard O., Jr., and Steven G. Medema (1998) "Ronald Coase, the British Tradition, and the Future of Economic Method." Pp. 209–38 in *Coasean Economics: Law and Economics and the New Institutional Economics*, edited by Steven G. Medema. Boston: Kluwer.

Index

The letter *n* following a page number indicates a note on that page.